Teaching Elementary
Physical Education

Teaching Elementary Physical Education

A Handbook for the Classroom Teacher

Robert P. Pangrazi
Arizona State University

Allyn and Bacon
Boston ◆ *London* ◆ *Toronto* ◆ *Sydney* ◆ *Tokyo* ◆ *Singapore*

Senior Editor: Suzy Spivey
Editorial Assistant: Lisa Davidson
Marketing Manager: Quinn Perkson
Manufacturing Buyer: Suzanne Lareau
Cover Designer: Hannus Design Associates

Copyright © 1997 by Allyn & Bacon
A Viacom Company
Needham Heights, MA 02194

Internet: www.abacon.com
America Online: keyword: College Online

Portions of this material first appeared in *Dynamic Physical Education for Elementary School Children*, Eleventh Edition, by Robert P. Pangrazi and Victor P. Dauer, copyright © 1995 by Allyn and Bacon.

Library of Congress Cataloging-in-Publication Data

Pangrazi, Robert P.
    Teaching elementary physical education: a handbook for the
 classroom teacher / Robert P. Pangrazi.
            p.   cm.
    Includes bibliographical references and index.
    ISBN 0-205-19362-5
    1. Physical education for children--Study and teaching
(Elementary)--United States--Handbooks, manuals, etc.   I. Title.
    GV221.P35 1997
    372.86'0973--dc20   96-24587
                                                          CIP

Printed in the United States of America
10 9 8 7 6 5 4 3 2 1   00 99 98 97 96

Contents

Preface   xi

Chapter ONE   **So You Want to Teach Physical Education**   **1**

You Can Teach Physical Education!   **3**
Objectives of Physical Education   **3**
The Development of Motor Skills   *3*
Health-Related Physical Fitness and Wellness   *4*
Social Skills and Positive Self-Concept   *4*
Lifetime Participation in Activity   *5*
Who Should Teach Physical Education?   **5**
How Does This Book Help?   *6*
Requisites for a Successful Program   **6**
Scheduling   *6*
Class Size   *7*
Equipment   *7*
Instructional Area   *10*
Successful Physical Education Programs   *10*
Reference and Suggested Reading   *11*

Chapter TWO   **Why Physical Education and Activity Are Necessary**   **12**

Physical Activity in the School Curriculum   **13**
Factors Controlling Physical Performance   **14**
Body Type Affects Motor Skill Learning   *18*
Maturity Strongly Influences Physical Performance   *19*
Boys and Girls Are Similar in Muscular Strength and Endurance   *20*
Strength and Body Size Affect Motor Performance   *20*
Aerobic Activity Periods for Children Should Be Short   *21*
Obesity Limits Performance in Aerobic Activities   *21*
Children in Sports Activity   **22**
Physical Maturity Influences Sport Skills Learning   *22*
Allow Youngsters to Learn All Positions in Sports   *22*
Avoid Identifying Gifted Athletes at a Young Age   *23*
Starting Young Does Not Make a Better Athlete   *23*

Guidelines for Exercising Children Safely   25
Use Moderation in Exercise   25
Use Care When Exercising in Warm Climates   26
Limit How Far Children Run   27
Use Caution When Running the Mile   28
Guidelines for Resistance (Weight) Training   28
References and Suggested Readings   30

Chapter THREE   Teaching Motor Skills   33

Motor Patterns Common to All Children   34
When Skills Should Be Taught   35
Maturity   35
Prior Learning Experiences   35
State of Readiness   35
How to Create a Desire to Learn   36
How to Give Feedback about Skill Performance   36
Knowledge of Results   37
Knowledge of Performance   38
How to Make Effective Use of Practice Time   39
Make Practice Learning Oriented   39
Decide on Whole versus Part Practice   40
*Determine the Length and Distribution of Practice
    Sessions   41*
Use Random Practice Techniques   42
Offer Variable Practice Experiences   42
Understand Transfer of Learning   43
Teach Skills in Proper Progression   44
Skill Performance Principles That Should Be Taught   46
Starting and Stopping the Body   46
Propelling Objects   47
Catching Objects   48
References and Suggested Readings   49

**Chapter FOUR   Implementing an Effective Physical Education
Lesson   50**

Before You Start the Lesson   51
Secure and Check Equipment   51
Maximize Learning in a Minimal Amount of Time   52
Vary the Size of the Teaching Space   53
Implement a Variety of Instructional Formations   54
Increase the Effectiveness of Instruction   56
Optimize Skill Learning through Planning   56
Effectively Use Practice and Activity Time   57
Use Drills That Facilitate Skill Development   58
Consider the Developmental Level of Students   59
Make It Challenging, Not Threatening   59
Teach to Improve Creative Responses   60
Encourage Cognitive Development   61
Develop Affective Skills and Outcomes   62
Demonstrate Skills to Expedite Learning   64
Demonstrations by Teachers   64
Student Demonstrations   64

**Use Instructional Cues to Improve Student
   Performance   65**
Develop Precise Cues   65
Use Short, Action-Oriented Cues   65
Integrate Action Cues   66
Maintain a Productive Class Environment   66
Create a Safe Environment   66
Effectively "Eyeball" the Class   67
Systematically Scan the Class   68
Minimize Talking and Maximize Activity   68
Maintain Instructional Focus   68
Maintain Focus on Educational Objectives   69
*Personalize Instruction by Showing Concern for
   Differences   69*
Provide Meaningful Instructional Feedback   70
Positive, Corrective, and Negative Feedback   70
Use Specific Feedback Statements   71
Distribute Feedback to All Students   72
Focus of Feedback: Individual or Group?   72
References and Suggested Readings   73

**Chapter FIVE   Management and Discipline Strategies in a Physical
   Education Setting   74**
Characteristics of a Well-Managed Class   75
Teach Class Management Skills   76
Stop and Start a Class Consistently   76
Deliver Instruction Efficiently   77
Move Students into Groups and Formations Quickly   77
Use Squads to Expedite Class Organization   78
Learn Students' Names   80
Establish Pre- and Postteaching Routines   80
Distribute Equipment Efficiently   81
Prevent Behavior Problems   82
Plan and Implement Rules at the Start of the School Year   82
Establish an Atmosphere That Encourages Learning   84
Create a Positive and Fair Environment   85
Modify and Maintain Desirable Behavior   86
Increase Desired Behavior with Positive Reinforcement   87
Prompt Desirable Behavior to Encourage New Behavior   90
Shape Desirable Behavior   91
Decrease Undesirable Behavior   92
Negative Consequences   92
Behavior Contracts   96
Minimize Criticism   96
Use Punishment Judiciously   97
Expulsion: Legal Considerations   99
References and Suggested Readings   99

Chapter SIX   Children with Disabilities   101
Screening and Assessment   102
Screening   103
Assessment   103

Procedures for Assuring Assessment Standards   *104*

Development of the IEP   105

Criteria for Placement of Children   108

Creating the Least Restrictive Environment   108

Mainstreaming   109

Teacher Behavior and the Mainstreaming Process   112

Utilizing Parental Support   113

Recruiting and Training Aides   113

**Modifying Participation for Children with
    Disabilities   114**

Understanding Specific Disabilities   117

Mental Retardation   117

Epilepsy   118

Visual Impairment   120

Auditory Impairment   121

Orthopedic Disabilities   122

Emotional Disturbances   124

Learning Disabilities   124

*Asthma, Cerebral Palsy, Cardiac Problems, and
    Diabetes   125*

References and Suggested Readings   126

Chapter SEVEN Legal Liability and Proper Care of Students   128

Torts   129

Negligence and Liability   129

Foreseeability   130

Types of Negligence   131

Malfeasance   131

Misfeasance   131

Nonfeasance   131

Contributory Negligence   132

Comparative or Shared Negligence   132

Common Defenses against Negligence   132

Act of God   132

Proximate Cause   132

Assumption of Risk   133

Contributory Negligence   133

Areas of Responsibility   133

Supervision   134

Instruction   135

Equipment and Facilities   138

Administration   138

Instructional Staff   139

The Sports Program   139

Mismatching Opponents   140

Waiver Forms   140

Medical Examinations   140

Preseason Conditioning   140

Transportation of Students   140

Safety   141

The Safety Committee   142

The Emergency Care Plan   143

**Personal Protection: Minimizing the Effects of a
    Lawsuit   145**
Liability Insurance   145
Recordkeeping   145
Safety and Liability Checklist   145
References and Suggested Readings   147

Chapter EIGHT   Physical Activity and Fitness   149

What Is Physical Fitness?   150
Health-Related Physical Fitness   150
Skill-Related Physical Fitness   151
Which Type of Fitness Should You Teach?   152
Are Today's Children Fit?   153
Why Do People Continue to Believe Children Are Unfit?   154
Can All Children Meet Similar Standards of Fitness?   154
Should Instruction Focus on Fitness or Regular Activity?   156
Create Positive Attitudes toward Activity   158
Individualize Fitness Activities   158
*Expose Youngsters to a Variety of Fitness Routines and
    Exercises   158*
*Give Students Meaningful Feedback about Their
    Performances   158*
Teach Physical Skills and Fitness   159
Be a Role Model   159
Be Concerned about the Attitudes of Children   159
Start Easy and Progress Slowly   160
Use Low-Intensity Activity   160
Encourage Lifetime Activity   160
Develop a Varied Approach to Fitness   161
Implementing Fitness Routines   161
**Fitness Activities for Children in Kindergarten through
    Grade 2   163**
Fitness Challenges   163
Animal Movements   167
Fitness Games   168
Miniature Challenge Courses   169
Parachute Fitness Routines   169
Walk, Trot, and Sprint   170
Jump Rope Exercises   170
Four-Corners Movement   170
Other Fitness Challenges and Routines   171
**Fitness Activities for Children in Grades 3
    through 6   171**
Harmful Practices and Exercises   172
Exercises for Developing Fitness Routines   174
Flexibility Exercises   174
Arm-Shoulder Girdle Exercises   177
Abdominal Exercises   180
Leg and Agility Exercises   183
Trunk-Twisting and Bending Exercises   184
Partner-Resistance Exercises   187
Developing Physical Fitness Routines   190

Student Leader Exercises   *190*
Squad Leader Exercises   *190*
Exercises to Music   *190*
Circuit Training   *191*
Continuity Drills   *194*
Hexagon Hustle   *194*
Astronaut Drills   *194*
Challenge Courses   *195*
Aerobic Fitness Routines   *195*
Aerobic Fitness and Partner-Resistance Exercises   *199*
Sport-Related Fitness Activities   *199*
Walking and Jogging   *201*
Continuous Movement Program   *202*
Interval Training Activities   *203*
Partner Fitness Challenges   *204*
References and Suggested Readings   **206**

Index   **209**

Preface

This handbook and the accompanying lesson plan books are designed for use by classroom teachers. The handbook offers content and guidelines for instructional methodology. It is used as a resource to supplement the lesson plans and to offer necessary information for program implementation. The following reflects the purpose for each chapter in this handbook.

- Chapter 1 offers information about the goals and objectives of an effective physical education program. Essential requisites for teaching physical education such as scheduling, equipment needs, class size, and characteristics of successful physical education programs are discussed.

- Chapter 2 explains the importance of activity and how it is essential for optimal growth and development. Guidelines for exercising children safely are included so teachers can implement activity and feel comfortable about their expectations.

- Chapter 3 offers basic principles for teaching motor skills. These are the guidelines for knowing how to offer effective practice and learning sessions. Motivating children to learn and giving proper feedback about skill performance is also included. Principles of movement are covered to assure that students are learning new skills properly.

- Chapter 4 deals with instructional strategies such as planning decisions to make prior to the start of the lesson. Increasing the effectiveness of instruction, offering meaningful instructional cues, and maintaining a productive class environment are emphasized in this chapter.

- Chapter 5 places strong emphasis on management and discipline. Students behave differently in a physical education setting as compared to a classroom environment. It is important to know how to manage in the physical education class. Learning how to find partners and make small groups is explained in detail. Dealing with deviant behavior is given strong coverage. A number of strategies for increasing positive behavior and decreasing undesirable behavior are listed.

- Chapter 6 offers instructional strategies for teaching children with disabilities. It covers a wide range of disabilities that commonly are found in a typical classroom. In addition, many ideas are offered for modifying physical activities so these students can successfully participate.

- Chapter 7 explains liability and safety issues. All teachers worry about providing a safe environment that protects the safety of their students. This chapter provides many guidelines for minimizing the possibility of a serious accident.

- Chapter 8 covers physical activity and fitness and offers many types of activities for students. This chapter is a reference chapter for the lesson plans. For example, many of the exercises are described in detailed in this chapter but not in the lesson plan book. Also, a new focus on activity for all youngsters is discussed, as well as understanding how all youngsters are unique in their abilities to exercise.

Three separate lesson plan books accompany this handbook and are presented in three levels—kindergarten through second grade, third and fourth grades, and fifth and sixth grades—allowing for a greater range of activity and ensuring that presentations are closely aligned to the maturity and experience of students. The lesson plan books can be ordered separately by calling 1-800-278-3525.

The lesson plans are comprehensive and include necessary information to implement a comprehensive physical education program. They provide movement experiences in a sequential and well-ordered manner. The lesson plans offer activities to be taught for an entire school year. They can be used as is or serve as a framework for modifying and developing a curriculum that is shaped to meet the needs of individual teachers. Many teachers take activities from the lesson plans and write them on 4" by 6" note cards. Writing the activities on cards helps teachers mentally organize the lesson and results in a more effective presentation.

In addition to the wealth of activities found in each of the lesson plan books, requisite teaching hints are offered. Teaching hints explain how to organize the lesson, what safety guidelines to follow, how to teach skills properly, and what instructional cues to deliver during skill learning. These plans reduce the amount of time required for planning a physical education lesson. In addition, all equipment needed and desired objectives for the lesson are included with each lesson plan.

As you implement physical education in your school, consider that a healthy mind can reside only in a healthy body. Without physical health and vigor, children have little opportunity to learn and mature at an optimum rate. It is my hope that these books will help you offer children a chance to do more than play. Play is not enough—it is random learning and rewards those who are the most gifted. Hopefully, these books will help you offer *all* children a chance to learn new skills and develop an active lifestyle that will serve them for a lifetime.

Happy Activity!

Chapter ONE

So You Want to Teach Physical Education

In this chapter, you will learn...

- *What physical education is*
- *What the three major goals of physical education are*
- *Why physical education is an important component of the total school curriculum*
- *That you can teach a quality physical education program*
- *About the objectives of a physical education program*
- *Who should teach physical education in an elementary school*
- *What equipment is requisite for a successful physical education program*
- *Why class size and scheduling strongly influence the effectiveness of physical education*
- *What instructional areas are needed*

What is physical education (PE, Fizz Ed, Gym)? Physical education has many different meanings. A physical education professional will describe it as an essential subject dedicated to learning physical skills and developing lifetime physical activity patterns. It is not the same as athletics or competitive sports. It is not recess or free-time play. Physical education places emphasis on learning and educating. It should educate all students and place particular focus on students who are less gifted. A common theorem is that physical education should provide educational sequences for the 70 percent of students who are less gifted and able. Why? Because those students who are gifted have many opportunities to learn new skills and improve existing abilities. They can take private lessons, join the myriad of sport teams, and compete with others of similar ability. Physical education in the elementary school is one of the last opportunities for students to learn skills. Therefore, a strong physical education component in the total school curriculum is to help students become competent and able movers.

The differences in perceptions of physical education are, no doubt, a result of the wide variety of experiences of different individuals. Most adults believe that physical activity is important for all. However, many children have not received an opportunity to learn in a physical education setting. National statistics (Ross, Pate, Corbin, Delpy, & Gold, 1987) indicate that only 50 percent of children in grades 1 through 4 receive physical education as often as three days a week. In grades 5 and 6, less than 50 percent of children receive physical education as often as three days a week.

Physical education is an integral part of the elementary school curriculum. It contributes to the activity and skill development needs of students. Too often, teachers assume that students will be able to develop physical skills without guidance. The assumption is that play is enough activity and all students are receiving a positive experience through recess-type activities. Unfortunately, what is true for adults is true for children. Many students will not exercise without a supportive system, and some will find the free activity situation to be threatening. This less than positive experience creates the need to help physically educate all children regardless of skill, ability, or genetic predisposition. Students must be given the opportunity to develop personal competence in a number of skills or else there is little chance they will take advantage of the opportunity as adults. Finally, teachers know that youngsters are physical in nature. Children do not like to sit still, walk in the halls, or move quietly. Physical education is the only time where students receive the opportunity to physically educate themselves. A few minutes a week seems a small contribution to the legacy of healthy and active children in the future.

Physical education is a part of the total educational program that contributes, primarily through physical activity, to the total growth and development of all children. *Physical education* is defined as education through movement and activity. It is difficult to conceive that an unhealthy student would be able to learn. The healthy mind/healthy body adage points out that learning in the academic world is not enough. Physical health is a requisite for learning. Energy and vitality are necessary if quality learning experiences are to continue throughout the school day.

You Can Teach Physical Education!

The outcomes of physical education are unique within the total school curriculum. There are three major things you need to teach. The first outcome is to develop a personalized physical fitness and increased activity level. Second is the development of personal competency in a variety of physical skills so students can function effectively in selected physical activities. The third outcome is to give students requisite knowledge related to motor skill performance and fitness maintenance. When these outcomes are not accomplished in physical education classes, they are not realized elsewhere in the curriculum. Classroom teachers can offer physical education experiences that will help students reach these outcomes. It is not an impossible task. When understood, physical education is not a difficult activity to teach. In fact, it can be rewarding and can offer classroom teachers and students a break from the rigors of the classroom.

Objectives of Physical Education

The objectives of physical education are straightforward and easy to reach. Much of learning in physical education requires repetition and refinement. A large part of teaching is developing an environment where students are comfortable and want to practice. Expecting yourself to be expert in teaching all skills and activities is unrealistic. When necessary, bring in someone (perhaps a student who is gifted) to help introduce skills and follow up by focusing on key points of instruction. All teachers, including trained physical educators, find areas where they feel incompetent. The objectives listed here are offered to give direction to the teacher.

Why are these activities being taught? What is the reason for including fitness in the lesson? What are long-term objectives of physical education? These and other questions are answered by an examination of the objectives.

The Development of Motor Skills

All people want to be skilled and competent in the area of motor performance. The elementary school years are an excellent time to teach motor skills because children have the time and predisposition to learn. The types and range of skills presented in physical education should be unlimited; youngsters must have the opportunity to encounter and experience many activities. Because children vary in genetic endowment and interest, they need opportunities to learn about their abilities in many different skill areas. These experiences allow students to develop personal competence in areas where they are able and to accept their limitations in areas where they are less capable.

Health-Related Physical Fitness and Wellness

Above all, physical education programs should provide children with opportunities to participate in regular physical activity. The focus of the physical fitness component is on the process of activity rather than the product of fitness (i.e., how many, how fast, or how far). Students need opportunities to learn about the importance of activity and how such choices will impact their health in adulthood. When students are responsible for participating in regular activity, whether at school or at home, physical fitness objectives have been accomplished and will last a lifetime.

A portion of each physical education lesson period should be allotted to fitness activities. Physical fitness must be experiential—students must participate in fitness activity to learn what is necessary for good health. It is not enough to learn facts about fitness; it must be a participatory experience in the elementary school years. Many people know facts about fitness but have not learned the habit of participating in regular activity. This is not to say that knowledge is unimportant, but that regular participation in activity designed to promote fitness is the priority in elementary school. Positive experiences in fitness activity assist students in developing attitudes that help ensure they will be active adults. What is gained if students develop high physical fitness levels in the elementary school years but leave school with a strong dislike of physical activity? Establishing a desire in children to maintain fitness and wellness throughout the adult years is the ultimate outcome.

Social Skills and Positive Self-Concept

Physical education classes contribute to an environment of effective social living. Children learn to internalize and understand the merits of participation, cooperation, competition, and tolerance through physical activity. Some terms, such as good citizenship and fair play, help define the desired social atmosphere. Through listening, empathy, and guidance, teachers help children differentiate between acceptable and unacceptable ways of expressing feelings. Youngsters can develop an awareness of how they interact with others, and how the quality of their behavior influences others' responses to them. If students do not receive feedback about negative behavior from teachers and peers, they may never perceive behaviors that are strongly resented by others.

Cooperative skills can be learned in an activity setting. Cooperation precedes the development of competition and should be emphasized in the school setting. If people do not cooperate, competitive games cannot be played. The nature of competitive games demands cooperation, fair play, and sportsmanship, and when these are not present, the joy of participation is lost. Cooperative games teach children that all participants are needed. As the nature of competition comes into clearer focus, teachers can help students temper the urge to win at all costs and come to the realization that not all participants can be winners.

How teachers feel and act contributes to the hidden curriculum. These feelings and actions often teach students more about the subject matter than spoken words. How teachers feel about physical education, how the lesson is organized, the types of activities presented, how teachers view students who are less successful, and how children with disabilities are treated send a number of hidden, but implied, messages to students. How teachers respond to children communicates that they are loved, capable, and contributing people. Not only must teachers understand learners, but students should understand themselves, for self-understanding has a powerful influence on human behavior. The self-concept that a child develops is vital to the learning process. It can make learning possible, or it can hinder or block the ability to learn. If children believe they belong, and are loved and respected, and if their successes outweigh their failures, the probability of developing a positive self-concept is high.

The ability to move with grace, confidence, and ease helps children regard themselves in a favorable light. Achieving satisfactory levels of skill competency and fitness can make students feel positive and assured. The self-concept is related to perceived physical skill competence. Self-perception dictates many of the decisions students illustrate with behavior. If students perceive themselves to be competent in an activity setting, they want to participate in activity outside the school setting. On the other hand, if they feel incompetent, they avoid activity at all costs in an attempt to maintain their self-esteem.

Lifetime Participation in Activity

The basic considerations for lifetime activity are several. Children must derive enjoyment through activity so they will seek further participation. To this end, children must become proficient in a variety of motor skills. Most adults do not participate in activities unless they have an adequate level of perceived competence. Because learning new motor skills takes a great deal of time and repetition, adulthood often prohibits busy adults from developing a level of skill competence to assure play without embarrassment.

Youngsters learn social skills through activities such as small-group games and sport activities. The burden of providing a broad orientation to skills, games, and fitness activities falls on the elementary school program. Less required physical education and more choices and options for meeting activity requirements (band, cheer squad, etc.) make it possible to complete high school with few opportunities for learning recreational and lifetime activity skills. Preparation in and orientation to many different activities during the elementary school years can provide a background to help students make choices for a lifetime of recreational enjoyment.

Who Should Teach Physical Education?

Most teachers agree that children need the opportunity to learn physical skills and participate in physical activity. At issue is who should teach the physical education class and how it should be taught. There is general agreement that physical education taught by a trained physical educator is the best alternative. However, many times, economics prevents the hiring of full-time physical education specialists. The following options are different solutions that can be used in an elementary school.

- A physical education specialist and classroom teachers share responsibility for the program. A common model includes having the physical education teacher present the first lesson of the unit while being observed by the classroom teacher. The classroom teacher then teaches the remainder of the classes in the unit. In most cases, planning is led by the physical education specialist while the classroom teacher assumes grading responsibilities.

- A physical education specialist trains the classroom teachers at the start of each week (or month). The emphasis is on showing the teachers how to present the material. The actual teaching and grading responsibilities belong to the classroom teachers.

- A classroom teacher assumes physical education teaching responsibilities. Through differentiated staffing, one teacher teaches physical education for a number of other classroom teachers who assume the social studies, math, reading, and so on, responsibilities of this designated teacher. The strength of this model is that a classroom teacher who enjoys teaching physical education is usually assigned to do it. The disadvantage is that the designated teacher does not have much contact with his or her students in an academic setting.

- Classroom teachers assume the responsibility to teach their own physical education. This is usually the least desirable model because it places much stress on a number of classroom teachers and includes some teachers who have little inclination toward activity instruction. The upside for a school district is that it is the cheapest model and does not require additional personnel. The downside is that instruction is done by the least qualified teachers and released time for planning is not available.

How Does This Book Help?

This book is designed for classroom teachers who are expected to teach in any of the preceding models. It assumes that a physical education specialist is not available and that little time is available for planning. The program of activities presented here demand a minimum of equipment for implementation. The activities offer a well-rounded program so all students have an opportunity for success. Emphasis is placed on activities that minimize the chance for injury.

Requisites for a Successful Program

Scheduling

Time must be scheduled for physical education. Too often, classroom teachers are expected to teach physical education but a scheduled time is not offered. This makes it difficult to know when the activity area is available and reduces the expectation for such instruction to occur. Scheduling time for each teacher places a clear expectation on instructors and helps assure that physical education will be taught. Time for activity should occur every day. However, at a minimum, 30 minutes of time should be scheduled for physical education three days a week. This implies 30 minutes of activity; changing shoes, traveling to the activity area, getting drinks, and so on, should not be included in the 30 minutes.

There are a number of ways to design a schedule. Teachers can meet and barter for different times and areas. Another way is to elect or assign a scheduling team who schedules all the facilities and instructional areas in the school. This involves scheduling music, art, and physical education so there are no conflicts. This is a time-consuming job. Some faculties prefer asking the administrator to design a schedule for their inspection and approval. Regardless of how it is done, the schedule has to consider the activities being taught in physical education. For example, football is best taught outdoors, whereas activities such as juggling, tossing and catching, and rhythms are best taught indoors. Scheduling subtleties can involve scheduling primary grades indoors while intermediate grades are involved in outdoor activities. Activities that demand little equipment might be placed outside so that equipment-intensive instruction could be done indoors. Another contingency to plan for is the rainy-day schedule, which might involve more than one class in the teaching area. However the schedule is designed, not having a schedule usually means not having physical education instruction.

Class Size

It is becoming increasingly more common to send two or more classes at one time to a physical education class. Teachers find themselves in a situation that is next to impossible to supervise. The noise level, the number of behavior problems, and the risk of accident increase geometrically with class size. Expecting teachers to find a sense of satisfaction in this setting is unrealistic. Class sizes for physical education should be the same as a self-contained classroom. Consider this interesting observation: Teachers constantly bargain for smaller classloads so they can be more effective teachers. At the same time, some advocate increasing the size of classes in physical education. An increased class size does not work; it makes instruction in physical education difficult, if not impossible. If the experience is going to be educational, normal class sizes must be maintained.

Equipment

Trying to teach physical education without equipment is like trying to teach academic subjects without books and other supportive materials. Some equipment is necessary if skills are going to be learned. The program delineated in this book minimizes equipment needs for a number of reasons. Equipment is expensive. If individuals are not held accountable for the equipment, it often disappears and needs to be replenished on a regular basis. This added cost factor needs to be considered when equipment budgets are assigned. Second, large apparatus and equipment is expensive and often goes unused by teachers if it needs to be moved out and put away each day. Finding a teacher who is willing to set up the equipment and put it away is difficult. Therefore, activities in this book (listed in the accompanying lesson plans) do not require large and expensive pieces of equipment.

Getting equipment ready for instruction is a time-consuming job. Classroom teachers often bring their classes to the teaching area and try to put out their equipment while youngsters are milling about. Equipment must be easy to carry, put out, and put away when finished. Activities in the lesson plans meet such requirements. A suggestion is to have students put out the equipment in the morning under the supervision of a teacher. If necessary, it can be put away during lunch. A team of students arrive after school to put away the equipment. It is much easier to teach if the desired equipment is in place when the teacher arrives.

The types of equipment for the program in this book are relatively inexpensive. Tables 1.1 and 1.2 show equipment lists that are suggested for a comprehensive program. When the quantity of 36 is listed, the assumption is that there will be one piece of equipment for each student. If the class is larger or smaller, more or less equipment will be required. The equipment is listed in priority of utility (i.e., what piece of equipment offers the greatest use in the physical education program). Table 1.1 shows equipment in the material and supplies category. This is small and inexpensive equipment that needs to be replaced periodically. Playground balls are listed first because they can be used for bouncing and dribbling, kicking and striking, tossing and catching, and many low-organized games. These balls are relatively inexpensive and offer a multitude of uses. Table 1.2 lists capital outlay items. They are more costly, but last for many years if cared for. Again, these items are listed in order of priority. The Robert Widen Company, P.O. Box 2075, Prescott, AZ, (800) 862 0761, can supply the equipment listed in Tables 1.1 and 1.2.

Storage of Equipment

Not only does the program require adequate equipment but there must also be a specified storage area. Within the storage area, equipment must be assigned to areas and stored properly. All teachers must adhere to the organizational system or it will be difficult to find the equipment and prepare for the lesson. Nothing is more distressing to teachers than to enter the teaching area, expect the equipment to be in place, only to find it missing or not put away properly. Many times, teachers will cancel physical education rather than try to piece together a lesson. The storage room must have labeled areas and proper receptacles designated.

It is important to identify equipment for physical education use only. When possible, buy equipment for physical education that can be easily distinguished from playground/general use equipment. If the equipment is not restricted to physical education use, teachers and students will begin to borrow it for playground use. Over time, physical education equipment will disappear. Thus, physical education equipment must be for physical education use only!

TABLE 1.1   Required Material and Supplies

Priority (Rank)	Description	Quantity
1	*8½-inch Playground Balls.* They come in many colors. A good idea is to specify a unique color for physical education balls. This prevents their use as general playgrounds balls.	36
2	*8-inch Foam Rubber Balls.* Good-quality foam balls are dense and bounce well enough to allow dribbling. A more expensive option is vinyl-covered foam-rubber balls, which bounce better and last much longer.	36
3	*6" × 6" Beanbags.* These should be made of soft canvas and filled with inert beads. Beans, peas, and other legumes should be avoided since they will get wet and rot.	36

4	*Jump Ropes.* Two major types are available: beaded ropes and speed ropes. The beaded ropes are easier for beginners to use, but the solid vinyl speed ropes are better for experienced jumpers. The following lengths are needed:
	   7-foot length
	   8-foot length
	   9-foot length (for teachers)
	   14- to 16-foot length (for long rope-jumping activities)
		
		18
		18
		6
		12

5	*Hula Hoops* (30-inch diameter). They can be purchased as a solid hoop or in segments. Segments allow the hoops to be repaired when bent or broken and are more colorful.	36
6	*Traffic Cones* (8- to 12-inch size). Smaller cones are easier to carry, but may not hold signs as well in the wind.	18
7	*Tambourine (or Tom-Tom).* Used to accentuate rhythmic movement activities. Can be used to stop a class with a loud double beat.	1
8	*Juggling Scarves.* These are excellent for teaching K–2 children throwing and catching skills. They move slowly, which allows youngsters to track them successfully. Also, youngsters can throw them a limited distance, which assures safety.	36
9	*Beachballs* (18 to 20 inches in diameter). These are excellent for catching and kicking skills. They can be used in games because they move slowly and will not hurt students.	36
10	*Pinnies* (four colors, 12 each). These are used to identify teams. Students should be able to put them on and take them off easily.	48
11	*Ball Bags.* Nylon see-through mesh is best so it is easy to see what is in the bags. These are necessary for moving and storing equipment.	12
12	*Bowling Pins.* These can be acquired from bowling alleys, usually at no cost.	24

TABLE 1.2   Required Capital Outlay Items

Priority (Rank)	Description	Quantity
1	*Tumbling Mats* (4' × 8' × 1¼" thick with Velcro fasteners on all four sides). The mats should fold and be lightweight so students can help move them.	8
2	*Cassette Tape Player*	1
3	*Parachute and Storage Bag* (24- to 28-feet diameter)	1
4	*Ball Carts.* Used for storing and moving all types of equipment. Particularly useful for moving equipment outdoors.	4
5	*Electric Ball Pump*	1

Instructional Area

A designated instructional area is a requisite for a successful physical education program. The instructional area should be off limits to others when it is in use. Whenever possible, an indoor area should be designated as the physical education "classroom." Few teachers want to go outside and fight the elements, other students at recess, airplanes, dogs, dirt, insects, cars, and the myriad of other problems that arise when instruction must occur outdoors. This is not to suggest that some lessons are not better taught outdoors. However, the vast majority of lessons are better taught in the multipurpose room. Equipment does not have to be moved in and out, the walls of the room confine equipment and students in an assigned area, and the noise factor is reduced.

Too often, the multipurpose room is used for purposes that are less educational in nature. Lunch hours are often extended beyond what is necessary because custodians do not want to rush and clean the area. Therefore, it is often unused for 3 to 4 prime-time hours. At other times, teachers want to practice a play or allow their students to recreate. If the physical education program is valued, it must have a teaching area similar to any other classroom or specialty area. Teachers will not move equipment outside and back in on a regular basis. If the weather is inclement, activity will be suspended and the list goes on and on. An indoor area is a requisite.

The indoor area (and an outdoor teaching surface) needs to be marked with lines on the floor for physical education instruction. Figure 1.1 offers suggested markings that make teaching all activities easier. The lines can be used for game activities of all types and make it easier to move students into formation.

Bulletin boards should be placed in the instructional area so youngsters can view upcoming activities, learn about new ideas, and receive instructional tips. An established location for the cassette player is necessary so teachers can easily retrieve it and plug it in for use. Doors on the instructional area should be kept closed so that noise and excitement will not bother other students and teachers.

Successful Physical Education Programs

Physical education programs succeed when teachers work in a climate that includes the following:

- Teachers, parents, and administrators value physical education and view it as a vital component in the total development of students.
- Equipment and facilities are available and valued as much as other resources in the school.
- A physical education schedule is in place so teachers and students know it will occur regularly.

FIGURE 1.1 **Floor Markings to Maximize Gymnasium Use**

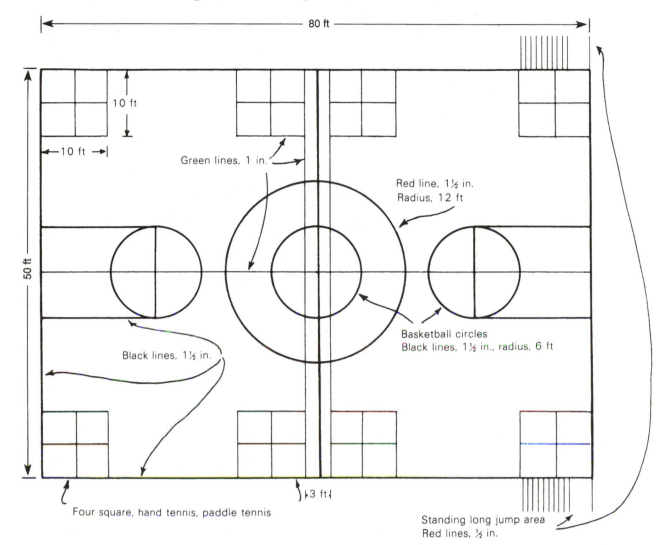

- Teacher evaluation systems include physical education as a part of the overall program.
- The physical health and vigor of children is valued as much as the basic skills.

Reference and Suggested Reading

Ross, J. G., Pate, R. R., Corbin, C. C., Delphy, L. A., & Gold, R. S. (1987). What is going on in the elementary physical education program? *Journal of Physical Education, Recreation, and Dance, 58* (9), 78–84.

Chapter TWO

Why Physical Education and Activity Are Necessary

In this chapter, you will learn...

◆ *The importance of activity in the development of healthy children*

◆ *About factors that control the limits of physical performance*

◆ *How growth patterns of children show large variations*

◆ *Why different types of bodies affect the ability to learn motor skills*

◆ *That preadolescent boys and girls are similar in physical performance traits*

◆ *Why children should exercise in short alternating bursts of aerobic and strength/flexibility activity*

◆ *How to treat obese youngsters in an activity setting*

◆ *How maturity influences motor skill learning*

◆ *The importance of not identifying outstanding athletes at an early age*

◆ *Safety guidelines for children in physical activity settings*

Physical activity contributes to the development of well and active children. During the past decade, the interest in physical activity and an increased awareness of the benefits derived from an active lifestyle have spawned a wide assortment of health clubs, a vast array of books and magazines concerning activity and fitness, a weekly smorgasbord of distance runs and triathalons, streamlined exercise equipment, and apparel for virtually any type of physical activity. Unfortunately, the nation's enthusiasm for physical activity has not trickled down to elementary school youngsters. A statement issued by the American Academy of Pediatrics (1991) reported that children from the ages of 2 to 12 watch about 25 hours of television per week—more time than they spend in school. Only about one-third of U.S. children and youth participate daily in school physical education programs nationwide (Ross, Pate, Corbin, Delpy, & Gold, 1987), and that amount is both declining and insufficient.

Physical Activity in the School Curriculum

The need for activity as an integral part of children's lifestyles is strong. Rather than encourage increased activity among children, schools have focused on physical fitness testing. This excessive concern about the fitness levels of children has resulted in a need to train children to pass fitness tests to meet district standards. When fitness results become more important than participation in regular activity, children learn the importance of short-term goals (fitness test results) rather than long-term lifestyle changes (daily activity). Health goals for the nation for the year 2000 (U.S. Public Health Service, 1990) are primarily based on increasing daily levels of physical activity, not fitness levels. Many of the goals directly target schools, or programs that can take place within the school setting. These goals are stated in terms of activity objectives rather than fitness objectives and emphasis is placed on reducing inactivity and increasing light to moderate physical activity.

Physical education programs should cause lifestyle changes in physical activity levels and improve health-related fitness (Simons-Morton, Parcel, O'Hara, Blair, & Pate, 1988; Sallis & McKenzie, 1991). Whereas fitness testing has anointed a few gifted children and failed the majority of others, developing programs that change the activity patterns of students allows all youngsters the opportunity for success and long-term health. Children should be recognized for their willingness to participate rather than their reticence to be tested.

One area of concern in dealing with children's health is heart disease. Common wisdom is that heart disease is of geriatric origin and manifests itself only in older adults. In a study by Glass (1973), 5,000 youngsters in the Iowa public schools were examined over a two-year period. Of these students, 70 percent had symptoms of coronary heart disease, including 7 percent who had extremely high cholesterol levels, a large percentage with high blood pressure, and at least 12 percent who were obese.

In examining the developmental history of heart disease in humans, a study by Rose (1968) showed the first signs appear around age 2. Wilmore and McNamara (1974) examined 95 boys, aged 8 to 12 years, in an effort to determine the extent to which coronary heart disease risk factors derived from an adult population were manifested in a group of young boys. They concluded that "coronary heart disease, once considered to be a geriatric problem, is now recognized as being largely of pediatric origin" (p. 531). Fortunately, an increase in activity plays an important role in combating the onset of such problems.

Other diseases and physical conditions are associated with a lack of activity in young children. One concern is the high incidence of obesity among youngsters. Depending on the source of statistics and the criteria used to define obesity, anywhere from 30 to 60 percent of U.S. children have been identified as obese. The need is clear: Physical education programs are needed to teach youngsters how to live active and healthy lifestyles.

Factors Controlling Physical Performance

Growth patterns are generally controlled by genetic makeup at birth. Although unhealthy parents or poor dietary practices can have a negative impact on proper growth and development, this section will examine normal maturation differences common to the majority of youngsters. All youngsters follow a general growth pattern; however, each child's timing is unique. Some children are advanced physically for their chronological age, whereas others are slow maturers. Only when aberration from the norm is excessive should teachers and parents become concerned.

Children grow at different rates throughout their developmental years. When heights and weights are plotted year to year, a distance curve can be developed (see Figure 2.1). These curves give an indication of how tall and how heavy children are expected to be during a specific year of life. Another method of examining growth patterns is to look at a velocity curve (see Figure 2.2). The velocity curve is useful because it reveals the rate of growth on a year-to-year basis.

FIGURE 2.1 Distance Curves for Height and Weight

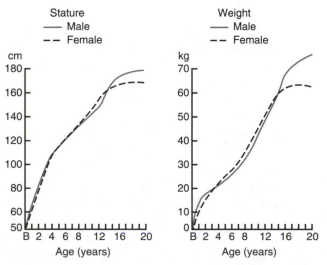

Source: Malina, R. 1975. *Growth and development: The first twenty years in man,* p. 19. Minneapolis: Burgess. Used with permission.

Children go through a rapid period of growth from birth to age 5. From age 6 to the onset of adolescence, growth velocity slows. A general rule of thumb for motor learning is that when growth is rapid, the ability to learn new skills decreases. Because the rate of growth slows during the elementary school years, it is an excellent opportunity to enhance motor skills. If motor skills are not practiced and learned during the elementary school years, the opportunity never reappears.

During adolescence, rapid growth occurs again until adulthood is reached. During the preadolescent school years, boys are generally taller and heavier. However, girls reach the adolescent growth spurt first and often grow taller and heavier than boys during the sixth- and seventh-grade years. Boys quickly catch up, however, and grow larger and stronger. Growth charts based on a large and recent sample of children have been developed by the National Center for Health Statistics (see Figures 2.3 and 2.4). These tables can be consulted to identify height and weight percentiles for children aged 2 through 18. The tables offer an opportunity to visualize the marked differences among children in a so-called normal population. In addition, they serve as excellent reference points for] discussing aberrant growth patterns with parents.

Young children (kindergarten through grade 2) have relatively short legs for their height. The trunk is longer in relation to legs during early childhood. The ratio of leg length (standing height) to trunk length (sitting height)

FIGURE 2.2 Growth Velocity Curve for Height

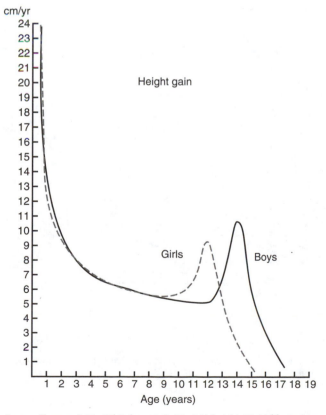

Source: Tanner, J. M., Whitehouse, R. H., & Takaishi, M. 1966. *Archives of Diseases in Childhood, 41,* 466. Used with permission.

FIGURE 2.3 Physical Growth Percentiles for Boys 2 to 18 Years

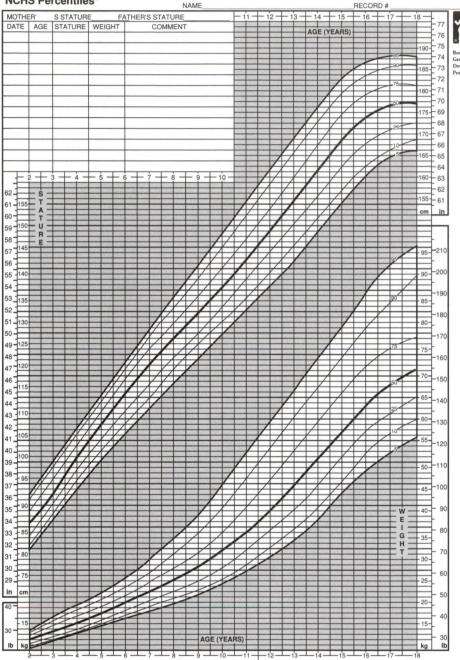

Sources: Adapted from Hamill, P. V. V., Drizd, T. A., Johnson, C. L., Reed, R. B., Roche, A. F., & Moore, W. M. 1979. Physical growth: National Center for Health Statistics percentiles. *American Journal of Clinical Nutrition, 32,* 607–629. Data from the Fels Research Institute, Wright State University School of Medicine, Yellow Springs, Ohio. Ross Laboratories, Columbus, Ohio. Used with permission of Ross Products Division, Abbott Laboratories, Columbus, OH 43216, from NCHS Growth Charts© Ross Products Division, Abbott Laboratories.

FIGURE 2.4   Physical Growth Percentiles for Girls 2 to 18 Years

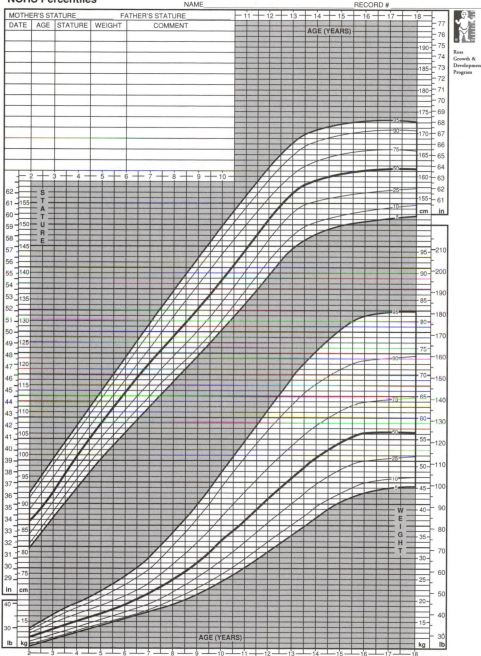

Sources: Adapted from Hamill, P. V. V., Drizd, T. A., Johnson, C. L., Reed, R. B., Roche, A. F., & Moore, W. M. 1979. Physical growth: National Center for Health Statistics percentiles. *American Journal of Clinical Nutrition, 32,* 607–629. Data from the Fels Research Institute, Wright State University School of Medicine, Yellow Springs, Ohio. Ross Laboratories, Columbus, Ohio. Used with permission of Ross Products Division, Abbott Laboratories, Columbus, OH 43216, from NCHS Growth Charts© Ross Products Division, Abbott Laboratories.

is similar for boys and girls through age 11. The head makes up one-fourth of the child's total length at birth and about one-sixth at age 6. Figure 2.5 illustrates how body proportions change with growth.

Because K–2 students have short legs in relation to their upper bodies, they are often "top heavy" when performing activities such as the curl-up and V-seat. They may fall more easily than adults, because their center of gravity is higher than it will be at maturity. Growth gradually lowers the center of gravity and gives children increased stability and balance.

Body Type Affects Motor Skill Learning

Sheldon, Dupertuis, and McDermott (1954) developed the original scheme for categorizing adults into three different types of body physiques; endo-morphic, mesomorphic, and ectomorphic. A similar system for classifying children (Petersen, 1967) is useful for helping teachers understand how body types affect physical performance. The first of these body types is the *meso-*

FIGURE 2.5 *Changing Body Proportions from Conception to Adulthood*

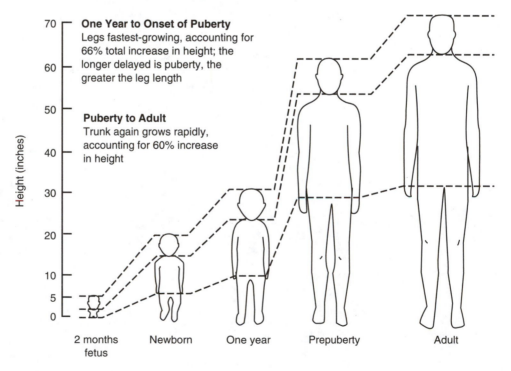

Changing Bodily Proportions

Conception to Birth
Head fastest-growing structure, completing 70% of its total growth

Birth to One Year
Trunk fastest-growing, accounting for 60% total increase in height

One Year to Onset of Puberty
Legs fastest-growing, accounting for 66% total increase in height; the longer delayed is puberty, the greater the leg length

Puberty to Adult
Trunk again grows rapidly, accounting for 60% increase in height

Height (inches)

70
60
50
40
30
20
10
5
0

2 months fetus   Newborn   One year   Prepuberty   Adult

Source: Whipple, D. 1966. *Dynamics of development: Euthenic pediatrics,* p. 122. New York: McGraw-Hill.

morph, which characterizes those youngsters having a predominance of muscle and bone who are often labeled "muscled." In general, children who possess a mesomorphic body type perform best in activities requiring strength, speed, and agility. These children usually perform well in most team sports, because such activities require strength, speed, and agility. A second body type is the *ectomorph,* which is identified as thin, with a minimum of muscle development, and usually characterized as "skinny." These children are less able in activities requiring strength and power, but do well in aerobic endurance activities such as jogging, cross-country running, and track and field. The third classification is the *endomorph,* a soft and round individual, with an excessively protruding abdomen. These children often perform poorly in many areas, including aerobic and anaerobic skill-oriented activities. Obese children are generally at a disadvantage in all phases of physical performance because of excess body fat. The importance of body type classification is to understand how dramatically children differ in body physique. Children vary widely in body types and these differences necessitate that instruction accommodate individual differences.

Maturity Strongly Influences Physical Performance

Teachers have long understood and discussed differences in maturity among students. Often, children are referred to as being immature or more mature than other students—usually in reference to the emotional maturity of youngsters. Another type of maturity—physical maturity—is important to teachers. Physical maturity has a strong impact on the student performance in physical education. A method used to identify physical maturity is to compare chronological age with skeletal age. Ossification (hardening) of the bones occurs in the center of the bone shaft and at the ends of the long bones (growth plates). The rate of ossification gives an accurate indication of a child's rate of maturation. This rate of maturation or skeletal age is identified by x-raying the wrist bones and comparing the development of the subject's bones with a set of standardized x-rays; it gives a truer sense of the child's physical maturity (Gruelich & Pyle, 1959; Roche, Chumlea, & Thissen, 1988). Children whose chronological age is ahead of skeletal age are said to be late (or slow) maturers. On the other hand, if skeletal age is ahead of chronological age, such children are labeled early (fast) maturers. This advanced or retarded skeletal age strongly impacts physical performance.

Studies examining skeletal age (Gruelich & Pyle, 1959; Krahenbuhl & Pangrazi, 1983) consistently show that a 5- to 6-year variation in maturity exists in a typical classroom of youngsters. For example, a class of third-graders who are 8 years old chronologically ranges in skeletal age from 5 to 11 years. Teachers would not think of asking a 5-year-old kindergarten child to perform tasks that 11-year-olds are expected to accomplish. Teachers need to monitor and adjust program activities to allow students to progress at a rate suitable to their levels of maturity.

Early-maturing children of both sexes are generally heavier and taller for their age than average- or late-maturing students. In fact, obese children (endomorphs) are often more mature for their age than normal-weight children. Early-maturing children also have larger amounts of muscle and bone tissue, due to their larger body size. However, the early maturer also carries a greater percentage of body weight as fat tissue (Malina, 1980). The motor performance of boys is related to skeletal maturity because more mature boys usually perform better than less mature boys on motor tasks (Clarke, 1971). For girls, however, motor performance is less related to physiological maturity. Among girls, a study by Malina (1978) showed that late maturation is commonly associated with exceptional motor performance.

Teachers often want students to learn at the same rate, even though this practice can be detrimental to the development of students who are developing at a faster or slower rate. Teachers may mistakenly expect all youngsters to be capable of performing the same activity at the same time, regardless of maturation. Since students do not mature at the same rate and are not at similar levels of readiness to learn, it is best they be allowed to progress at individual rates.

Boys and Girls Are Similar in Muscular Strength and Endurance

In the elementary school years, muscular strength increases linearly with chronological age (Malina, 1980; Beunen, 1989). A similar yearly increase occurs until adolescence, at which time a rapid increase in strength occurs. Strength is related to body size and lean body mass. Preadolescent children show few strength differences between the sexes. Boys and girls can be expected to perform similarly in strength activities such as push-ups and sit-ups. In the past, teachers have accepted lower performances from girls, even though they are capable of more. Expectations should be similar for preadolescent boys and girls.

Strength differences do occur among children of widely differing weight and height, regardless of sex. Differences in weight and height should be considered when pairing children for competitive activities such as running together, physical contact, or games that require strength. Problems occur when a student is paired with someone who is considerably taller and heavier (or more mature) and therefore stronger.

Strength and Body Size Affect Motor Performance

Strength is an important factor in performing motor skills. A study by Rarick and Dobbins (1975) identified and weighted factors that contribute to the motor performance of children. The factor identified as most important was strength or power, or both, in relation to body size. High levels of strength in relation to body size helped predict which students were most capable of performing motor skills. Deadweight (fat) was the fourth-ranked factor in the study and was weighted negatively. Obese children were less proficient at learning and performing motor skills. Deadweight acts negatively on motor performance by reducing the child's strength in relation to body size. Obese children may be stronger than normal-weight children in absolute terms, but they are less strong when strength is adjusted for body weight. This lack of strength in relationship to body size makes it more difficult for obese children to perform a strength-related task (e.g., push-up or curl-up) compared to normal-weight children. The need for varied and personalized workloads is important to assure all youngsters the opportunity for success in strength-related activities.

Aerobic Activity Periods for Children Should Be Short

Maximal aerobic power is an individual's maximum ability to use oxygen in the body for metabolic purposes. The oxygen uptake of an individual, all other factors being equal, determines the quality of endurance-oriented performances such as waking, running, or biking. Adults often train to improve their aerobic performance and think children should be trained in a similar manner. However, the adult model appears to be inappropriate for youngsters; training appears to have little or no impact on aerobic performance. A recent study (Payne & Morrow, 1993) analyzed 28 studies dealing with the impact of exercise on aerobic performance in children. The results showed training caused little, if any, increase in aerobic power in prepubescent children. If there is improvement in running performance in young children, Bar-Or (1983) has postulated that it may occur because they become more efficient mechanically or improve in anaerobic metabolism. Another theory is that young children are active enough to make intergroup differences negligible (Corbin & Pangrazi, 1992).

Aerobic activities for children should be presented in a manner that maintains motivation and love of movement. Youngsters fatigue quickly and recover rapidly from strenuous exercise; this rapid recovery rate should be used to full advantage. Since youngsters are resistant and usually dislike long-duration activities, exercise bouts should be interspersed with restful stretching and strength development activities. Interval training (strenuous activity alternated with less strenuous recovery activity) is a particularly effective training method to use with children because it allows for rest and recovery.

Obesity Limits Performance in Aerobic Activities

Depending on the criteria used to evaluate bodyfat, 25 to 35 percent of youngsters have been identified as being overfat or obese. Obesity restricts children's motor performance because of the greater metabolic cost of the obese child's exercise (Bar-Or, 1983). Obese children require higher aerobic capacities compared to normal-weight youngsters to perform a given task. Obesity takes a toll on a child's aerobic power because obese children must perform at a higher percentage of their maximal oxygen uptake. Usually, their maximal uptake values are lower than those of lean children. This gives obese children less reserve capacity and causes them to perceive higher exertion (Bar-Or & Ward, 1989) when performing a task. This increased exertion causes them to perceive aerobic tasks as demanding and unenjoyable. These reactions contribute to the well-known perception among teachers that "obese children don't like to run." Teachers should bear this in mind when they ask obese children to try to run as far and as fast as normal-weight children. The task is more demanding for obese children. Understand that obese children are working harder than normal-weight children and need workloads adjusted to their abilities. There is no acceptable premise, physiological or psychological, for asking all children to run the same distance regardless of ability or body type.

When designing aerobic workloads, base the dosage on time rather than distance. Lean and efficient runners should be expected to move farther than obese youngsters during a stipulated time period. All children do not and should not have to do the same amount of exercise. Just as one would not expect kindergarten children to perform the same workload as that of fifth-graders, it is unreasonable to expect obese children to be capable of workloads similar to those of lean, ectomorphic youngsters. Exercise programs for obese subjects should be designed to increase caloric expenditure rather than improve cardiovascular fitness (Rowland, 1991). The intensity of the activity should be secondary to the amount of time the student is involved in some type of moderate activity. For weight control, long moderate bouts of activity are always preferable to short intense bouts of exercise.

Children in Sports Activity

Sports and related activities are ever-present in most physical education programs. Too often, these programs are administered by persons who have little, if any, training and understanding of young, immature children. It is important to teach sports in a manner that considers the capabilities and developmental characteristics of participants.

Physical Maturity Influences Sport Skills Learning

Maturity plays an important role in dictating which position a child will learn to play in a sport. Will a youngster be a pitcher or a right fielder, play in the line or be a quarterback? Often, these questions are answered for young children by teachers and coaches—a decision that may not allow youngsters an opportunity to realize their potential. In a study by Hale (1956), skeletally mature athletes were found to be playing in the skilled positions in the Little League World Series. Chronologically, all players were 11 years old, with a skeletal age range similar to that described earlier. The most mature were pitchers and catchers, and the least mature played at less skilled positions. This study shows that skeletally mature children are often assigned to skilled positions and receive more opportunity for throwing practice at an early age (through pitching and catching). These youngsters become better throwers due to the large number of opportunities they receive when throwing in games and practice. In contrast, children who are immature are forced to play right field and receive limited throwing or catching opportunities. Because these less mature children receive much less throwing practice, it is improbable they will ever have the chance to close the skill gap and develop adequate skill competency.

Allow Youngsters to Learn All Positions in Sports

Another issue related to skill development is allowing youngsters to play all positions in sport activities. If the best athletes are assigned to skilled positions, the rich get richer and the poor get poorer. Because all children deserve equal opportunity to learn sport skills, it should be a mandate that all children play all positions and receive similar amounts of practice time.

In addition, reinforcement schedules should be similar for children regardless of their current skill level. Children participate in activities that offer them reinforcement; it is easy to become discouraged if little encouragement and praise are given to participants trying to learn new skills and positions. Physical education is one of the few opportunities where teachers can allow all participants equal opportunity to learn about sports. When they enter the competitive sports field, they will have little say about what positions they want to play.

Avoid Identifying Gifted Athletes at a Young Age

The willingness to try new experiences and participate in activities is driven by how people feel about their ability levels—their perceived competence. Perceived competence becomes more specific as students mature. In other words, very young students think they are good and competent at everything. As they become older (third or fourth grade), they start to realize that other students are better in some areas. If these students are not given the chance to succeed in physical education, they may lack perceived competence about their ability to perform physical skills. This "learned helplessness" (Harter, 1978) eventually results in the student disliking and dropping out of physical education. There is a strong possibility that less able students will leave school with negative feelings about developing an active lifestyle. Dropping out of physical education commonly occurs at the middle and high school level or as soon as students have the opportunity to make a choice. Unfortunately, the process of feeling incompetent begins in the elementary school years. Elementary school youngsters are often characterized as gifted (or not gifted) at a young age. This creates a self-fulfilling prophecy, with students identified as gifted receiving more feedback and being expected to reach higher levels of performance. Less able students receive less feedback and expectations remain low.

Even though teachers and parents make early judgments about students, it is difficult to identify outstanding athletes by viewing their performance in the elementary school years. In a study by Clarke (1968), athletes identified as outstanding in elementary school were seldom outstanding in junior high school, and predictions based on elementary school performance were correct only 25 percent of the time. Most people would not risk discouraging a youngster if they knew they were going to be wrong 75 percent of the time. However, youngsters are often labeled at early age, even though three out of four such predictions are incorrect. All children should be treated as if they have the potential to become successful. It is not the purpose of a physical education program to develop athletes, but rather to help all students develop physical skills within the limits of their potential. A physical education program should not allow athletically gifted students to excel and prosper at the expense of the less talented youngsters.

Starting Young Does Not Make a Better Athlete

There is no evidence to support the notion that starting a child at a young age creates an outstanding athlete (see Figure 2.6). In fact, many excellent athletes, particularly in basketball, did not even play the sport until their high

FIGURE 2.6   An Early Start Does Not Guarantee Success

school years. One reason many parents and coaches push to have children start competing in a sport at an early age is that it gives them the perception that a better athlete has been developed by the age of 8 or 9. Participating children may seem more gifted compared with nonparticipants because they have been practicing skills for four or five years. The "early starter" looks advanced compared with a child who has not been in an organized program. In most cases, however, genetically gifted children quickly catch up and surpass "early superstars" in one to three years. As Shephard (1984) stated, "Any advantage that is gained from very prolonged training probably lies in the area of skill perfection rather than in a fuller realization of physical potential."

There is concern that children who have been pushed into documented programs at an early age burn out at an early age. A documented program is one that offers extrinsic rewards. Examples of such rewards are trophies, published league standings, ribbons, and excessive parental involvement (keeping score, giving rewards, etc.). Evidence shows that using extrinsic motivation may decrease intrinsic motivation, particularly in children age 7 years and older. Researchers (Thomas & Tennant, 1978; Whitehead & Corbin, 1991) found that younger children (age 5) perceived rewards as a bonus, which added to the joy of performing a throwing motor task. However, this effect decreased with age, and by the age of 9, the reward was seen as a bribe; intrinsic motivation was undermined. There is no substitute for allowing young children to participate in physical activity for the sheer enjoyment and excitement involved in moving and interacting with peers.

If starting youngsters early creates early burnout, why do parents feel pressured to force their children into a sport program? One reason is that they compare their children to other children. Parents see other children participating and practicing sport skills in an organized setting. They worry their child will be unable to "catch up" if they do not get them involved in a similar program immediately. Even though this is not true, parents need reassurance and facts. Teachers can help parents find programs that minimize pressure and focus on skill development. A key is to find programs that allow youngsters to participate regardless of ability and to have fun while playing. Most children consider having fun and improving their skills to be more important than winning (Athletic Footwear Association, 1990). Many children drop out of sport activities, but would probably continue to participate if given the opportunity (Petlichkoff, 1992). Unfortunately, programs become elitist and start eliminating and "cutting" less gifted players. It is difficult to justify this approach at the elementary school level. All children should be given the opportunity to participate if they choose to do so.

Another reason given for starting children at a young age is tied to the commodity that only children have: free time. Parents know they have little time in their lives to learn new skills. They feel their youngsters have an abundance of free time that can be devoted to practice. If a child shows promise, greater emphasis is placed on increasing practice time since it becomes necessary to ensure that "all this talent is not lost." It is important to remind parents that life includes more than athletic development and that many youngsters have been maimed by excessive emphasis on sports at the expense of intellectual and social development. Participation in activity should be self-selected. It should be internally driven rather than motivated by external factors. Similarly, students should have the opportunity to withdraw from participation in an activity if they choose. Withdrawal should be child controlled rather than externally controlled (Gould, 1987). In other words, participants should not be forced out of the program due to cost, limitation of participants, or injury. On the other hand, if youngsters choose to withdraw, they should be allowed that opportunity without pressure.

Guidelines for Exercising Children Safely

Use Moderation in Exercise

As is usually the case, moderation helps ensure that children grow up enjoying different types of physical activity. Moderate exercise, coupled with opportunities to participate in recreational activity, helps develop a lasting desire to move. Some educators are concerned that a child may be harmed physiologically by too much or too vigorous activity. To date, there is no evidence that a healthy child can be harmed through vigorous exercise. However, a more important consideration is whether the youngster is psychologically turned off to activity. Just because a child can exercise strenuously does not mean he or she should be forced to do so (see Chapter 8).

There was concern at one time that the large blood vessels do not grow in proportion to other body parts. It was theorized that this placed the heart and the circulatory system under stress during strenuous exercise. Research has now established that fatigue causes healthy children to stop exercising long before any danger to health occurs (Shephard, 1984). In addition, the child's circulatory system is similar in proportion to that of an adult and is not at a disadvantage during exercise.

Use Care When Exercising in Warm Climates

Care should be used when youngsters exercise in warm climates. Hot days do not mean that exercise must stop, but certain measures should be used to avoid heat-related illness. Children are not little adults, and they do not adapt to extremes of temperature as effectively as adults do for the following physiological reasons (Bar-Or, 1983; American Academy of Pediatrics, 1991):

1. Children have higher surface area/mass ratios than those of adults. This allows a greater amount of heat to transfer between the environment and the body.
2. When walking or running, children produce more metabolic heat per unit mass than adults produce. Youngsters are not as efficient in executing movement patterns, so they generate more metabolic heat than do adults performing a similar task.
3. Sweating capacity is not as great in children as in adults, resulting in a lowered ability to cool the body.
4. The ability to convey heat by blood from the body core to the skin is reduced in children due to a lower cardiac output at a given oxygen uptake.

These physiological differences put children at a distinct disadvantage compared with adults when exercising in an environment where the ambient air temperature is higher than skin temperature. Individuals acclimatize to warmer climates. However, children appear to adjust to heat more slowly (up to twice as long) than adults (Bar-Or, 1983). Also, children do not instinctively drink enough liquids to replenish fluids lost during exercise. The American Academy of Pediatrics Committee on Sports Medicine (1991) offers the following guidelines for children who exercise in hot climates:

1. The intensity of activities that last 30 minutes or more should be reduced whenever relative humidity and air temperature are above critical levels. Table 2.1 shows the relationship between humidity and air temperature and when activity should be moderated.
2. At the beginning of a strenuous exercise program or after traveling to a warmer climate, the intensity and duration of exercise should be

TABLE 2.1   Hot Weather Index

Humidity Level (%)	Air Temperature (°F)
40	90
50	85
60	80
70	75
80	70
90	65
100	60

restrained initially and then increased gradually over a period of 10 to 14 days to acclimatize to the effects of heat.

3. Children should be hydrated 20 to 30 minutes before strenuous activity. During the activity, periodic drinking (e.g., 5 ounces of cold tap water every 30 minutes for a child weighing 88 pounds) should be enforced. If youngsters are hydrated before going to a 30-minute physical education class, it probably is not necessary to drink until the end of the class period unless conditions are unusually severe.

4. Clothing should be lightweight and limited to one layer of absorbent material to facilitate evaporation of sweat and to expose as much skin as possible. Sweat-saturated garments should be replaced by dry ones. Rubberized sweatsuits should never be used to produce weight loss.

The committee identifies children with the following conditions as being at a potentially high risk for heat stress: obesity, febrile (feverish) state, cystic fibrosis, gastrointestinal infection, diabetes insipidus, diabetes mellitus, chronic heart failure, caloric malnutrition, anorexia nervosa, sweating insufficiency syndrome, and mental retardation.

Limit How Far Children Run

The question often arises as to how much and how far children should be allowed to run, particularly in a competitive or training-for-competition setting. The answer is complex, and long-term effects may not be seen for many years after the running program has started. The American Academy of Pediatrics Executive Committee (1991) has identified a number of concerns. Lifetime involvement in running often depends on the type of early participation and gratification gained. Psychological problems can result from unrealistic goals for distance running by children. A child who participates in distance running primarily for adult approval may tire of this after a time and quit, or the child may continue while chafing under the pressure. In either case, psychological damage may be done, and the child may be discouraged, either immediately or in the long run, from participating in future activity. A prepubertal child should be allowed to participate for the enjoyment of running without fear of adult or peer rejection or pressure. A child's sense of accomplishment, satisfaction, and appreciation by peers, parents, and teachers will foster involvement in running and other sports during childhood and in later life.

The International Athletics Association Federation (IAAF) Medical Committee (1983) stated, "The danger certainly exists that with over-intensive training, separation of the growth plates may occur in the pelvic region, the knee, or the ankle. While this could heal with rest, nevertheless definitive information is lacking whether in years to come harmful effects may result." In view of this danger, it is the opinion of the committee that training and competition for long-distance track and road-running events should not be encouraged. Up to the age of 12, it is suggested that not more than 800 meters (one-half mile) should be run in competition.

Use Caution When Running the Mile

Running the mile to test aerobic fitness has been used for years in the school setting. Unfortunately, the mile run test has probably done more to turn students off to lifetime activity than any other single practice in physical education. Teachers often test children at the start of the school year in the one-mile run/walk. This practice should be discontinued, since many children do not have ample conditioning to participate safely in the activity. In addition, in many parts of the country, the start of the school year is hot and humid, adding to the stress placed on the cardiovascular system. If the mile run is used, the recommendation is to test only at the end of the school year after youngsters have had an opportunity to be conditioned. If this is not possible, allow youngsters at least four to six weeks to condition themselves. Rowland (1990) has recommended starting with a one-eighth mile run/walk and gradually building to a mile run/walk over a four-week period.

A better alternative is to avoid using the mile run as a test item. Fortunately, a new test has been designed called the PACER aerobic fitness test* (Copper Institute, 1992) that can be administered indoors. This test involves running back and forth between two lines 20 meters apart within a certain time limit, and it can be stopped when the minimal health level is reached. This contrasts dramatically with the mile run, which requires that the entire mile be run before the level of performance can be determined.

Guidelines for Resistance (Weight) Training

The term *resistance (weight) training* is used here to denote the use of barbells, dumbbells, or machines as resistance. It is in sharp contrast to weight lifting or power lifting, which is a competitive sport for the purpose of determining *maximum* lifting ability. There is strong agreement among experts that resistance training is acceptable for children, but weight lifting is highly undesirable and may be harmful. In a statement of strength training recommendations, the American Orthopaedic Society for Sports Medicine (AOSSM) (Duda, 1986) stated, "(1) competition is prohibited, and (2) no maximum lift

---

* The PACER test is part of the Fitnessgram that is available from the Cooper Institute for Aerobic Research, 12330 Preston Road, Dallas, TX 75230. Call (800) 635-7050 to order test materials.

should ever be attempted." In addition, AOSSM recommends a physical exam, proper supervision by knowledgeable coaches, and emotional maturity on the part of the participating youngster.

Safety and prevention of injury are paramount considerations for those interested in resistance training for children. Serious consideration also has to be given as to whether weight training is an appropriate activity for a typical group of children in a physical education class. When injuries are reported, most are due to inadequate supervision, lack of proper technique, or competitive lifting. The majority of weight-lifting injuries were caused by the major lifts, the power clean, the clean and jerk, the squat lift, or the dead lift (Tanner, 1993). These lifts often are competitive and performed in an uncontrolled (ballistic) manner; they should not be used with preadolescent children. If knowledge and expertise are limited, weight-training programs for children should be avoided. A knowledgeable instructor is required to provide an effective and safe program.

Resistance training for preadolescent children has generated a great deal of concern among educators. Many worry about safety and stress-related injuries, and others question whether such training can produce significant strength gains. Accepted thinking for some time has been that prepubescents are incapable of making significant strength gains because they lack adequate levels of circulating androgens. Research evidence is continuing to build that contradicts this point of view. A study by Cahill (1986) demonstrated significant increases in strength among 18 prepubescent boys. A study by Servedio and colleagues (1985) showed significant strength gains in shoulder flexion. Weltman and Associates (1986) conducted a 14-week, three times a week program using hydraulic resistance training (circuit training using 10 different stations) in 6- to 11-year-old boys. Results showed an 18 to 37 percent gain in all major muscle groups.

It seems that strength can be increased through resistance training in prepubescent youngsters. However, the way prepubescent children gain strength differs from how adolescents and adults do (Tanner, 1993). In preadolescent children, it appears that strength gains occur from motor learning rather than muscle hypertrophy. Youngsters develop more efficient motor patterns and recruit more muscle fibers, but show no increase in muscle size (Ozmun, Mikesky, & Surburg, 1991).

There are no studies that examine the long-term effects of strength training in children. In addition, many experts worry about highly organized training programs that place great emphasis on relative gains in strength. When used, a resistance training program should be only one component of a comprehensive fitness program for children. The National Strength and Conditioning Association (NSCA) (1985) has recommended that 50 to 80 percent of the prepubescent athlete's training must include a variety of different exercises such as agility exercises (e.g., basketball, volleyball, tennis, tumbling) and endurance training (e.g., distance running, bicycling, swimming).

When a variety of physical activities are experienced in elementary school physical education, there probably is little need for resistance training within the school curriculum. However, such training may have a place on an individual basis with parental approval in a club setting. If a decision is made to develop a resistance training program for children, it should be done in a thoughtful and studied manner. Proper supervision and technique are key ingredients in a successful program. Program prescription guidelines recommended by AOSSM and NSCA are as follows:

1. Training is recommended two or three times a week for 20- to 30-minute periods. High repetitions at low resistance appear to be most safe for elementary school-age children.

2. No resistance should be applied until proper form is demonstrated. One set equals 6 to 15 repetitions; one to three sets per exercise should be done.

3. Weight or resistance is increased in 1- to 3-pound increments after the prepubescent does 15 repetitions in good form.

4. Maximal lifts should not be performed until youngsters are at least 16 to 17 years old.

References and Suggested Readings

American Academy of Pediatrics. (1991). *Sports medicine: Health care for young athletes (2nd ed.).* Elk Grove Village, IL: American Academy of Pediatrics.

Athletic Footwear Association. (1990). *American youth and sports participation.* North Palm Beach, FL: Athletic Footwear Association.

Bar-Or, O. (1983). *Pediatric sports medicine for the practitioner.* New York: Springer-Verlag.

Bar-Or, O., & Ward, D. S. (1989). Rating of perceived exertion in children. In O. Bar-Or (Ed.), *Advances in pediatric sport sciences.* (Vol. 3). Champaign, IL: Human Kinetics.

Beunen, G. (1989). Biological age in pediatric exercise research. In O. Bar-Or (Ed.), *Advances in pediatric sport sciences.* (Vol. 3). Champaign, IL: Human Kinetics.

Cahill, R. R. (1986). Prepubescent strength training gains support. *The Physician and Sportsmedicine, 14*(2), 157–161.

Clarke, H. H. (1968). Characteristics of the young athlete: A longitudinal look. *Kinesiology Review, 3,* 33–42.

Clarke, H. H. (1971). *Physical motor tests in the Medford boys' growth study.* Englewood Cliffs, NJ: Prentice-Hall.

Cooper Institute for Aerobics Research. (1992). *The Prudential Fitnessgram test administration manual.* Dallas: Cooper Institute for Aerobics Research.

Corbin, C. B., & Pangrazi, R. P. (1992). Are American children and youth fit? *Research Quarterly for Exercise and Sport, 63*(2), 96–106.

Duda, M. (1986). Prepubescent strength training gains support. *The Physician and Sportsmedicine, 14*(2), 157–161.

Glass, W. (1973, May/June). Coronary heart disease sessions prove vitally interesting. *California AHPER Journal,* 7.

Gould, D. (1987). Understanding attrition in children's sport. In O. Bar-Or (Ed.), *Advances in pediatric sport sciences* (Vol. 2). Behavioral issues. Champaign, IL: Human Kinetics.

Gruelich, W., & Pyle, S. (1959). *Radiographic atlas of skeletal development of the hand and wrist* (2nd ed.). Stanford, CA: Stanford University Press.

Hale, C. (1956). Physiological maturity of Little League baseball players. *Research Quarterly, 27,* 276–284.

Harter, S. (1978). Effectance motivation revisited. *Child Development, 21,* 34–64.

International Athletics Association Federation. (1983). Not kid's stuff. *Sports Medicine Bulletin, 18*(1), 11.

Krahenbuhl, G. S., & Pangrazi, R. P. (1983). Characteristics associated with running performance in young boys. *Medicine and Science in Sports, 15*(6), 486–490.

Malina, R. M. (1978). Physical growth and maturity characteristics of young athletes. In R. A. Magill, M. H. Ash, & F. L. Smoll (Eds.), *Children and youth in sport: A contemporary anthology.* Champaign, IL: Human Kinetics.

Malina, R. M. (1980). Growth, strength, and physical performance. In G. A. Stull & T. K. Cureton (Eds.), *Encyclopedia of physical education, fitness, and sports.* Salt Lake City, UT: Brighton.

National Strength and Conditioning Association. (1985). Position paper on prepubescent strength training. *National Strength and Conditioning Association Journal, 7*(4), 27–31.

Ozmun, J. C., Mikesky, A. E., & Surburg, P. R. (1991). Neuromuscular adaptations during prepubescent strength training (abstract). *Medicine and Science in Sports and Exercise, 23*(4), S31.

Pate, R. R., Dowda, M., & Ross, J. G. (1990). Associations between physical activity and physical fitness in American children. *American Journal of Diseases of Children, 144,* 1123–1129.

Payne, V. G., & Morrow, Jr., J. R. (1993). Exercise and VO$_2$max in children: A meta-analysis. *Research Quarterly for Exercise and Sport, 64*(3), 305–313.

Petersen, G. (1967). *Atlas for somatotyping children.* The Netherlands: Royal Vangorcum Ltd.

Petlichkoff, L. M. (1992). Youth sport participation and withdrawal: Is it simply a matter of fun? *Pediatric Exercise Science, 4*(2), 105–110.

Rarick, L. G. (Ed.). (1973). *Physical activity, human growth and activity.* New York: Academic.

Rarick, L. G., & Dobbins, D. A. (1975). Basic components in the motor performances of children six to nine years of age. *Medicine and Science in Sports, 7*(2), 105–110.

Roche, A. F., Chumlea, W. C., & Thissen, D. (1988). *Assessing the skeletal maturity of the handwrist: Fels method.* Springfield, IL: Thomas.

Rose, H. E., & Mayer, J. (1968). Activity, calorie intake, fat storage and the energy balance of infants. *Pediatrics, 41,* 18–29.

Rose, K. (1968). To keep people in health. *Journal of the American College Health Association, 22,* 80.

Ross, J. G., & Gilbert, G. G. (1985). The national children and youth fitness study: A summary of findings. *Journal of Physical Education, Recreation, and Dance, 56*(1), 45–50.

Ross, J. G., Pate, R. R., Corbin, C. C., Delpy, L. A., & Gold, R. S. (1987). What is going on in the elementary physical education program? *Journal of Physical Education, Recreation, and Dance, 58*(9), 78–84.

Rowland, T. W. (1990). *Exercise and children's health.* Champaign, IL: Human Kinetics.

Rowland, T. W. (1991). Effects of obesity on aerobic fitness in adolescent females. *American Journal of Disease in Children, 145,* 764–768.

Sallis, J. F., & McKenzie, T. L. (1991). Physical education's role in public health. *Research Quarterly of Exercise and Sport, 62,* 124–137.

Servedio, F. J., Bartels, R. L., Hamlin, R. L., Teske, D., Shaffer, T., & Servedio, A. (1985). The effects of weight training, using Olympic style lifts, on various physiological variables in prepubescent boys. Abstracted. *Medicine and Science in Sports and Exercise, 17,* 288.

Sheldon, W. H., Dupertuis, C. W., & McDermott, E. (1954). *Atlas of men: A guide for somatotyping the adult male at all ages.* New York: Harper & Row.

Shephard, R. J. (1984). Physical activity and child health. *Sports Medicine 1,* 205–233.

Simons-Morton, B. B., Parcel, G. S., O'Hara, N. M., Blair, S. N., & Pate, R. R. (1988). Health-related physical fitness in childhood: Status and recommendations. *American Review of Public Health, 9,* 403–425.

Tanner, S. M. (1993). Weighing the risks: Strength training for children and adolescents. *The Physician and Sportsmedicine, 21*(6), 105–116.

Thomas, J. R., & Tennant, L. K. (1978). Effects of rewards on changes in children's motivation for an athletic task. In F. L. Smoll & R. E. Smith (Eds.), *Psychological perspectives in youth sports.* New York: Hemisphere.

U.S. Public Health Service. (1990). *Health people 2000: National health promotion and disease prevention objectives.* Washington, DC: U.S. Government Printing Office.

Weltman, A., Janney, C., Rians, C. B., Strand, K., Berg, B., Tippitt, S., Wise, J., Cahill, B. R., & Katch, F. I. (1986). The effects of hydraulic resistance strength training in pre-pubertal males. *Medicine and Science in Sports and Exercise, 18,* 629–638.

Whitehead, J. R., & Corbin, C. B. (1991). Effects of fitness test type, teacher, and gender on exercise intrinsic motivation and physical self-worth. *Journal of School Health, 61,* 11–16.

Wilmore, J. H., & McNamara, J. J. (1974). Prevalence of coronary disease risk factors in boys, 8 to 12 years of age. *Journal of Pediatrics, 84,* 527–533.

Chapter THREE

Teaching Motor Skills

In this chapter, you will learn...

◆ *About normal motor development patterns among children*

◆ *When children are ready to learn motor skills*

◆ *How to get students to want to learn new skills*

◆ *What type of feedback helps youngsters learn motor skills*

◆ *The most effective ways to use practice time for maximum learning*

◆ *Why variable learning experiences are important when learning motor skills*

◆ *How transfer of learning affects new skills to be learned*

◆ *Why it is important to teach skills in proper progression*

◆ *What skill performance principles youngsters should know*

The learning process involved in mastering motor skills can be made more productive when teachers understand basic motor learning research. The applications vary with the stage of learning, the activity presented, and the maturity of the children. A key issue to remember is that the elementary years are a time for children to learn the proper way of performing skills. The product or outcome (making a basket, etc.) is much less important than learning correct skill technique. Learning motor skills demands repetition and refinement; children sould be allowed to practice over and over. The following sections offer direction for creating an environment of understanding and support for optimal learning.

Motor Patterns Common to All Children

The development of motor skills is an individual matter, and wide variation occurs among children of similar chronological age. However, the developmental sequence of skill among youngsters is similar and progresses in an orderly fashion. Three developmental patterns typify the growth of elementary school children.

1. Development, in general, proceeds from head to foot (cephalocaudal); that is, coordination and management of body parts occur in the upper body before they are observed in the lower. If youngsters lack coordination in the upper body, they may find it difficult to perform foot and leg skills that demand agility and coordination. Children can throw before they can kick; toss and catch before they can jump rope, and dribble a ball with their hands before they can dribble a soccer ball with their feet.

2. Development occurs from inside to outside (proximodistal). For example, children control their arms before they learn to control their hands. They can reach for objects before they can grasp them. This implies youngsters will be better able to catch large objects such as a beachball because they can catch it with their arms rather than their hands. A smaller object such as a beanbag not only moves more quickly but it also requires catching with the hands and fingers.

3. Development proceeds from the general to the specific. Gross motor movements occur before fine motor coordination and refined movement patterns. As children learn motor skills, nonproductive movement is gradually eliminated. One clear sign of motor learning at any age is the ability to eliminate wasteful and tense movement and concentrate on reproduction of a smooth and consistent product. This stage implies youngsters need to learn large-muscle movements when they are young and immature, such as running, jumping, and hopping. As they mature, they can refine their movements and do folk dances and sports requiring complex footwork, as well as catch objects moving in a somewhat unpredictable fashion.

When Skills Should Be Taught

One role of the teacher in teaching skills is to ascertain the time when children are capable and ready to learn, and then to design a learning environment that promotes the most effective development of the skills. A number of factors affect readiness, among them maturity level, previous practice, prerequisite skills, body management skills, and state of fitness. Interest in an activity also plays a role in readiness, because people do things that interest them. If youngsters do well at an activity, they want to learn more about the activity. People usually want to do well because of the social rewards that accompany success.

Maturity

Maturity level is defined as the gross physical and neural body management competencies necessary for a child to have a basis for success and to be challenged by the selected movement pattern. For example, children must have the ability to track a moving object before they can become proficient in catching skills. If children lack the capability to perform a task, the activity should be modified in a progressive manner. For instance, if children cannot catch a small, rapidly moving object, asking them to play a game involving softball skills results in failure. Increase the chance for success by using a large, brightly colored, and slower-moving object, such as a beachball, for practice sessions.

Prior Learning Experiences

Previous experience and prerequisite skills strongly impact the ability to learn new skills. A second-grader who began rope jumping in kindergarten would be ready for advanced activities that would frustrate an inexperienced student of similar age. *Prerequisite skills* refer to fundamental competencies needed for success in a later unit. For example, dribbling, trapping, and kicking skills are necessary prerequisites for successful participation in the game of soccer. In addition, physical health affects a child's readiness to learn. Children strong enough to perform skills, resist fatigue, and sustain the rigors of skill practice are more likely to achieve than are those with an inadequate fitness level.

State of Readiness

A learner's optimum state of readiness is the time when learning occurs most efficiently and with the least difficulty. Whenever possible, identify the optimum state for each student. This state of readiness will occur at different ages because students mature at different rates. When selecting learning activities for children, two questions should be asked: Are students ready for the activity? At what level of difficulty in activity progression should instruction begin? In an activity unit, use a start-and-expand approach. Begin at an entry level where all children are successful and expand the sequence of activities to a point where difficulty in execution is encountered by a majority of the class. At this point, arrange a learning situation for the development of new skills. Regardless of the perceived entry level for students, allow youngsters to practice at a level that is within their learning capabilities.

How to Create a Desire to Learn

Arousal is the level of excitement stress produces (Schmidt, 1991). The level of arousal can have a positive or negative impact on motor performance. The key to proper arousal is to find the "just right" amount. Too little arousal and the youngster is uninterested in learning. Too much arousal makes stress and anxiety a problem. High arousal fills youngsters with concern, worry, nervousness, and indecision. This results in an inability to learn, since high anxiety results in a decrease in motor performance. The goal is to arouse youngsters to a level where they are excited and confident about participation. The more complex the skill, the more easy it is for arousal to disrupt learning. On the other hand, if a skill is simple, such as skipping or running, a greater amount of arousal can be tolerated without causing a reduction in skill performance.

With children, competition should be used sparingly since it adversely affects the arousal levels of children. When competition is introduced in the early stages of skill learning, stress and anxiety reduce a child's ability to learn. On the other hand, if competition is introduced after skills have been overlearned, it improves the level of performance. Most children in elementary school have not overlearned skills, therefore minimize competitive situations when *teaching* skills. An example illustrates the point: The teacher's goal is to teach basketball dribbling. The teacher makes an instructional decision to place youngsters in squads and run a relay where they have to dribble to the opposite end of the gym and return. The first squad finished is the winner. The result: Instead of concentrating on proper dribbling form, students show more concern about winning the relay. They are overaroused and determined to run as quickly as possible. Dribbling is done poorly (if at all), the balls fly out of control, and the teacher is dismayed by the end result. The competitive situation overaroused youngsters who had not yet overlearned the dribbling skill.

How to Give Feedback about Skill Performance

Feedback is important when teaching skills because it reflects what is to be learned, what should be avoided, and how the performance can be modified. *Feedback* is any kind of information about skill performance. There are two types of feedback: intrinsic and extrinsic. *Intrinsic* feedback is internal and inherent to the performance of the skill and travels through the senses such as vision, hearing, touch, and smell. *Extrinsic* feedback is external and comes from an outside source such as a teacher, a videotape, a stopwatch, and so on. Teachers can control extrinsic feedback and decide whether and when to use it. When using feedback, it should be positive or constructive, given frequently, and contingent on performance or (preferably) effort. There are two major types of performance feedback: knowledge of results and knowledge of performance.

Knowledge of Results

Knowledge of results can be extrinsic or intrinsic. Intrinsic feedback occurs when the child watches a successful attempt occur, such as making a basket or striking a ball. Regardless of whether knowledge of results is extrinsic or intrinsic, no learning takes place without some type of feedback. Knowledge of results is a requisite for learning new motor skills. Teachers cannot manipulate intrinsic feedback, but they can regulate extrinsic feedback that offers students insight about improved results. Knowledge of results is most often verbal information about the performance of a goal—for example, telling players when they have succeeded at a task (see Figure 3.1). Following are some key points about knowledge of results:

FIGURE 3.1 *Students Need Knowledge of Results from Teachers*

1. Learners must be aware of errors they are making or practice will not improve skill performance. In many cases, both extrinsic and intrinsic feedback is similar and obvious (e.g., the teacher says a basket was made [extrinsic] and the student sees the ball go in the hoop [intrinsic]. However, in situations where children are unskilled, they need to know that successful results are occurring when the ball is hit farther or thrown more accurately. They need to be told they are approximating the desired goals.

2. Extrinsic feedback more quickly improves skill performance than intrinsic feedback in beginners. Verbal feedback is motivating for most youngsters.

3. Knowledge of results can be taught to learners so they know when they have made a successful approximation of the skill. The opposite side of the coin is that they must also know when they have made an error.

Knowledge of Performance

This type of feedback is similar to knowledge of results because it is usually verbal, extrinsic in nature, and occurs after skill performance. Whereas knowledge of results focuses on the outcome of a skill, knowledge of performance relates to the process of how the skill or a part of a skill was performed. Using this type of feedback requires reference to specific aspects of the learner's behavior (e.g., "I like the way you kept your chin on your chest" or "That's the way to step toward the target with your left foot"). Knowledge of performance is particularly effective with elementary children who are trying to learn new motor patterns. Since it is difficult for learners to evaluate their performance, they need extrinsic feedback from the teacher.

Knowledge of performance increases a youngster's motivation because it provides feedback about improvement of skill technique. Many youngsters become easily frustrated because they find it difficult to discern improvement. Teacher feedback provides a lift and a rededication to continued practice. Knowledge of performance is a strong reinforcer, particularly when the instructor mentions something performed correctly. This motivates youngsters to repeat the same pattern, ultimately resulting in improved performance. A most important aspect of feedback is to provide information for future patterns of action. Some suggestions for effectively giving knowledge of performance are:

1. Keep feedback about performance short and concise.

2. Feedback should be content filled and specific. It should tell the youngster exactly what was correct or incorrect (e.g., "That was excellent body rotation").

3. Feedback should not contain more than one key point because it confuses youngsters and makes concentration on performance difficult. Imagine a youngster who is told, "Step with the left foot, rotate the trunk, lead with the elbow, and snap the wrist on your next throw!" Excessive feedback confuses anyone trying to learn a new skill.

4. If choosing between knowledge of results and knowledge of performance, focus on knowledge of performance. Using knowledge of results to focus on the outcome without concern for the process of skill performance leads children to believe that learning to perform a skill correctly is unimportant and that only the outcome counts.

5. Focus knowledge of performance on performing a skill correctly with little emphasis on the outcome. A child who manages to get the ball into a basket might believe that the skill performance was performed correctly because of the outcome, even though the technical points of the shot were performed incorrectly.

6. Allow time for the youngster to internalize the feedback. Often, teachers tell a youngster something and at the same time ask them to "try it again." It is possible that the same mistake will be repeated since the youngster does not have time to concentrate on the feedback. Offer feedback about performance and move to another youngster.

7. Concentrate on a positive approach by praising progress and proper performance. Take care to assure that the praise reinforces specific phases of the performance. If a teacher praises simply by saying "Good job" to a child, there is a great deal of latitude for misinterpretation. For example, if the child was performing a forward roll, the teacher may have been praising foot position while the child thought head placement was the focus of the praise. Dwelling on criticism and identifying performances of poor quality encourage peer rejection. Make enough equipment available so each child is occupied in a movement task and has no time to observe and ridicule less skilled children. Total student involvement helps reduce stress and anxiety, as it decreases the child's concern that everybody is watching and waiting for him or her to fail.

How to Make Effective Use of Practice Time

Practice is the key to motor learning. For effective motor learning to take place, emphasis must be given to the quality and amount of practice. It is not enough that students receive the opportunity to practice, but they must also receive the maximum amount of practice in a physical education class and the practice must emphasize quality of movement (practicing correctly). This section will help you design practice sessions that optimize motor learning.

Make Practice Learning Oriented

Teachers generally have two interrelated goals when designing practice sessions. One is performance, which involves asking students to meet an outcome (product focused) such as hit 10 balls or make 5 baskets. The second goal focuses on proper learning of motor skill patterns (process focused). Reinforcing the process encourages students to modify their skill performance and to find the best possible way to perform the skill. This leads to a product/process conflict. Students who think the teacher is interested in how well they accomplish a product (e.g., make a basket) will be unwilling to take chances to properly learn the skill. To make practice learning oriented, place emphasis on searching for the best pattern and encouraging experimentation. With elementary school children who have learned few skills, emphasis on outcome decreases a student's desire to take risks and practice proper ways of performing a skill.

A way for teachers to avoid this conflict is to separate their goals for the practice sessions. If the focus of the lesson is to allow students an opportunity to learn, communicate this goal and reinforce students who are involved in experimentation and error correction. If the goal is to measure how much students have learned, indicate that the practice session is a test. Place emphasis on performing "your best" and rewarding students for their performance. A final note here: Most elementary school children are learning motor patterns, and excessive pressure to perform may stifle their willingness to try (especially less gifted children).

Decide on Whole versus Part Practice

The *whole method* of teaching skills refers to the process of learning the entire skill or activity in one dose. The *part method* first breaks learning into parts of the whole activity and then combines the parts into a unified whole. For example, in a rhythmic activity, teachers might teach each step in a dance and then put them together. A simple gymnastics routine could be broken into component parts and put back together for the performance.

The choice of the whole or the part method depends on the complexity and organization of the skill or activity to be learned. *Complexity* refers to the number of individual skills or components in a task. *Organization* defines how the parts are related to each other. High organization means that the parts of the skill are strongly related to each other, making it difficult to separate them. An example of a highly organized and complex skill is throwing, whereas a low-organized skill might be a folk dance. Generally, if the skill is high in complexity but low in organization, it can be taught in parts. If it is low in complexity but high in organization, it is best taught as a whole (see Figure 3.2). A final consideration is the duration or speed of the skill. If the skill is of short duration—such as throwing, batting, or kicking—trying to teach the skill in parts is probably futile. Imagine trying to slow down kicking while trying to teach it part by part. The performer would be unable to develop proper timing.

Another criterion for deciding whether to teach a skill in parts is to analyze the relationship of the parts. If each part can be performed independently of the others, the skill probably is conducive to part instruction. Even this is not as simple as it sounds, since the component skill may be dependent on the skill performed before it. For example, in a gymnastics routine, a student may be able to perform the activities separately, but find difficulty when sequencing them. Regardless, the ultimate goal is to perform the skill as a whole. Teaching a skill in parts is done only when it will optimize the amount of learning in a practice session.

FIGURE 3.2   *Practicing a New Motor Pattern*

Determine the Length and Distribution of Practice Sessions

Practice sessions that last a shorter time and involve relatively fewer repetitions usually produce more efficient learning than do longer sessions with more repetitions. This is probably due to physical and mental fatigue. Using varied approaches, challenges, and activities to develop the same skill helps maintain teacher and student motivational levels. For example, using many different types of beanbag activities offers novelty, which helps maintain motivation yet continues the focus on tossing and catching skills.

Another way to gauge the length of practice sessions is to examine the tasks being practiced. If the skill causes physical fatigue, demands intense concentration, or is simple and boring, practice sessions should be short and frequent with an adequate rest pause between intervals. In some cases, with elementary school children, it is effective to stop practicing the desired skill and play a game until youngsters regain their enthusiasm for learning. On the other hand, practice sessions can be longer and less frequent if the tasks contain much variety or are unique and novel.

Practice sessions offered over a longer time period are more effective than many sessions crowded into a shorter period. For example, trying to teach all skills at the start of the unit will probably decrease the amount learned. More effective learning occurs if skills are taught over a period of weeks or days. Combining practice and review effectively enhances skill learning. Activities can be taught in a short unit and practiced in review sessions spaced throughout the school year. In the initial stages of skill learning, it is particularly important that practice sessions be distributed in this way. In later stages, when increased success becomes self-motivating, individual practice sessions can be lengthened.

Use Random Practice Techniques

There are two basic ways to organize the presentation of activities to be taught. The first is *blocked practice*, where all the practice trials are completed before moving on to the next task. The other method is *random practice*, where the order of task presentations are mixed, assuring the learner never practices the same task twice in succession. Goode and Magill (1986) showed that random practice is the most effective approach to use when learning skills. Blocked practice gives the best results when skills are first introduced; however, students who learned through random practice demonstrated a higher level of retention over time.

The reason random practice results in increased learning is thought to be related to mental generation of solutions. When the same task is practiced over and over, not only do youngsters become bored but they do not think about the task to be learned. Since the same motor program is used over and over to complete the task, little effort or thinking is required. In contrast, students learning through random practice never practice the same task back to back. Therefore, they forget the motor program used and have to consciously re-create the solution to be successful. The application of random practice makes sense to teachers of children. Because youngsters become bored quickly when doing the same task over and over, random practice assures boredom will be minimized. Students learn more when a variety of tasks are built into lessons. Another drawback to blocked practice is that it gives learners false feedback about their performance. Since blocked practice is effective during practice (without lasting effects), learners might improve rapidly but not learn how to fine-tune each repetition. When the skill is then applied in a natural setting, the performance level is lower and youngsters feel discouraged about their decreased competency.

Is blocked practice ever effective? Blocked practice can be used during the early stages of learning a skill. The rapid improvement will enhance performance quickly and students will be motivated by their progress. After the initial learning of the skill, the switch can be made from blocked to random practice to assure learned skills are better retained.

Offer Variable Practice Experiences

Motor tasks are grouped into classes of tasks. For example, throwing is a collection of a class of movements. Throwing a ball in a sport setting requires many different adjustments, such as different speeds, different trajectories, and varying distances. Even though the throwing tasks are all different, the variations have fundamental similarities. Movements in a class usually involve the same body parts and have similar rhythm, but differ in the parameters of the skill. These differences in parameters form the basis of variable practice. Variable practice is important to use because it causes an increase in skill performance in a variable setting.

Just as practice should be random rather than blocked, variation should be introduced into practice sessions through variable practice sessions. This contrasts with constant practice, which focuses on similar experiences within a class of movements. Variable practice offers many different experiences within a movement class. Applied to a teaching situation, this implies having students practice *within* a skill class (throwing, kicking, etc.) with as many different experiences as possible. For example, instead of practicing shooting a number of baskets from the same spot, have students shoot from as many different angles and distances as possible. Even though the movement class is shooting, the variable shooting practice assures learned skills will be better retained.

Schmidt (1975) developed the schema concept, which explains why success occurs when a novel response is dictated. A *novel response* is defined as one that has not been performed in exactly the same manner in previous practice situations. It is almost impossible to practice all the possible responses that might occur in a game situation (e.g., different throwing positions, batting balls thrown at differing speeds and levels, etc.). How do you prepare students for the unlimited number of responses they will have to make as they participate in a number of activities? The schema theory offers a solution.

The schema theory implies that a motor skill should be learned under a variety of conditions and should be practiced in as many situations as possible to assure practice variability. Developing a broad set of experiences upon which a response foundation can be built allows youngsters to respond to the widest possible range of novel situations. To prepare children for novel responses, practice sessions should contain both a large amount of practice on the skill in a movement class and a variety of situations and parameters in which the skill is performed. One note: If the skill to be learned primarily involves a fixed way of performing it (a "closed" skill), such as placekicking a football or shooting a free throw, variability is much less important. However, most skills are "open," and responses are somewhat unpredictable, thereby making variability in practice the usual mode of operation. Fortunately, in this scenario, the theory coincides with the characteristics of children: They like variety and will practice longer when allowed to practice skills in different settings.

Understand Transfer of Learning

Transfer of learning is the effect that previous acquisition of skills and concepts has on the student's ability to learn new skills. Teachers want students to learn skills and be able to generalize them to the different situations they face throughout life. This ability to apply skills learned in practice to game situations is known as *generalization*. Transfer is most obvious and effective when a learner is just beginning to learn a skill. As the skill becomes learned, transfer becomes less important because the skill becomes more specific and has less in common with other similar skills. For example, a volleyball serve and a tennis serve may seem similar to a beginner and could facilitate early learning of the tennis serve. However, as the tennis serve becomes learned, it becomes more distinct and unique.

This discussion leads to the principle of *specificity*. There does not appear to be a general athletic trait that allows one student to excel in all areas. Therefore, when one skill is learned, it does not assure that other skills will be easily learned. Do not use performance in one skill area to predict success in another. Transfer of learning is quite specific. Learning to shoot a basketball does not make a student a better football passer. There is some transfer from fundamental movement skills (e.g., walking, hopping, jumping) to specific skills that incorporate these components.

Transfer is not automatic; rather, it occurs more readily when the novel skill pattern closely resembles a previously learned skill pattern. A learner may not cognitively recognize the similarity between skill patterns. It is important to make a conscious effort to discuss and apply generalizations about skills and skill applications in similar situations. In addition to transfer among similar tasks, transfer is more probable if the learner has a good understanding of the movement principles involved in the original task and has learned that task well. Throughout the program, the relevance of pertinent movement principles should be stressed when they are applicable. The following points should be considered to increase the probability for transfer of learning:

1. Try to identify common skill patterns among activities. For example, throwing a softball and hitting a volleyball might be similar. Serving a tennis ball and throwing are similar, and this could be pointed out in a tennis unit. Transfer occurs most when a well-learned skill can be used in a new setting.

2. Many specialized sport skills form the basis of later games and activities. Provide a variety of situations for students to practice these skills. The use of lead-up games is excellent if they focus and concentrate on specific skills in a gamelike setting. It is important to tell students how skills learned in the lead-up activities can be transferred to the actual sport.

3. When introducing a new skill, identify similarities with previous skills that youngsters have learned. Identify key points of performance among skills; this helps students transfer previously learned movement patterns to the new skill being practiced.

4. Discuss mechanical principles (see the next section of this chapter) that are basic to a class of skills students understand. For example, there are principles that are common to all situations involving propelling objects (e.g., opposition, weight transfer, development of torque, and follow-through).

Teach Skills in Proper Progression

Progression is defined as moving the learning process through ordered steps from basic to more challenging facets of an activity. The ideal starting point is a task that is one step beyond the student's present ability level, since this offers challenge and the opportunity for success. Youngsters develop at different rates and any single progression will not satisfy everyone's requirements.

Motor skills can be ranked in a hierarchy from simple to complex. Complex skills are difficult, if not impossible, to attain when fundamental skills have not been learned. The learning of fundamental motor skills requires considerable time and practice for refinement to take place. Fundamental skills must be overlearned so they can be performed automatically and without conscious effort. Eventually, this allows the child's thought processes to be directed toward learning new, complex movements or to thinking about strategy while performing sport activities.

Progression involves reviewing previously learned steps before proceeding to new material; further, the concept includes the development of prerequisite skills before experiencing a more complex activity. When teaching a new skill, it can be simplified by eliminating the locomotor parts in order to concentrate on the fine motor aspects of the skill. For example, a skill performed in place should precede the same skill performed while moving. A basketball dribble is simpler when done in place; later, it can be made more complex by adding locomotor movements. A further progression could be practiced by asking the dribbler to retain control while moving and being guarded.

Developmental Levels and Progression

To help teachers present skills in proper sequence, various activities have been listed in the lesson plans in progression from simple to complex. Activities for kindergarten through second-grade children are the least complex and form the foundation for more complex skills. The majority of these skills are performed individually or with a partner so as to increase the success of primary-grade children. Examples might be tossing and catching, striking a stationary object, and playing games that simply incorporate fundamental locomotor movements. The number of complex decisions to make while performing the skill is minimized so youngsters can concentrate on the skill at hand. As youngsters mature and progress into grades 3 and 4, the tasks become more difficult and many are performed individually or within small groups. More environmental factors such as different speeds of objects, different sizes of objects, and games requiring locomotor movements and specialized skills (throwing, catching, etc.) are introduced at this level. When students reach grades 5 and 6, students incorporate learned skills in a number of sport and game situations. Simple skills previously learned are sequenced into more complex motor patterns. Cognitive decisions about when to use a skill and how to incorporate strategy into the game are integrated into the learning experiences at this level.

Children learn skills in a natural progression, but not at the same rate. When progression is considered in the skill-learning process, youngsters are allowed to progress at a rate best suited for them. This means all children learn within a category of skills (throwing, striking, etc.) but progress at different rates and practice different skills within the category. This premise forms the basis for the current curriculum emphasis to offer a "developmentally appropriate physical education program" (Barrett, Williams, & Whitall, 1992).

Skill Performance Principles That Should Be Taught

Teaching physical skills to students requires knowing a few principles that are basic to groups of similar activities. For example, when throwing an object—whether it is a football, basketball, or softball, the same principles apply. When stopping the body—whether in a tag game, basketball activity, or gymnastics—similar skill performances can be applied. The following principles apply to these generic groups of skills.

Starting and Stopping the Body

The following general principles can be applied to starting and stopping the body in any activity.

The Ready Position
The ready position is used when preparing to catch an object, guard another player, or any other activity where movement in an unexpected direction must be taken. In the ready position, the feet are spread to shoulder width. For most skills, one foot is placed ahead of the other. The knees are bent slightly, the toes are pointed forward, and the weight is carried on the balls of the feet. In this position, the body can be moved equally well in any direction. The back should be reasonably straight, the head up, and the hands up ready for quick movement (see Figure 3.3).

Fast Starts
When a fast start in a known direction is desired (e.g., in a race or running with the ball in football), the feet are spread and pointed in the direction of the desired motion with the body leaning in the direction of the proposed movement. The center of gravity is moved forward (almost to the point of being off balance) and lowered somewhat by forward body lean and increased bending at the knees. This enhances a rapid shift of body weight in the direction of movement.

Stopping Forward Movement
When the body is stopped quickly, force must be absorbed to prevent falling. Primary-grade youngsters often fall forward when they stop because they fail to lower the center of gravity and widen the base of support (by spreading the feet apart). Bending at the ankles, knees, and hips and leaning back slightly will allow force to be absorbed over as long a period of time as possible. An important skill is to be able to stop without falling.

Changing Direction of Movement
Changing direction quickly is similar to stopping rapidly. Forward force must be absorbed and redirected in another direction. To effectively change direction without falling, youngsters should lower the center of gravity by bending at the ankles, knees, and hips and spreading the feet to make a wide base of support. As soon as the body is under control, forward movement continues in the desired direction.

FIGURE 3.3   Ready Position

Propelling Objects

Throwing, striking, kicking, and batting skills involve applying force to an object. Regardless of the specific skill, when trying to apply force to an object, the following principles help assure optimum performance.

Visual Concentration on the Object
In object propulsion, the eyes focus on some point, fixed or moving, depending on the skill. When striking an object, children should watch the ball. In shooting a basket or in bowling, performers should fix their gaze on the target. If kicking an object, children should keep their head down and watch the ball.

Opposition of Body Limbs
Opposition refers to the coordinated use of the arms and legs. When walking or running, leg movement is coordinated with arm movement on the oppo-site side of the body. For example, correct walking occurs when the right foot goes forward with the left arm moving forward. When performing a right-handed throw, a forward step toward the target is taken with left foot. Almost all skills that generate force to an object will demand opposition (i.e.,

a serve or throw with the left arm should be coordinated with a forward step with the right foot).

Transfer of Body Weight in the Direction of the Propelled Object

The transfer of weight from the back to the front foot (in line with the direction of the projectile) is a critical element in throwing, batting, and striking skills. Initially, the body weight is on the back foot, with the transfer of body weight occurring during execution of the skill. It is important to note that the weight is transferred to the forward foot just prior to the release of the ball in throwing skills, and just prior to batting or striking the object. It is nearly impossible to transfer body weight if opposition of body limbs does not occur.

Developing Body Torque

Development of torque involves the coordination of a series of body actions. Usually, the force is generated from the core of the body to the limb where force is applied. For example, in throwing, body torque begins by twisting the trunk away from the desired direction of the throw and then quickly untwisting to develop force. Since trunk muscles are strong, a great deal of torque can be generated by this untwisting motion. In throwing or batting, children should start with a forward motion of the hip and then rotate the trunk, thus adding force to the thrown or batted ball. This generation of body torque can separate good throwers from less able throwers. Youngsters who throw primarily with their arm will not be able to generate much force, which will result in weak throws.

Follow-Through

Follow-through refers to a smooth ending of the already-initiated movement. The principle is vitally important in throwing, striking, batting, and kicking skills. In kicking, the instruction is to kick through the ball, not at it. In batting, the normal swing must be fully completed, not arrested after a hit. When throwing, the arm must not be stopped, but continue until the force has diminished.

Catching Objects

Catching is an important skill in many activities and should be practiced with different objects, as each type presents a different challenge. Catching is a more difficult skill for children to learn since it requires visual tracking. Most youngsters, if given ample opportunity for practice and proper instruction, can achieve a mature pattern of catching by the age of 8. Mature catching form usually does not occur for another year or two, around the ages of 9 to 10 years.

Visually Focusing on the Moving Object

To catch a moving object, youngsters must learn to visually focus on the object until it is caught (also called *tracking*). In addition, hand-eye coordination is critical to assure that the youngster is able to move the hands into the path of the projectile. Primary-grade youngsters often focus on the thrower rather than the object. When teaching young children to catch, throwers should wave the object (a large ball or beachball) until the catcher is looking at the projectile. As children become more proficient, they can begin to track faster-moving (smaller) objects. The size and speed of the object is a critical element in catching. Fear of an object (because it is hard, small, and fast moving) will often slow the development of catching skills. Use soft, large, and slow-moving objects with beginners.

Moving the Body into the Path of the Object
The body should be positioned directly in line with the incoming object, and the weight should be transferred from the front to the rear foot as the object is caught. This helps spread the force of impact over time. Bending the knees as the catch is made will aid in absorbing the force and making the catch easier. Spread the feet to increase body stability.

Absorbing the Force of the Object with the Hands
Youngsters should reach for the object and then draw the object toward the body as the catch is made. This is known as *giving*. Giving with the hands and arms allows force to be absorbed over a longer period of time and helps prevent the object from rebounding out of the hands. The catch should be made with the pads of the fingers, which are spread and relaxed.

References and Suggested Readings

AAHPERD. (1987a). *Basic stuff, series I.* Reston, VA: AAHPERD.

AAHPERD. (1987b). *Basic stuff, series II.* Reston, VA: AAHPERD.

Barrett, K. R., Williams, K., & Whitall, J. (1992). What does it mean to have a "developmentally appropriate physical education program"? *The Physical Educator, 49*(3), 113–117.

Goode, S., & Magill, R. A. (1986). The contextual interference effects in learning three badminton serves. *Research Quarterly for Exercise and Sport, 57,* 308–314.

Schmidt, R. A. (1975). A schema theory of discrete motor skill learning. *Psychological Review, 82,* 225–260.

Schmidt, R. A. (1991). *Motor learning and performance: From principles to practice.* Champaign, IL: Human Kinetics.

Chapter FOUR

Implementing an Effective Physical Education Lesson

In this chapter, you will learn...

- ◆ *How to prepare and distribute equipment for a lesson*
- ◆ *How to make effective use of class time*
- ◆ *About the size of the teaching space and its impact on effective management*
- ◆ *Different teaching formations used in physical education instruction*
- ◆ *How to plan lessons that optimize skill learning*
- ◆ *Ways to enhance learning during practice sessions*
- ◆ *How to facilitate cognitive development through physical education*
- ◆ *Ways to develop positive attitudes and values toward activity*
- ◆ *Instructional cues and how they help students learn physical skills*
- ◆ *Ways to maintain an effective class environment*
- ◆ *Methods of delivering feedback in ways that stimulate learning*

Planning is an integral part of effective teaching that assures a sequential and creative lesson is implemented. Designing an effective presentation involves planning prior to the start of the lesson. Preinstructional planning makes teaching less stressful and reduces unexpected events.

Before You Start the Lesson

Preinstructional decisions include selecting teaching styles, effectively using allotted time and teaching space, and arranging students in an instructional formation. Next follows the actual design and implementation of the lesson plan, using a format that is flexible and meaningful. It has been estimated that teachers make up to 200 decisions a minute while teaching. The complexity of teaching is simplified when as many decisions as possible can be made prior to the actual lesson presentation. A number of decisions that need to be made prior to the lesson are discussed in the following sections.

Secure and Check Equipment

Prior to the lesson, teachers need to know exactly what equipment is available and in working condition. Rolling out a cart of basketballs only to find that half of them are not inflated results in a deflated teacher and a rough start to the lesson. Before beginning, determine how much equipment is available; this, in turn, will define the structure of the lesson and how students will be grouped. For example, if there are only 16 paddles and balls for a class of 30, some type of sharing or station work will have to be organized.

How Much Equipment Is Necessary?
How much equipment is enough? If it is personal equipment—such as beanbags, jump ropes, paddles, or balls—there should be one piece of equipment for each student. If it is group-oriented equipment, such as tumbling mats, there should be enough to assure waiting lines of no more than four students. Sometimes, teachers settle for less equipment because they teach as they have been taught. An often-observed example finds an instructor teaching volleyball with plenty of available equipment but using only a small amount of it. Rather than have students practice individually (each with a ball) against the wall or with a partner, the teacher divides them into two long lines and uses one or two balls. The majority of equipment remains on the sidelines and most of the instruction time is spent waiting in line rather than practicing skills.

If equipment is limited, it is necessary to adapt instruction for the time being. Be careful, however, about accepting limited equipment without expressing concern—many administrators believe that teachers can "make do." Communicate with the educational leader on a regular basis, explaining that instruction could be much more effective if more equipment were available. Ask parent-teacher groups to conduct fund-raisers to help purchase necessary equipment. Math teachers are not expected to teach math without a book for each student, and physical education cannot be done without adequate equipment. If you settle for less, you end up with less.

Teaching with Minimal Equipment

What are temporary alternatives when equipment is lacking? A common solution is to teach using the station format. This involves dividing students into small groups so each group has enough equipment. For example, in a softball unit, some students might practice fielding, others batting, others making the double play, and so on. Another approach is to divide the class in half and allow one group to work on one activity while another is involved in an unrelated activity. For example, due to a shortage of beanbags, half of the class is involved in practice while the other half is jumping rope. This approach is not as educationally sound and it increases the managerial and instructional demands made on the instructor.

Another approach is the peer review technique. While one student practices an activity, a peer is involved in offering feedback and evaluation. The two share the equipment and take turns being involved in practice and evaluation. The final approach is to do what is most commonly done— design drills that involve standing in line and waiting for a turn. In most cases, this is the least acceptable from an educational standpoint.

Distribute Equipment Quickly

When using equipment, the initial arrangement of the equipment can facilitate a quality lesson. An effective method for distributing individual equipment is to place it around the perimeter of the area. It is the fastest approach and allows students to assume personal responsibility for quickly acquiring a piece of apparatus. Time spent getting a piece of equipment is time unavailable for learning. Large apparatus should be placed in the safest possible manner. This implies arranging it so that all pieces are visible to the teacher from all angles. The initial setup of equipment depends on the focus of the lesson. For example, the height of the basket can be reduced to emphasize correct shooting form. The height of the volleyball net can be lowered to allow spiking. Nets may be placed at different heights to allow different types of practice. Equipment and apparatus should be modified to best suit the needs of the learner. There is nothing sacred about a 10-foot basket or regulation-sized ball. If modifying the equipment improves the quality of learning, change it.

Maximize Learning in a Minimal Amount of Time

Several decisions need to be made about time management prior to instruction. How the time allotted for the total lesson is utilized has been discussed previously. The amount of time allowed for fitness and skill development directly influences what is accomplished in a physical education program. For example, assume a teacher decides to use 10 additional minutes per lesson for fitness development. The end result is an increase of nearly 30 hours of time devoted to physical fitness during the school year. How time is used greatly affects whether program objectives are met.

Another advantage of programming how lesson time is used lies in accountability. Assume that evaluation shows student performance in throwing is subpar. If a stipulated amount of time is not consistently apportioned for the development of throwing skills, it is difficult to ascertain whether insufficient time was the reason for the lack of progress.

Pace the Lesson to Increase Learning

The pace of a lesson is related to time. Know when to terminate practice sessions and move on to new activities. For example, students become bored and begin to display off-task behavior if practice sessions are excessively long. Knowing the right time to refocus their attention on a varied task is important. In most cases, it is better to err on the short side rather than allow practice to the point of fatigue and boredom and the ensuing class management problems.

Timing the pace of a lesson is difficult since it involves a certain "feel" about the class. A rule of thumb is to refocus or change the task when five or more students are off task. If it is necessary to stay on the current task, a few options for extending the length of the practice session are available.

1. *Refocus the class.* This is accomplished by asking the class to observe a specific student's performance. Another method is to explain the importance of the skill and how it helps develop skills the children can use in games and sports.

2. *Refine or extend the task.* Stop the class and ask the children to improve their technique by improving a phase of their performance or adding a more difficult variation. This approach redefines the challenge as a more difficult variation of the skill they were practicing.

3. *Stop and evaluate.* Stop the class and evaluate the youngsters' performances. Students can work with a partner and check for key points. Place emphasis on evaluating and correcting the performance. Practice can resume after a few minutes of evaluation.

Another impact on pacing is whether the lesson is teacher or student directed. When a teacher directs the pace, timing is controlled by the instructor, and students are expected to perform the same task at the same time. Determining whether a presentation should be teacher or student paced depends on the type of skill being taught. If the skill is closed in nature (only one way to perform or respond), teacher pacing is most effective. Teacher pacing can be accompanied by verbal cues and modeling behavior. Teacher pacing is effective in learning skills that are novel or new to the learner because the cues and visual imagery help the learner develop a conception of the pattern to be performed. Student pacing allows learners to progress at their own rate. It is effective when open skills are being learned and a variety of responses are preferred or encouraged.

Vary the Size of the Teaching Space

A common mistake is to take a class to a large practice area, tell the children what task to accomplish, and fail to define or limit the space where it should be performed. The children spreads out in an area so large it makes it impossible to communicate with and manage the class. The size of the space is dictated by skills being practiced and the ability of the teacher to control the class. Delineating a small area for participation makes it easier to control a class. As students become more responsive, the size of the area can be enlarged. Regardless of the size of the space, the practice area must be defined. An easy way to mark the participation area is to set up cones or marking spots around the perimeter. Chalk lines, evenly spaced equipment, or natural boundaries can also be used to signal restraining lines.

A factor that affects the size of the practice area is whether or how much feedback needs to be administered. If students are learning a closed skill and need feedback and redirection regularly, it is important they stay in proximity to the instructor. An effective approach is to establish a smaller area where students move on signal for instruction and then return to the larger area for practice. If this approach is used, care must be taken to prevent wasting time moving between areas.

Another way to effectively use space is to divide it into smaller areas to maximize student participation. For example, a volleyball game where only 12 students can play on one available court may leave many students waiting. In most cases, it is more effective to divide the area into two courts to facilitate a greater number of students. A related consideration when partitioning space is safety. If the playing areas are too close together, it is possible that players from one area might run into players in the other area. For example, it is unsafe in a softball setting if a player on one field can hit a ball into another playing field. In most cases, the safety of students can be ensured by careful planning.

Implement a Variety of Instructional Formations

Different instructional formations or arrangements can be used to facilitate learning experiences. Different formations are needed for activities in place (nonlocomotor), activities in which children move (locomotor), and activities in which balls, beanbags, or other objects are thrown, kicked, caught, or otherwise received (manipulative activities). Selecting a formation should focus on assuring maximum activity for all students. When small groups are used, no more than four students should be placed in a squad. This minimizes the amount of time spent standing and waiting for a turn. The following are some of the more common formations used when teaching physical education.

Mass or Scattered Formation
By far, the most common and most useful formation is the scattered formation. Children are scattered throughout the area in random fashion so each student has personal space. This formation is useful for in-place activities and when individuals need to move in every direction. From the beginning, emphasis should be placed on not bumping into or interfering with other children. Scattered formation is basic to personal equipment activities such as wands, hoops, individual rope jumping, and individual ball skills.

Extended Squad Formation
Extended squad formation is a structured formation based on squad organization. In formal squad formation, members stand about 3 feet apart in a col-

FIGURE 4.1   Regular and Extended Squad Formation

Regular Ⓛ **X X X X X X**

Extended Ⓛ **X X X X X X**

FIGURE 4.2   Partner Formation

umn. In extended formation, the squad column is maintained with more distance (10 to 15 feet) between members. Figure 4.1 shows a regular and an extended squad formation.

Partner Formation

Partner formation is most important in throwing, catching, kicking, and receiving activities. One ball or object is needed for each pair. On the playground, where there is sufficient room, pairs can scatter. Indoors, keeping pairs aligned in somewhat parallel fashion minimizes problems with moving projectiles (see Figure 4.2).

Small Groups

The small-group formation is similar to the partner arrangement but includes a few more children. Children work together on either a fundamental movement problem or ball skills.

Lane or File

Lane, or file, arrangement is the basic relay formation (see Figure 4.3). It can be used for locomotor activity, with those in front moving as prescribed and then taking their place at the rear of the lane.

Squad Formation with Leader

Squad formation with a leader (or lane-plus-one formation) is useful for fitness activities. It is useful for throwing and catching skills. Each leader is positioned a short distance in front of the squad (see Figure 4.4).

FIGURE 4.3   Lane, or File, Formation

X X X X
X X X X
X X X X
X X X X
X X X X
X̲ X̲ X̲ X̲

FIGURE 4.4   Squad Formation with Leaders

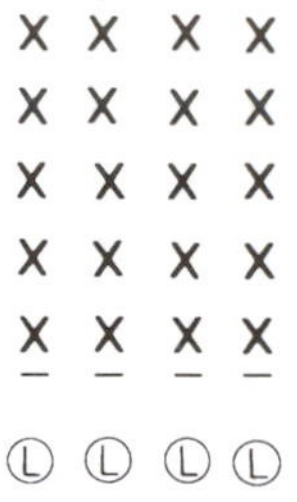

X X X X
X X X X
X X X X
X X X X
X X X X

Ⓛ Ⓛ Ⓛ Ⓛ

Increase the Effectiveness of Instruction

The importance of planning a lesson cannot be overemphasized. It is possible to present a lesson without planning, but the quality of the lesson can, in almost all cases, be improved through preparation and a well-sequenced plan. A strong case for planning can be made if a teacher wants to be creative and develop the ability to interact with students. Teachers, regardless of their experiences and abilities, have many elements to remember while teaching. When presenting a lesson, situations occur that are impossible to predict—for example, dealing with discipline problems; needing to modify the lesson spontaneously; relating to students by name; and offering praise, feedback, and reinforcement. If the content of the lesson is planned, written, and readily available, energy and concentration do not have to be focused solely on the content of the presentation. Competency determines the depth of the lesson-planning effort. More research and reading has to be done for an activity when the teacher has little experience. The scope of the curriculum is limited by an unwillingness to prepare and learn new skills and knowledge.

A major reason for planning is to assure the instructional presentation results in student learning. If students do not learn, teachers are failing. If the ball is rolled out of the closet and students are left on their own, little learning, if any, occurs. Allowing students to choose sides and play games without the input of a teacher leaves learning to chance. The following points can be used to develop an effective lesson plan that facilitates and maximizes student learning.

Optimize Skill Learning through Planning

A major objective of physical education is to improve skill performance. Students expect to be physically educated. If they go to a math class, they expect to learn math. Teachers owe students an educational experience rather than a recreational one. A well-developed lesson plan answers the following questions.

1. Is there a purpose to the lesson? The lesson should be designed to improve the skill performance of students. What is the purpose of the total program and the lesson plan? If the lesson presentation does not contribute to the fitness and skill development of participants, it is difficult to justify. Know why an activity is taught and how it fits into a developmental scheme designed for optimal student growth.

2. Is instruction part of the lesson? Instruction should be an observable action. There are many different methods for accomplishing instructional goals, but there must be instruction. Instruction can take many forms, such as working individually with students, evaluating a student's progress on a contingency contract, developing task cards, and conducting group instruction. Regardless of the method used, physical education instruction must occur as a regular and consistent part of the lesson. It is difficult to justify a program that concentrates only on recreational aspects. The recreational approach allows the rich to get richer and the poor to get poorer. For example, if the ball is rolled out for basketball games, the skilled players will handle the ball more and dominate the less skilled players. Under the pressure of competition, unskilled students find it difficult to think about technique and proper performance. Therefore, game situations usually benefit students who have already learned the basic skills.

3. How does the lesson integrate with past and future instruction? It is important to know the types of experiences students have participated in prior to the current lesson. Elementary school teachers must be cognizant of activities that have been presented at other grade levels so they can integrate their instruction with these past experiences.

4. Are the lessons planned to assure skill instruction and pratice occur throughout the unit? Skill development activities should be evenly spread throughout a unit so instruction is sequential and regular. Offering skill instruction only during the first day or two of a unit makes it difficult for students to develop new motor skill patterns. The opportunity for practice and learning new skills must be presented in many short sessions throughout the entire unit.

Your teaching philosophy plays a large part in determining whether planning will take place. Do you believe youngsters must learn on their own and that the total responsibility for learning lies on the students' shoulders? Or do you believe that student and teacher share the burden of learning in an environment where both are determined and dedicated to educational goals? How planning for skill development is done strongly influences what students learn. If you do not assume the responsibility for assuring that students learn new skills and refine old ones, who will?

Effectively Use Practice and Activity Time

Students can listen to an instructor, read books, and watch gifted athletes and still not improve their motor skill performance. Without practice sessions emphasizing skill development, participants will demonstrate little improvement in their level of performance. American society has a fetish for buying books that discuss how to improve everything from aerobics to Zen. Many people spend a great deal of money for private lessons and never practice on their own. Students do not learn new skills if the lesson does not include effective practice sessions. Of all the elements that go into learning new skills, *correct practice* is the most critical and necessary. Plan a lesson that assures necessary instruction and maximizes the amount of productive practice time for the learner.

Maximize Practice Time

Analyze reasons students do not receive the maximum amount of activity in a lesson. Perhaps there is a limited amount of equipment, and students have to wait to take their turn. Consider how much time can be wasted standing in line waiting for a turn. Contemplate the following example: Students are organized into groups of nine to practice basketball shooting skills. Unfortunately, there is only one ball available for each group of nine students. Assume that it takes 20 seconds to shoot three shots and recover the ball. Each student in the group will have to stand in line nearly 3 minutes before receiving a turn. If the drill continues for 15 minutes, each student receives little more than 1 minute of productive practice. Small wonder youngsters do not learn skills when such drills are used.

Effectively Involve All Students

Another factor that may limit practice time is class organization. Organize two or more games rather than rotate youngsters in and out of a game. Use activities that maximize participation and that do not eliminate students. Often, the least gifted student is eliminated first and stands on the side waiting for a new game or activity. Students learn little, if anything, standing in line or waiting on the sidelines to return to an activity.

Avoid Embarrassing Students

Another point to consider when organizing lessons for maximum practice is the type of environment in which the practice takes place. Drills should provide private and sensitive practice settings. Students should not be placed in a setting where they have to exhibit their mistakes and errors in front of peers. Not all of this can be prevented, but much can be done to enhance the quality of the setting. For example, students have friends who might accept their errors without comment. Many drills are best done with a friend in a one-on-one setting. Another alternative is to assign individual homework or to allow students to work at a personalized pace with the guidance of a contingency contract. Whenever possible, try to ease the burden of learning new skills by reducing the fear of failing in front of peers.

Use Drills That Facilitate Skill Development

Quality control within practice sessions are necessary to help students learn skills correctly. Drills in practice sessions must be related to the desired skill outcome. Poorly designed drills result in students learning skills incorrectly. For example, assume students are learning to dribble a basketball. To teach dribbling in a different context, students are organized into squads for a dribbling relay that requires them to dribble the length of the floor, make a basket, and return. Odds are this drill will result in improper skill development because students concentrate on other things beside dribbling. Some students worry about making the basket, others are more concerned about speeding down and back, and still others are preoccupied with failing in front of their peers. Few students focus on dribbling the ball under control with proper form. The result is a situation where little effective and correct dribbling practice takes place.

When developing drills, eliminate as many distracting factors as possible. Identify elements that prevent students from correctly practicing the skills. Is the drill designed to offer effective and productive practice, or is it just a way of keeping students busy? What stipulations have been made to assure students practice correctly? Does the drill serve as a lead-in to actual use in an activity, or is it useful in and for itself? Examine each drill and modify it accordingly when it appears desired skill outcomes are not being enhanced.

Consider the Developmental Level of Students

To make instruction effective, present activities in a manner consistent with the developmental level of students. Even though students develop in a consistent pattern, there is great variability among individual children as to when they will be capable of mastering certain skills. Approach instruction in a flexible and caring manner, knowing that instruction needs to be as varied and unique as students in the class. Because an activity is designed for fourth-grade students does not mean all fourth-graders will be able to accomplish it (see Chapter 2 regarding maturity). When necessary, present activities that best suit individual students regardless of the recommended level.

Make It Challenging, Not Threatening

Deciding on a best way to arrange activities for instruction is difficult because schools group children by chronological age and grade rather than by developmental level. Classroom teachers, responsible for a graded group of youngsters, find it difficult to understand how to adjust for developmental levels. Take into account the past experiences of students to assure that the type of experiences offered help them reach educational outcomes. Design drills and activities that are challenging but not threatening. An important key is to understand that an activity is challenging or threatening based on the student's perception, not the instructor's. An activity is challenging when the learner believes it is difficult but achievable. It is threatening when the learner perceives it to be an impossible task. The same drill can be challenging to some students and threatening to others. This is what makes teaching a difficult task—trying to sort out how students perceive various activities.

A well-planned lesson allows students to progress at different rates of learning. This does not have to be done at all times, since students can stand a certain amount of failure. On the other hand, if they are fed a steady diet of failure, they come to believe they are failures, leaving little reason for trying. The more opportunities allowed for individual or partner practice, the greater the chance for self-paced learning. In most cases, when students find an activity too difficult, they will avoid it. The percentage of students off task increases quickly, illustrating the need to modify the activity. If students complain loudly, the activity should be carefully reviewed. If given the opportunity, students will offer productive and effective modifications.

A final word on customizing activities to developmental skill levels: Students need to succeed a majority of the time if they are going to develop positive feelings about activity during adulthood. An instructor is in the position of being able to force (through punishment or embarrassment) students to do just about anything within the educational setting. If they are forced into activities that result in a great deal of failure, students will probably dislike and avoid activity for all their lives. If you are concerned with giving students lifetime skills and attitudes, try to monitor and adjust lesson activities regularly. One of the most serious errors committed by teachers occurs when they lose their sensitivity to the learners' perceptions and feelings.

Teach to Improve Creative Responses

To develop creativity, you must integrate originality and personality into the teaching process. Some personalities are better suited to such emphasis and methods than others. Through creativity, a child is stimulated to become a self-propelled learner, to develop habits of discovery and reflective thinking, and to increase retention of concepts. When children discover cognitive elements by themselves, the concepts are better retained and more easily retrieved for future use.

Allow Time for Creativity

An approach for encouraging creativity is to set aside time at the beginning of a movement experience, before instruction, and allow youngsters to explore creatively. For example, youngsters can be given a hoop and told, "Experiment with the different kinds of things you can do with it." Some educators believe strongly in this practice. They maintain that direction stifles creativity and that children should have the opportunity to try, become familiar, and explore the range of movement possibilities before more defined instruction occurs. Opposing this viewpoint are those who believe that a rudimentary level of learning occurs without direction and that more productive and creative activity is possible when the teacher transmits simple basics before experimentation begins.

Provide creative opportunity during appropriate segments of the instructional sequence. This can take the form of asking children to add on to a movement progression just presented or to expand it in a new direction. Time for creativity can be allowed in the lesson plan to allow for creativity at teachable moments. Allowing an opportunity for creativity after a few progressions have been taught gives breadth to movement responses. Creativity is furthered by the judicious use of movement factors, particularly sequence building and continuity.

Allow Students to Demonstrate Their Creations

The creative process can be stimulated by show-and-tell demonstrations. After a period of exploration, discussion centers on what types of movement patterns are possible to create. Children naturally observe others when they reach a block or are stymied in their thinking. Although concentration should be on developing unique patterns, ideas from others can be a base for devising alternatives.

Encourage Cognitive Development

Learning can be enriched by encouraging students to discover ways of improving techniques or remedying problems they are having in skill performance. They can be given opportunities to help each other diagnose and improve techniques. Strategies for game situations can be developed through group discussions and planning. The point is not to detract from skill learning and performance, but to enrich and enhance learning situations so students can internalize them in a more personalized and meaningful manner. A golden rule does not have to be taught in every lesson, but little will be learned if teachers fail to offer integrated presentations regularly.

Accept Student Input

Cognitive development can be enhanced by allowing student input into instructional activities. This is not meant to suggest students will decide what, when, and how learning will take place, but rather that students can help improve the structure of learning tasks. There are many advantages to involving students in the instructional process, including the following:

- Students usually select experiences that are in line with their abilities and skill levels.
- Youngsters feel better about an environment in which they have some input. Positive self-concepts are the result of situations where learners help determine their own destinies.
- When lessons fail because incorrect decisions were made, students shoulder some of the responsibility if they offered input. This helps develop decision-making skills that focus on personal responsibility.

Decision making and involvement in the learning process are learned. People need an opportunity to make decisions and be placed in situations where they can realize the impact of their decisions. This means an opportunity to make incorrect as well as correct decisions. There is no decision making involved if only correct decisions are accepted and approved by the teacher. Soon, students begin to choose not to make decisions at all rather than risk making an incorrect choice.

Encourage Students to Make Decisions

Responsibility is learned. When students are allowed to begin making decisions at a young age, the stakes are much less compared to when they grow older. Allow children to make decisions and choose from alternatives. Making choices should be done in a gradual and controlled manner by using some of the following strategies.

1. Present a limited number of choices. This still gives you ultimate control of the situation, but offers students a chance to make deci-

sions about how the outcome will be reached. This may be a wise choice when learners have had little opportunity for decision making in the past. An example is to permit students the choice of practicing either a drive or a pass shot in a hockey unit. The outcome is to practice striking the puck, but students make the choice about which one they want to practice.

2. Allow students the opportunity to modify an activity. In this setting, learners are allowed to modify the difficulty or complexity of the skill being practiced. If used effectively, it allows learners to adapt the activity to suit their individual skill levels. Involving them in this process reduces the burden of the teacher, who no longer has to decide about exceptions and student complaints that "it is too hard to do" or "I'm bored." It becomes the student's responsibility to personalize the task. Options allowed could be to change the rules or to change the implement being used. It might mean changing the number of players on a team or using a ball that moves slowly. Some examples are:
   a. Using a slower-moving family ball rather than a handball
   b. Increasing the number of fielders in a softball game
   c. Lowering the basket in a basketball unit
   d. Decreasing the length of a distance run or the height of hurdles

3. Offer tasks that are open ended. This allows children the most latitude to make decisions about the content of the lesson. In this situation, tell them the task and make it their responsibility to decide how it will be reached. The teacher determines the educational outcome while the student decides the means used to reach it. As students become adept in using this approach, they learn to develop alternatives. Examples that might be used at this level are as follows:
   a. "Develop a game that requires four passes before a shot at the goal."
   b. "Plan a floor exercise routine that contains a forward roll, backward roll, and cartwheel."
   c. "Design a long-rope jumping routine that involves four people and two pieces of manipulative equipment."

This problem-solving approach has no predetermined answers. Students do not have to worry about offering the wrong alternative. The technique is effective for teaching students to apply principles they have learned previously and to transfer previously learned skills to new situations. Ultimately, the problem is solved through a movement response that has been guided by cognitive involvement.

Develop Affective Skills and Outcomes

The performing arts (physical education, music, and drama) offer a number of opportunities for affective domain development. There are many occasions to learn to share, express feelings, set personal goals, and function independently. Teamwork—learning to be subordinate to a leader, as well as being a leader—can be learned. Realize the importance of teaching the whole person rather than teaching just physical skills. It is a sad commentary when one overhears teachers saying, "My job is just to teach skills. I'm not going to get involved in developing attitudes. That's someone else's job." Educators have an excellent opportunity to develop positive attitudes and values. The battle may be won but the war will be lost if teachers produce youngsters with well-developed skills but negative attitudes toward physical activity and participation.

How youngsters feel about a subject determines their levels of motivation to learn. It also effects the long-range effectiveness of instruction. It is possible to design experiences that enhance the development of positive attitudes and values. When developing a lesson plan, analyze whether the planned experiences result in a positive experience for students. Few people develop positive feelings about an activity when they are embarrassed or fail miserably. Ponder the following situations and attitudes that could be developed.

- A teacher asks everyone to run a mile. Overweight students are obviously going to run slower and take longer. Faster students will wait for them to finish—a rather embarrassing situation. Obese students cannot change the outcome of the run even if they wanted to. Failure and belittlement occur every day. It is a small wonder such students dread coming to class.

- How do students feel when asked to perform in front of the rest of the class even though the teacher knows they are unskilled? The added stress probably results in a poorer than usual response.

- What feelings might a student have when asked to pitch in a softball game, only to find herself or himself unable to throw strikes? Might the student do everything possible to avoid having this situation occur in the future?

Students expect teachers to care and avoid placing them in embarrassing situations. Sometimes, teachers have the idea that caring for students indicates weakness. This is seldom the case. Teachers can be firm and demanding as long as they are fair and considerate. Knowingly placing students in an embarrassing situation is never justified and results in negative student attitudes.

It is not the content of the lesson plan that improves positive development of the affective domain. Rather, attitudes and values are formed based, in part, on how students were treated by teachers and peers. How instructors teach is more important than what they teach. Students must be acknowledged as human beings with needs and concerns. They should be treated in a courteous and nonderogatory manner. Feelings should be discussed. When teachers fail to sense how students feel, they are unable to make positive adjustments in the learning environment. More often than not, the best way to discover how students feel is to ask them. The majority will be honest and tell it as it is. If you can accept student input without taking it personally, the result is an atmosphere that is conducive to the constructive development of positive attitudes and values.

Demonstrate Skills to Expedite Learning

Most students learn physical skills best by seeing them demonstrated or modeled. Demonstrating skills can illustrate variety or depth of movement, show something unique or different, point out items of technique or approach, illustrate different acceptable styles, and show progress. Demonstrations should increase the understanding of skills presented and encourage students to observe critically and analyze what they have seen. Demonstration should immediately be followed by a period of practice.

Demonstrations by Teachers

Because of physical limitations, some teachers cannot demonstrate skills effectively. This is to be expected, since few teachers can perform all physical activities well. The inability to demonstrate does not mean instruction is ineffective. At times, even a skilled teacher needs to devise alternatives to personally demonstrating activities. An understanding and knowledge of activities can be developed through reading, study, analysis of movement, and other devices. Even if performing the activity is personally impossible, the teacher may verbalize how the activity should be done. In addition, visual aids and media can be used to offer meaningful orientation.

When the choice is made to demonstrate, be certain that all children can see and hear the performance. Briefly explain the technique and identify one or two key performance points. Show the proper starting position and demonstrate the skill once or twice. The more complex a skill is, the more demonstration is needed.

For creative and open-ended movement patterns, demonstrations may not be desirable because they often lead to imitative behavior, which reduces creativity. When teaching movement skills, a goal is to develop movement variety and versatility; thus, demonstrations are used infrequently. Instead, children are given the opportunity to develop individual approaches rather than imitating the style of another. Questions can be raised during the demonstration, but the question-and-answer period should be minimized.

Student Demonstrations

When students are asked to demonstrate, care must be taken to assure they can correctly demonstrate the skill. Rotating demonstration duties among students is not always a sound practice, as it can result in embarrassment for students who cannot perform the skill. If they desire, however, children should have the chance to demonstrate. An effective method is to observe students who are performing the skill during practice sessions and ask them if they would be willing to demonstrate. If they choose to demonstrate, they make the choice to do so and are usually able to accept the risk of failure.

Student demonstration is an effective teaching technique because it interjects children's ideas into the lesson sequence. As students practice and move, the class can be stopped to let individual children show what they have done. Make comments positive in nature, not derogatory. If a demonstration is unsatisfactory, go on to another child without comment or reprimand, saying only, "Thank you, Janet. Let's see what Carl can do," or simply direct the class to continue practicing.

Use Instructional Cues to Improve Student Performance

Instructional cues are words that quickly and efficiently communicate proper technique and performance of skills or movement tasks. The lesson plans contain many specific instructional cues that are used when teaching skills. Children learning new skills need a clear understanding of the critical skill points because motor learning and cognitive understanding of the skill must be developed simultaneously. Often, teachers carefully plan skill and movement activities yet fail to determine instructional cues they are going to use during the presentation. Meaningful instructional cues help students learn proper technique and key points of performance. Instructional cues for a wide variety of skills are listed in the accompanying lesson plan book. These cues refer to key points of performance. When using instructional cues, consider the following points.

Develop Precise Cues

Cues are short, descriptive phrases that call to the learner's attention key points of skill technique. To help the learner perform a skill correctly, a cue must be precise and accurate. It should guide the learner and be part of a comprehensive package of cues that enhance the quality of learning. Different cues should complement each other and make it easy for the learner to sequence a number of new motor patterns. Study an activity and design cues that focus student learning on correct performance of skills. All teachers must instruct activities they know little about. Few, if any, teachers know everything about all activities. Teachers cannot be expected to possess a vast library of learning cues, but they should possess an acceptable level for initial teaching experiences. Fortunately, instructional cues are offered in the accompanying lesson plans and can be immediately implemented during skill presentations.

Use Short, Action-Oriented Cues

Cues should be short and to the point; avoid making them more comprehensive and lengthy than necessary. A common model is to tell students everything they need to know at the start of the unit and let them practice the rest of the time. This assumes the learners can comprehend and remember a long list of skill instructions and techniques. This is seldom the case; most learners can remember only one or two key points at a time.

To avoid confusing and overwhelming the learners, choose a small number of cues to be presented during each lesson. The cues should contain key words and be short so they encourage the children to focus on one phase of a skill during practice. For example, if learning to throw, a cue might be, "Begin with your throwing arm away from the target." This cue prevents the students from facing the target and precludes trunk rotation in later phases of the throw. Other examples of throwing cues might be: "Step toward the target," "Keep your eye on the target," and "Shift your weight from the rear to the front foot."

A way to examine the effectiveness of cues is to see if they communicate critical points of a skill. Cues should focus on only one phase of a skill, as most beginners can best concentrate on only one thing at a time. Action-oriented words are most effective with children, particularly if they have an exciting sound—for example, "Pop up at the end of the forward roll," "Twist the body during the throw," or "Explode off the starting line." In other situations, the voice can strongly influence the effectiveness of the cue. If a skill is to be done smoothly and softly, speak in a soft tone and ask students to "let the movement floooooow" or to "move smooooothly across the balance beam." Cues are most effective when voice inflections, body language, and action words are used to signal the desired behavior.

Integrate Action Cues

Integrate cues to put the parts of a skill together and give the children a set of words that focus on the skill as a whole. These cues depend on prior cues used during the presentation of a skill and assume that the learners understand the concepts delineated in earlier phases of instruction. Examples of integrating cues are: "Step, rotate, throw," "Run, jump, and forward roll," and "Stride, swing, follow through." The first cue ("Step, rotate, throw") is a set of action words that serve to help students with timing involved in sequencing the parts of the skill. The second set of words ("Run, jump, and forward roll") helps children in primary grades remember the sequence of movement activities to perform. Integrated cues help learners remember proper sequencing of skills and form mental images of the performance. Depending on the rhythm of the presentation, cues signal the speed and tempo of the skill performance. In addition, they serve as specialized language that allows the students and teacher to communicate effectively.

Maintain a Productive Class Environment

Instructional behaviors can be used that ensure the activity area is safe and productive. Planning for each of these areas assures students an opportunity to learn skills in a positive and safe setting. Each of the areas discussed here should be considered carefully prior to presentation of the lesson.

Create a Safe Environment

Do not underestimate the importance of a safe environment. To say the least, it is uncomfortable to have an accident occur due to faulty planning and foresight. Injuries are inevitable in physical education classes, but if they are due to poor planning and preparation, teachers may be found liable and responsible for such injuries (see Chapter 7). Foresee the possibility of hazardous situations that could result in student injury. Rules dictating safe and sensible behavior need to be taught and practiced. For example, if students are in a tumbling unit, they need instruction and practice in developing proper methods of absorbing momentum and force. It may be necessary to practice safety procedures such as taking turns, spotting, and following directions.

Another way to make sure the environment is safe is to offer instructional presentations in proper progression. Injuries can be prevented when students refrain from performing activities for which they are not prepared. A written curriculum expresses to a safety committee or court of law that proper progression and sequencing of activities were used in the lesson presentation. In addition, proper progression of activities gives students confidence because they feel they have the requisite skills to perform adequately.

Schedule safety inspections at regular intervals. When apparatus has not been used for a while, it should be inspected prior to the lesson. This confirms a lesson will not have to be stopped to fix the equipment, causing unnecessary delays. Equipment such as tumbling mats, beanbags, and benches should be kept clean to prevent the spread of disease.

In spite of the foregoing precautions, accidents do happen. Try not to avoid activities that have a certain degree of risk, as one of the most important outcomes of a physical education program is to offer students an opportunity to take risks and overcome fear. If students feel adequate safety precautions have been taken, they will be less hesitant to learn new activities that involve risk.

Effectively "Eyeball" the Class

Observing class performance helps determine that students stay on task and practice activities correctly. A key for any observation approach is to be in a position where eye contact can be maintained with all students. Students stay on task if they know someone is watching them. Be unpredictable when positioning yourself throughout the teaching area. If students can predict where you will be, some of them will move to an area away from you. It is common to find students who enjoy being near the teacher and students who like to move as far away as possible. Random movements assure contact and proximity with all students in the class.

An assumption made by some teachers is that they must move to the same place in the area when giving instructions to students. It is assumed that students will listen only when the teacher is on or near this "instructional spot." Not only is this untrue, but it can result in some rather negative consequences. Students who choose to exhibit deviant or off-task behavior usually move as far away from the instructor as possible. If you always instruct from the same place, deviant students move as far from you as possible, making it difficult to observe them. In addition, it is possible that you may never move near certain students, resulting in a lack of reinforcement for those students. Deliver instruction from the perimeter of the area and vary the location regularly.

Teacher movement, coupled with effective observation skills, helps keep students on task. Moving into position to observe skill performance enhances a teacher's ability to improve student learning. For example, if you are observing kicking, it is best to stand to the side rather than behind the student. A judgment that needs to be made when observing performances is how long to stay with a student. Becoming overly involved with one student may cause the rest of the class to move off task. On the other hand, if contacts are short and superficial, it is possible students will not benefit from the interaction. Usually, the best advice is to give a student one or two points on which to concentrate and then move to another student. Follow up later in the lesson to check student progress.

Systematically Scan the Class

There are times when teachers can *look* at students but not *see* them. In other words, they look at a class, but they do not see how students are performing. If you do not have a systematic plan designed for observing and monitoring behavior, you will find it difficult to recall student behavior. To keep students on task, implement a monitoring plan. Scanning the class from left to right at regular intervals and observing the number of students who are performing the assigned task gives a quick indication of compliance. When teaching a class of 25 to 35 students, it usually takes four to six seconds to scan an entire class. If done faster, the teacher cannot internalize the results of the scan.

Minimize Talking and Maximize Activity

It is easy to become engrossed in instruction and lose sight of student interest. Most students enter the activity area expecting to be involved in movement. If you immediately sit the class down and talk for three to four minutes, students lose interest and motivation. In most cases, instructional episodes should be kept to 30 seconds or less. When episodes are longer, they are filled with more information than students can comprehend in one sitting. Most students in elementary school are capable of remembering one or two key points. Beyond this, they forget and move off task.

Teachers sometimes become angry about misbehavior and spend two or three minutes talking about the need to be model students. Much of the "sermon" is general in nature and reflects the instructor's anger. Lecturing students has little impact. If misbehavior has occurred, speak to it, do something about it, and resume instruction. Often, a whole class is lectured when only a few students were at fault. This forces the majority of students to have to sit and listen to verbalization that has little or no meaning to them. Keep in mind that time spent talking is time spent away from meaningful skill practice. Minimize excessive talking and maximize productive and on-task practice.

Maintain Instructional Focus

When teaching, it is easy to become sidetracked. During practice sessions, a student may try to explain what he did at the park yesterday, or express that she has done this activity before, or state that Johnny is not paying attention. The problem is knowing how to deal with the situation without losing instructional focus. The situation usually demands a quick acknowledgment followed by encouragement to get on task. If you are helping a student and others arrive on the scene with something to say, tell youngsters that you will discuss it in a minute and ask them to return to on-task behavior.

A concern of many teachers is that they will miss important student feedback if they do not listen to everything. This is the type of situation on which tattletale students thrive. If they can gain your immediate attention by telling you about other students who are misbehaving, they have met their immediate need for attention. Acknowledging this type of behavior only makes it occur more often. A solution is to consider the source of the interruption and the seriousness of the misbehavior being reported. In most cases, it is best handled by giving youngsters a gentle reminder that you are responsible for student misbehavior and would appreciate it if your students would be concerned about staying on task rather than wasting their time speaking to you about the behavior of others.

Maintain Focus on Educational Objectives

It is easy to become derailed when an interesting event occurs in class. Lesson plans are designed to guide the instruction toward desired objectives. If the teacher constantly is sidetracked by students to more interesting topics, it is doubtful predetermined goals will be reached. Effective teachers maintain their momentum toward objectives and still show concern for student ideas. There are times when it is necessary to deviate from planned objectives and to take advantage of the "teachable moment." However, this should be the exception, not the rule. Students are well aware that teachers are responsible for guiding the content of the lesson and they expect it.

Personalize Instruction by Showing Concern for Differences

A difficult task is personalizing instruction to better meet the individual needs of students. Even though the majority of instruction is conducted as a group activity, it is obvious, even to the least experienced teacher, that the ability levels of students vary widely. As students mature, this range of ability increases, multiplying the challenge. In addition, many students participate in extracurricular activities such as Little League baseball, Youth Basketball, private tutoring in gymnastics, and so on. This range of experiences places greater responsibility on the instructor to modify tasks so that all students can find success. The following are methods for personalizing instruction to facilitate learning in spite of developmental differences among youngsters.

1. *Modify the conditions.* Tasks and activities can be modified to allow children opportunities for success. For example, move partners closer together if they are learning to catch, use a slower-moving object such as a beach ball or balloon, increase the size of the target,

change the size of boundaries or goal areas, allow students to toss and catch individually, or increase the size of the striking implement. An optimum rate of success should be the goal of personalized instruction. When students find little success, they exhibit off-task behavior to draw attention away from their subpar performance. This behavior is a clear indicator that the error rate is too high and is preventing learning from occurring.

2. *Offer more challenging tasks.* When learning tasks are too easy, students become bored and avoid continued practice. Increase the challenge by asking gifted performers to accomplish higher levels of performance, use a faster-moving object, or increase the distance or decrease the size of the goal. Students respond best to challenges; a task is a challenge when it is slightly above the current skill level.

3. *Offer different task challenges.* Students can work on different tasks simultaneously. It is desirable to have a number of tasks of varying complexity so students of all skills learn to develop personal challenges. Task cards and station teaching allow students the opportunity to learn at an optimum rate. In cases where specialized sport skills are being learned, offer different tasks. For example, students who have limited upper body strength would find inverted balances to be difficult, if not impossible. Balance activities utilizing the legs could be substituted, allowing all students to work on balance skills through different activity challenges.

4. *Encourage higher levels of performance.* Another solution for personalizing instruction is to refine the performance of skilled individuals. Fine points of technique can be used to offer greater challenge. For example, during throwing instruction, less gifted students can be learning proper footwork while skilled throwers are working on distance, accuracy, or velocity of throws.

Provide Meaningful Instructional Feedback

Offering students feedback is an important part of instruction. Used properly, it can enhance a student's self-concept, improve the focus of performance, increase the rate of on-task behavior, and improve student understanding. The following points give direction for improving the quality of feedback used during instruction.

Positive, Corrective, and Negative Feedback

A majority of teachers concentrate on corrective feedback that focuses on rectifying student performance. Outright negative feedback (e.g., "That was a lousy throw") is seldom used by teachers. Instead, corrective feedback is offered, focusing on inaccurate phases of the performance. Some of this type of feedback is expected by students; however, if it is the only feedback offered, youngsters perceive the teacher as negative. A danger of overusing corrective feedback is that it results in a climate where students worry about making errors for fear the instructor will embarrass or belittle them. In addition, many youngsters will surmise that no matter what they do correctly, their efforts will never be recognized.

A more effective approach is to focus on positive points of student performance. This creates a positive atmosphere where students are more willing to accept a challenge and risk error or failure. Teachers who use positive feedback usually feel better about their students because they look for strengths in performance and use this as a foundation for skill improvement. This is not to suggest that corrective feedback should never be used; in fact, Siedentop (1991) suggested that a 4:1 ratio of positive to corrective feedback is desirable. Because many teachers have been taught in a setting where most feedback was corrective, they often perceive it to be the best way to teach others. Most teachers find it necessary to consciously increase the amount of positive feedback and decrease the amount of corrective feedback shared with students.

Use Specific Feedback Statements

Many teachers develop patterns of interaction that are positive yet habitual. For example, statements such as "Nice job," "Way to hustle," "Much better," "Right on," and "Great move" are used over and over. When used indiscriminately, students soon "tune out" and fail to find feeling in comments. In addition, since these comments contain little specific information or value content, there is a strong possibility of misinterpretation by the learner. For example, after a student performs a forward roll, the teacher applauds with a "Nice job" comment. The teacher reinforced the performance because the student's head was tucked. However, the student thought the teacher was pleased because the legs were bent. This results in the wrong or incorrect behavior being reinforced by the teacher.

Adding specific information or value to the feedback improves desired student behavior. The value content of a feedback statement tells students why it is important to perform a skill in a certain manner. Examples of positive feedback with *value content* are as follows:

- "Good throw. When you look at your target, you are much more accurate."
- "Excellent catch. You bent your elbows while catching, which created a soft home for the ball."
- "That's the way to stop. When you bend your knees, you always stop under control."

Examples of feedback with *specific content* are as follows:

- "That's the way to tuck your head on the forward roll."
- "Wow! Everybody was dribbling the ball with their heads up."
- "I'm impressed with the way you kept your arms straight."

These examples focus on verbal behavior; nonverbal behavior can also be used, such as demonstrating how the arms were held correctly, the bat was in proper position, and so on. In any case, students clearly understand why their performance was positive and can build on the reinforced behavior.

Distribute Feedback to All Students

Because there are a number of students in class, teachers have to make decisions about the length of feedback episodes as well as the number of students to contact. It is a decision that may depend on the skill being taught. For example, if a skill is learned quickly, it is usually best to move quickly from student to student, assuming there are no major dysfunctions. This fast-moving approach allows contact with all students a number of times during the lesson. In addition, it helps keep students on task since they know the teacher is moving and "eyeballing" the class regularly. The drawback to this approach is that there is little opportunity for in-depth feedback. If skills are complex and refinement is a goal, it is more effective to take additional time with students. This involves watching a student long enough to offer specific and information-loaded feedback. The end result is high-quality feedback to a fewer number of students.

When offering instructional feedback to students, avoid close scrutiny of the children at the completion of the feedback. Many students become tense if a teacher tells them how to perform the skill correctly and watches to see if they do it exactly as they were instructed. Most students are willing to try new and risky ways of performing if they are allowed to practice without being closely observed by the teacher or class. Observe carefully, offer feedback, move to another student, and recheck progress at a later time.

Focus of Feedback: Individual or Group?

In elementary school settings, much feedback is group oriented; a common method used is to stop the class and offer feedback to all youngsters. This is an expedient method, but it also allows the most room for misinterpretation. Some students may not understand the feedback, while others may not listen because it does not seem relevant to them. A more effective way is to direct feedback (positive only) to a youngster so the rest of the class can hear it. This allows the feedback to ripple throughout the class, offering instructional feedback for the class and a positive experience for the student identified. In addition, the student can demonstrate the skill and serve as a model for the rest of the class. Care must be taken to avoid giving negative or corrective feedback in this manner. The ripple effect with negative feedback can be a debilitating experience for youngsters. All negative or corrective feedback should be administered quietly to the individual so that only the teacher and the involved student are privy to the discussion. This avoids resentment that might build due to embarrassment or humiliation in front of peers.

Feedback should focus on the desired task. For example, if students are asked to "give" while catching a ball thrown by a partner, it clouds the issue if the teacher offers feedback on the quality of the throw being made. If catching is the focus, feedback should be about the technique of catching so that students concentrate on catching. An example of feedback in this setting is, "Watch the way Rachel is reaching out and 'giving' when catching the ball." A final clarification: It is not necessary to have students watch other students accomplish the desired outcome. In fact, watching is effective only if the performer is capable of showing the skill correctly. If this approach is used exclusively, less skilled (or shy) performers will never have an opportunity to receive classwide feedback. It is just as effective to tell the class how well a student was doing and move on—for example, "Mike always keeps his head up when dribbling."

Deliver feedback to students as soon as possible after a correct performance. If delayed feedback is offered, allow the opportunity for immediate practice so students can apply the information. Little is gained and much is lost if students are told how to improve but are not allowed a chance to practice before leaving class. If the end of class is approaching, it is best to limit feedback to situations that can be practiced immediately.

References and Suggested Readings

Gabbard, C., Leblanc, E., & Lowy, S. (1987). *Physical education for children.* Englewood Cliffs, NJ: Prentice-Hall.

Gallahue, D. L. (1987). *Developmental physical education for today's elementary school children.* New York: Macmillan.

Johnson, D. W., & Johnson, F. (1987). *Joining together: Group theory and group skills* (3rd ed.). Englewood Cliffs, NJ: Prentice-Hall.

Johnson, D. W., Johnson, R. T., & Holubec, E. J. (1990). *Circles of learning: Cooperation in the classroom* (3rd ed.). Edina, MN: Interaction.

Mosston, M., & Arnsworth, S. (1993). *Teaching physical education* (4th ed.). New York: Merrill/Macmillan.

Nichols, B. (1994). *Moving and learning: The elementary school physical education experience* (3rd ed.). St. Louis: C. V. Mosby.

Pangrazi, R. P., & Dauer, V. P. (1995). *Dynamic physical education for elementary school students* (11th ed.). Boston: Allyn and Bacon.

Pangrazi, R. P., & Dauer, V. P. (1995). *Lesson plans for dynamic physical education for elementary school students* (11th ed.). Boston: Allyn and Bacon.

Rink, J. E. (1993). *Teaching physical education for learning* (2nd ed.). St. Louis: C. V. Mosby.

Siedentop, D. (1991). *Developing teaching skills in physical education* (3rd ed.). Mountain View, CA: Mayfield.

Siedentop, D., Mand, C., & Taggart, A. (1986). *Physical education: Teaching and curriculum strategies for grades 5–12.* Palo Alto, CA: Mayfield.

ChapterFIVE

Management and Discipline Strategies in a Physical Education Setting

In this chapter, you will learn...

◆ *About the characteristics of a well-managed class*

◆ *How to prevent behavior problems*

◆ *Techniques to use at the start of the physical education year*

◆ *Methods of teaching class management skills through activity*

◆ *Ways to effectively teach students in an activity setting*

◆ *How to modify undesirable behavior and maintain desirable behavior*

◆ *Effective implementation of different types of positive reinforcement*

◆ *About using the time-out procedure to reduce undesirable behavior*

◆ *That behavior contracts can be used to deal with difficult students*

◆ *The importance of using punishment judiciously*

Successful teachers effectively manage student behavior. Skills vary among teachers in emphasis and focus, but collectively, they characterize quality teaching. Effective teachers take guidance from three assumptions: Teaching is a profession, students are in school to learn, and the teacher's challenge is to promote learning. These assumptions imply a responsibility to teach a range of students, both those who accept instruction and those who do not. Teachers must maintain faith that students who have not yet found success will eventually do so. Instructing the majority of children in a class is relatively easy, but making appreciable gains among low-aptitude and indifferent students is the mark of an effective teacher.

Some classroom teachers are hesitant to teach physical education because children are difficult to manage in an activity setting. Youngsters who are relatively quiet in the classroom suddenly become filled with energy and the ability to make a great deal of noise. Management and discipline strategies that work well in the classroom are not as effective in the gymnasium or outdoors. This chapter offers a number of strategies for effectively teaching and managing students in physical education.

Characteristics of a Well-Managed Class

A well-managed class results when effective teachers and disciplined students assume the basic responsibility of directing learning toward target goals. Effective teachers vary presentations and select instructional strategies appropriate to the capabilities of students and the nature of activity sequences. How teachers teach, more than the characteristics of a particular teaching style, determines what students learn. Effective class management and organizational skills create a comfortable environment that offers students freedom of choice in harmony with class order and efficient teaching procedures. Management techniques include the mechanics of organizing a class, planning meaningful activities, and enhancing the personal growth of students. Because skillful instructors have the ability to prevent problems before they occur, they spend less time dealing with deviant behavior. In short, teachers who fail to plan, plan to fail.

As a teacher, you must be aware of the impact your behavior has on students, since teaching reflects your personality, outlook, ideals, and background. A successful teacher provides high-quality learning experiences and communicates a zest for movement that is contagious. Personal habits and attitudes affect youngsters. Proper dress, a sound fitness level, and the willingness to participate with students are examples of teacher behavior that has an impact on the profession and the subject. A basic requisite is to model behavior you desire from students—for instance, moving quickly if you demand that students hustle, listening carefully to students, and performing required fitness activities. Modeling desired behavior has a strong impact on students. The adage "Actions speak louder than words" has significant implications for teachers.

Successful teachers communicate to students a belief that youngsters are capable, important, and self-sufficient. Stressing a positive self-concept and offering experiences to promote success are invaluable aids to learning. Make clear to students what the expectations are for learning and behavior. Well-managed classes function with little wasted time and disruption. They run smoothly and are characterized by routines that students expect and follow. The climate in a productive class setting is work oriented, yet relaxed and pleasant.

Teach Class Management Skills

Class management skills are a prerequisite to effective instruction. Moving and organizing students quickly and efficiently requires comprehension of proper techniques and student acceptance of those techniques. When a class is unmanageable, it is unteachable. Teaching management skills should not be viewed as a negative or punishing proposition. Most students and teachers enjoy a learning environment that is organized and efficient and that allows a maximum amount of class time to be devoted to learning skills.

Class management skills should be taught to students in a manner similar to physical skill teaching. All skills are learned through practice and repetition until they become second nature. Just as students make mistakes when performing physical skills, they sometimes perform management skills incorrectly. A simple statement such as, "It appears that you forgot how to freeze quickly. Let's practice," is more positive than indicting a class for its carelessness and disinterest. Class management skills must be practiced many times with the understanding that student performance will vary.

Stop and Start a Class Consistently

Teaching cannot begin if the teacher cannot start and stop the class. A voice command should be used to start the class. (See the following discussion on using a keyword.) It does not matter what the stop signal is, as long as it always means the same thing. Use both an audio signal (such as a whistle blast) and a visual signal (such as raising the hand overhead), as some youngsters may not hear the audio signal if they are engrossed in activity. Regardless of the signal used to indicate a stop, it is best to select a different signal than the one used to start the class. If children do not respond to the signal to stop, practice the procedure and repeat the expectations. Asking a class to freeze on signal is effective practice; youngsters should be positively reinforced when they do it well. Too often teachers reinforce skill performance but fail to reinforce management behavior. Expect your class to freeze, put down equipment, and prepare to listen in a short time. A class should take no longer than five seconds to freeze and get ready for the next command.

Expect 100 percent cooperation when asking students to stop. If some students stop and listen to directions and others do not, class morale soon degenerates. Students begin to wonder why *they* have to stop but *other* students don't. Scan the class to see if all students are stopped and are ready to respond to the next set of directions. If a teacher settles for less than full attention, students will fulfill those expectations.

Deliver Instruction Efficiently

If students are not listening when instructions are given, little learning will occur. Instructions should be delivered in small doses, focusing on one or two points at a time. The instructions should be specific and as clear as possible and seldom last longer than 30 seconds. This implies alternating short instructional episodes with periods of activity (in contrast to the common practice of delivering long and involved technical monologues on skill performance). In a series of spoken items, people usually remember only the first and the last items; most students are able to remember only one or two points during skill practice. Minimizing the amount of content per instructional episode helps eliminate student frustration and allows clear focus on stated goals. This is not to suggest that information should not be delivered to students, but that the tell-it-all-at-the-start-style should be replaced with a more effective input, practice, feedback model.

Tell students *when before what.* Tell the class *when* to perform an activity before stating *what* the activity is. An effective way to implement "when before what" is to signal starting an activity by using a keyword, such as *Begin!* or *Start!* Implement instructions by a statement similar to, "When I say 'Go!' I'd like you to…." For example, you might explain, "When I say 'Go!' I want you to jog to a beanbag, move to your own space, and practice tossing and catching." Since the keyword is not given until all directions have been issued, students are not to begin until they hear the selected keyword (Go!).

Move Students into Groups and Formations Quickly

Students routinely must be moved into small groups and instructional formations. Simple activities can be used to accomplish this in an enjoyable and rapid fashion.

Find a Partner Quickly

An enjoyable activity, *Toe to Toe,* can be used to teach children to find partners quickly. The goal of the game is to get toe to toe with a partner as fast as possible. Students without a partner nearby are instructed to go to the center of the teaching area (marked by a cone or spot) immediately and find someone else without a partner. This gives students a designated spot to assume, as opposed to feeling unwanted while running around the area looking for a partner. Emphasize rapid selection of the nearest person to keep children from looking for a favorite friend or telling someone that he or she is not wanted as a partner. If students insist on staying near a friend, tell the class to move throughout the area and find a different partner each time "toe to toe" is called.

Other suggestions for finding partners are to ask students to find a partner wearing the same color, with a birthday during the same month, with a phone number that has two similar numbers in it, and so on.

Create Small Groups Quickly

Another effective activity for arranging students in groups of a selected size is *Fast Groups*. When the whistle is blown a certain number of times, students form groups with students near them (without looking for friends) corresponding to the number of whistles and sit down to signify that they have the correct number in their group. Students who are left out go to the center of the area, find the needed number of members, and move to an uncrowded area. Once this skill is mastered, students move quickly into properly sized groups. If students have trouble hearing the whistle blasts, hand signals can also be used to show the size of the groups to be made.

Another way to arrange students in equal-sized groups is to place an equal number of different-colored beanbags or hoops on the floor. Students move throughout the area. On signal, they sit on a beanbag (or inside a hoop). All students with a red beanbag (hoop) are in the same group, green beanbags (hoops) make up another group, and so on.

Divide the Class into Two Equal Groups

To divide a class into two equal groups, have students get toe to toe with a partner. One partner sits down while the other remains standing. Those standing are asked to go to one area: those sitting are asked to go to another. Getting into groups is a skill that needs to be learned and practiced regularly.

Make Circles or Single-File Lines on the Move

An effective technique for moving a class into a single-file line or circle is to run randomly throughout the area until a signal is given. On the signal to "fall in" (or whatever your keyword is), students continue to jog, move to the perimeter of the area, and fall in line behind someone until a circle is formed. This exercise can be done while students are running, jogging, skipping, or walking. As long as students continue to move behind another person, the circle will form automatically. The circle can be made larger or smaller on the move.

Another method of moving a class into formation is to ask students to get into various formations without talking. This helps prevent the behavior of calling out for friends. Students can offer visual signals but cannot ask someone verbally to move. Groups can compete against each other to see which forms the desired formation faster. Teachers can hold up a shape drawn on a large card to signal the desired formation. Young students can learn to visualize various shapes through this technique.

Use Squads to Expedite Class Organization

Organizing students into squads helps some teachers manage a class effectively. Squads offer a place for students to meet, keeps certain students from sitting with each other, and can be used to place students into prearranged teams that are equal in ability. The following are guidelines for using squad formation to maximize teaching effectiveness.

1. Do not select squads or groups in a manner that embarrasses a child who might be chosen last. In no case should this be a popularity contest, where leaders look over the group and visibly pick those whom they favor. A fast way to group youngsters into squads is to use the *Fast Group* technique, described previously.

2. Designate a location where students assemble into squad formation. When students are signaled to their squads, they should move to the predesignated area, with squad leaders in front and the rest of the squad behind.

3. Squads provide opportunities for leadership and followership among peers. Make maximum use of squad leaders so that youngsters regard being a leader as a privilege entailing certain responsibilities. Examples of leadership activities are moving squads to a specified location, leading squads through exercises or introductory activities, and appointing squad members to certain positions in sport activities.

4. The composition of squads can be predetermined by the teacher. It may be important to have equal representation by gender on each squad. Squad makeup may be determined by ability level to facilitate organizing games with teams of similar ability. Squads can also be used to separate certain students so they do not have the opportunity to disrupt the class. Squad leaders should be changed every three weeks, and members should be altered every nine weeks. Each youngster must be offered an opportunity to lead.

5. In most cases, an even number of squads should be formed. This allows the class to be broken quickly into halves for games. Having a class of 30 students divided into six squads of five members places a small number of students on each piece of apparatus and makes for less waiting in line during group activities.

6. Squads should be an exciting, worthwhile activity, not an approach that restricts movement and creativity. For example, cones can be numbered and placed in different locations around the activity area. When students enter the gym, they are instructed to find their squad number and assemble. The numbers might be written in a different language or hidden in a mathematical equation or story problem. Another enjoyable experience is to spread out task cards in the area that specify how the squads are to arrange themselves. The first squad to follow instructions correctly is awarded a point or some acknowledgment from the rest of the class. Examples of tasks for squads might be positioning themselves in a circle, sitting with hands on head, or arranging themselves in crab position in a straight line facing northwest. Task cards can be used to specify what children are to do for an introductory activity, or where they should go for the fitness development activity.

7. Allow youngsters to name their squads. This helps them feel part of a select group, and that feeling makes the activity more enjoyable for

both teacher and students. Youngsters should be encouraged to develop pride in their squad.

Learn Students' Names

Effective class management requires learning the names of students. Praise, feedback, and correction go unheeded when you address students as "Hey, you!" Develop a system to expedite learning names. One approach is to memorize three or four names per class period. Write the names on a notecard and identify those students at the start and throughout the period. At the end of the period, identify those students one more time. After the first set of names has been memorized, a new set can be learned. The next time this class meets, review those names learned previously and identify those students.

Tell students you are trying to learn their names. Asking them to say their names before performing a skill or answering a question will speed the process. Once learned, you may precede the question or skill performance with the student's name. For example, say, "Mary, it's your turn to jump." Another effective way to learn names is to take a photo of each class in squads and identify students by keying names to the picture. With students in squads, it is easier to identify them, as they will consistently be in the same location. Identify those students you know and do not know before the start of the period.

Establish Pre- and Postteaching Routines

Children enjoy the sense of security that comes from knowing what to do from the time they enter the instructional area until they leave the area. There are a number of procedures that should be conducted in a systematic and routine manner. The following are situations that need to be planned for prior to the lesson.

Nonparticipating Students
An efficient system should be devised for dealing with the names of children who are not to participate in the lesson, primarily because of health reasons. This decision is best made before children arrive at the lesson area. When possible, youngsters who are not feeling well should be sent to the school nurse and excused from physical activity. A form can be completed that states whether the youngster is to sit out or to take part in modified activity. The information should be accepted at face value. This avoids the time-consuming procedure of questioning students on the sidelines to determine what the problem is and what the solution should be.

Entering the Teaching Area
Nothing is more difficult than trying to start a class that has not entered the teaching area in a quiet, orderly fashion. Stop the class at the door and explain how the youngsters should enter the area and what they are supposed to do. Another common method is to have the class enter the area and begin jogging around the area. When told to freeze, the day's activities are briefly described.

Another method is to have youngsters enter the area and sit in squads behind their respective cones or floor markers. Instruction starts when all students are in position. Regardless of the method used, students should enter the area under control and know where they are supposed to meet.

Discussing the Content of the Upcoming Lesson

Students enter the activity area expecting to move. Take advantage of this desire to move by having them participate in some activity before discussing the content of the lesson. Youngsters are willing to listen after they have participated in vigorous activity. Allow them to try the activity before working on points of technique. Students are more willing to listen to instruction after they have tried an activity and found it difficult to perform. Trying the activity first also gives you an opportunity to assess the ability level of the students.

Closing the Lesson

A routine for closing the lesson is important for teachers and students. Some type of closure related to the instructional content of the lesson is educationally sound. After a closure discussion, follow a routine for leaving the teaching area. This may be lining up at the door, returning to squads, or kneeling in a semicircle. Using a routine at the end of the lesson tends to calm and quiet youngsters in preparation for the classroom environment.

Distribute Equipment Efficiently

Equipment should be distributed to students as rapidly as possible. When children have to wait for a piece of equipment, time is wasted and behavior problems occur. Often, leaders are assigned to get the equipment for a squad. This results in a situation where the leaders are assigned a task, while other students sit and wait (and may become discipline problems). The easiest and fastest method is to have the equipment prearranged around the perimeter of the area. On signal, youngsters move to a piece of equipment, pick it up, move to their own space, and immediately begin practicing an assigned skill. (This takes advantage of the natural urge to use the equipment and reinforces those students who procure equipment quickly.) The reverse procedure can be used for putting equipment away. Notice that this procedure is in complete contrast to the practice of placing equipment in the middle of the area in a box and telling students to "run and get a ball." This approach often results in youngsters being knocked or pushed down.

Regardless of the method used, waiting for all students to get a piece of equipment before allowing any student to use it places control in the hands of the slowest and least cooperative student. Avoid this potential problem by telling students, "When I say 'Go,' I want you to get a jump rope and practice fast-time jumping." This reinforces the fastest-moving students, keeps students on task, and allows the teacher time to prompt students who are slow and less cooperative.

Equipment should be placed in a "home" position when the class is called to attention. For example, beanbags might be placed on the floor, balls placed between the feet, and jump ropes folded and placed behind the neck.

Placing equipment in its home position avoids the problem of youngsters striking one another with equipment, dropping it, or practicing activities when they should be listening.

Prevent Behavior Problems

Many class management and discipline problems can be prevented through anticipation and planning. Anticipate the types of problems that will occur and know how to deal with them when they do occur. Figure 5.1 lists key points for dealing with students in a proactive manner, thereby preventing behavoir problems. Teachers often worry that a situation will occur that they will not know how to handle. Anticipating and preparing for problems gives confidence and peace of mind.

Plan and Implement Rules at the Start of the School Year

Determine Rules and Procedures for the School Year

Most teachers want students to be respectful; it is not unreasonable to expect students to behave. If teachers cannot manage students, they cannot teach them. Managing students is a necessary and important part of teaching; in fact, it may be more important (or a requisite to) than delivery of content. Teachers are often judged by administrators according to how well students are managed. When writing rules, select general categories of behavior instead of specific behaviors. For example, "respect your neighbor" could mean many things, from not pushing to not swearing at another student.

FIGURE 5.1   Preventing Behavior Problems

- Anticipate and explain rules rather than wait for them to be broken.
- Talk with students' parents and ask for suggestions for dealing with misbehavior.
- Avoid placing students in situations that give rise to misbehavior, such as pairing up the "wrong students."
- Be aware of individual students' tolerance for failure. Some students are never willing to fail in front of peers.
- Call attention regularly to desirable behavior.
- Talk with students and try to better understand their feelings. For example, you may find that they feel that you, the teacher, do not like them.
- If feasible, give problem students added responsibility they are capable of handling. For example, make them student helpers or teacher's assistants.
- As a teacher, model behavior you expect students to emulate. For example, ask students to do things politely and discuss problems in a caring manner.

Generic, broad-based rules help students learn the importance of generalizing behavior across many different situations. Rules should be posted in the teaching area where all students can easily read them. The following are examples of general rules:

- *Stop, look, and listen.* This implies freezing on signal, looking at the instructor, and listening for instructions.
- *Take care of equipment.* This includes caring for the equipment, distributing and gathering it, and using it properly.
- *Respect the rights of others.* Usually, this means not pushing others, leaving their equipment alone, and not fighting and arguing.

The number of rules should be restricted to three to five; more than this number makes it difficult for students to remember all the details and makes you appear overly strict. Rules should be guidelines to desired behavior rather than negative statements that tell students what they *cannot* do. The following list summarizes points to consider when designing rules:

1. Select major categories of behavior rather than a multitude of specific rules.
2. Design rules that deal with observable behavior. This makes it easy to determine whether a person is following the rule and it does not involve teacher judgment.
3. Make rules reasonable for the age level of students. In addition, if rules are general, they can cut across ages and be used throughout the elementary school years.
4. Use no more than three to five rules.
5. State rules briefly and positively. It is impossible to write a rule that covers all situations and conditions. Make the rules brief yet broad.

Determine the Consequences of Breaking Rules

When rules are broken, students must learn the consequences of their behavior. Consequences should be listed and posted within the teaching area and discussed with the class. If students are going to make conscious decisions about their behavior, they must know clearly what consequences occur. Rules and consequences should be applied consistently to all students. A primary reason for listing rules and consequences is to avoid punishing students excessively or unfairly. For example, a teacher may favor one student more than another and inadvertently punish the two differently for the same misbehavior. This quickly leads students to believe the teacher is unfair.

Students and teacher should review the rules and come to a consensus regarding the necessity and fairness of the rules. When the consequences have been mutually agreed upon, teachers do not have to feel guilty because they have disciplined. The student chose to break a rule; the teacher is just administering predetermined consequences in an unemotional and concerned manner. Anger and guilt are avoided and both teacher and students will feel better about each other.

Practice Rules Systematically

Rules should stipulate expected behavior within the physical education class setting. If a rule is in place for proper care of equipment, students should have the opportunity to practice how the teacher wants equipment handled. If a rule deals with stopping and listening to the teacher, they should practice such behavior and be reinforced for proper response. Behavior will not always be correct, regardless of rules. It is common to hear teachers tell students, "I told you before not to do that." This assumes that telling students once results in perfect adherence to the rule. Obviously, this is not the case. Remember: Management behavior needs to be practiced throughout the school year.

Determine Routines for Students

Students feel most comfortable when they know what is expected of them. They *expect* to follow routines. Discuss the routines with students so they understand why the chosen procedures are used. Examples of routines that teachers often use are the following:

- How students are supposed to enter the teaching area
- Where and how students and teachers should meet (e.g., sitting in squads, moving and freezing on a spot, sitting in a semicircle, etc.)
- What students should do if equipment is located in the area
- What signal the teacher uses to freeze a class
- How students procure and put away equipment
- How the teacher will group students for instruction

Once routines are established and practiced, both teacher and students will be able to work together comfortably. Practicing the routines on a regular basis is important to assure efficient use of classtime.

Establish an Atmosphere That Encourages Learning

There are a number of things that can be done at the start of the year to assure physical education takes off on the right foot. The first few days of school require communication of expectations in a manner that leaves students with a positive first impression. Students want to develop a positive relationship with you, and a meaningful start can leave them confident and excited about the experience. The following points should be covered.

Be a Leader, Not a Friend

Students want a teacher who is knowledgeable, personable, and a leader. They are not looking for a new friend; in fact, most students feel uncomfortable if they perceive the teacher wants to be "one of them." Let students know what they will learn during the semester and that it will be an exciting year. Do not look to be a part of their personal discussions. There must be a comfortable distance between teacher and students. This is not to say you should not be friendly and caring. It is important to be concerned about students, as long as it is expressed in a professional manner. Being a leader means knowing where to direct a class. As the teacher, you are responsible for what will be learned and how it will be presented. Student input is important, but ultimately, it is your responsibility to lead the class to desired objectives.

Use Activities That Involve the Entire Class

To minimize class management problems, select instructional activities that demand that the entire group be involved in a simultaneous activity. As rapport is developed, different styles of teaching and class organization can be used. Group instruction allows you to view the entire class and see how students respond to the physical education setting. Less directed teaching styles and different organizational schemes can be implemented after class management skills have been developed. Station teaching, peer teaching, and other approaches are most effective when the teacher and students have developed a feeling of mutual respect.

Pick Interesting Activities to Teach

In all likelihood, selecting interesting activities implies teaching content you feel confident in presenting. Even though you have a curriculum to follow, it is difficult to justify presenting only activities in which you feel competent. However, during the first few weeks of school, most teachers feel stressed by having to learn names, develop routines, implement management skills, and teach content. Selecting instructional content that is easy to present encourages student enjoyment and helps generate a positive experience for both students and teacher. After initial routines have been established, instruction is guided by the curriculum guide rather than personal preferences.

Communicate High Standards

Students generally perform to the teacher's expectations—that is, if a teacher expresses the need for students to perform at a high level, the majority of them strive to do so. A common expression is "You get what you ask for." If you ask and expect students to perform to the best of their abilities, they probably will do so. On the other hand, if you act like you do not care whether they try, most students will do as little as possible.

Create a Positive and Fair Environment

Enforce Rules Consistently

One of the best ways to earn students' respect is to treat them all in a fair and caring manner. Most students are willing to accept the consequences of their misbehavior if they think they will be treated in a manner consistent and equal to how other students are treated. Animosity occurs when students sense the teacher has favorites. It is common to favor gifted athletes and students who are physically attractive; be aware of such behavior and to prevent its occurrence when possible. One of the reasons for defining consequences prior to misbehavior is to assure equitable application of the rules. This takes the pressure off the teacher, as it is clearly the student's misbehavior that has triggered the consequences. Once a student chooses to break a rule, the teacher should enforce the rule without making a judgment about the character and worth of the student.

Give Positive Group Feedback

Positive feedback delivered to a class develops group morale. A class must see itself as a unit that works together and is rewarded when it meets group goals. Students will work within groups in adulthood, so learning now about group cooperation and pride in accomplishment helps assure a smoothly running class.

Discipline Individually and Avoid Group Negative Feedback

When negative feedback is delivered, it should be done privately and personally to individual students. Few people want to have negative comments delivered globally for others to hear. All students should not be punished for the behavior of a few misbehaving youngsters. Group negative feedback can have contrary results. Teachers who criticize students in front of others will lose the respect and admiration of students who were behaving properly.

Give Clear and Specific Instructions

There are situations when students misbehave because they did not understand the instructions. Give students clear instructions and proceed with the activity. If some of the students do not perform correctly, it may be that they did not understand. Clarify the instructions and proceed. This two-tiered approach helps assure directions were clear and ample opportunity was given for all to understand.

Modify and Maintain Desirable Behavior

Managing student behavior is an important task in teaching. New teachers, especially, often question themselves in terms of their ability to control and manage a classroom of youngsters. A class of children is really a group of individuals, each of whom must be uniquely treated and understood. Why is instructional discipline necessary? The most basic of reasons is that it allows children to learn effectively without encroaching on the rights of others. Our society is based on freedom hinged to self-discipline. Americans have personal freedoms as long as they do not encroach on the rights of others. In a similar fashion, children can enjoy freedoms as long as their behavior is consistent with educational objectives and does not prevent other students from learning.

The majority of children choose to cooperate and participate in an educational setting. In fact, the learner is largely responsible for allowing the teacher to teach. No one can be taught who chooses not to cooperate. Effective management of behavior means maintaining an environment where all children have the opportunity to learn. It is your responsibility to fashion a learning environment where all children can learn and feel comfortable. Students who are disruptive and off task infringe on the rights of other students.

If you have to spend a great deal of energy working with youngsters who are disorderly, those students who want to learn are shortchanged.

The purpose of this section is to help teachers develop an action plan for modifying and maintaining desired behavior. There are three phases to such a program: (1) increasing desired behavior, (2) eliminating undesirable behavior, and (3) maintaining desirable behavior. A discipline program should focus on positive and constructive approaches designed to teach children responsible behavior. Figure 5.2 offers a condensed list of suggested strategies for modifying student behavior.

Increase Desired Behavior with Positive Reinforcement

Behavior that is followed by appropriate positive reinforcement will occur more often in the future. This principle is the guiding star for changing and improving student behavior. The strength of this simple principle is that it focuses on positive, desired educational outcomes. Effective reinforcement requires deciding what to use as reinforcers, selecting those that effectively reinforce individuals, and properly using the reinforcers. Three types of reinforcers are used in a physical education class. A discussion of each follows.

Social Reinforcers

This class of reinforcers is most often used by teachers. Most children have been involved in an environment filled with social reinforcers prior to attending school. Parents use praise, physical contact, and facial expressions to acknowledge desired behavior in their children. The following are examples

---

FIGURE 5.2   *Strategies for Modifying Misbehavior*

- Discuss with the student the problem his or her behavior causes.
- Reinforce proper behavior exhibited by other students.
- Use time out from reinforcement.
- Use a behavior contract.
- Talk with the student and parents about the problem.
- Ask the student to perform activities that are failure proof.
- Substitute one behavior for another; for example, ask a student who does not listen carefully to explain to others how to perform an activity, or make that student a leader.
- Use the Premack principle: If you stay on task for 10 minutes, you can have the last 5 minutes for free-time activity.
- Focus reinforcement on something the student does well.
- Use prompts to remind students when they are off task or misbehaving.
- If feasible and the behavior does not disrupt the class, ignore the behavior.

---

of social reinforcers that can be used with students in a physical education setting:

Words of Praise

Great job!	Nice going!
Exactly right!	I really like that job!
Perfect arm placement!	That's the best one yet!
Way to go!	Nice hustle!

Physical Expressions

Smiling	Winking
Nodding	Clenched fist overhead
Thumbs up	Clapping

Physical Contact

Handshake	High five

To make effective use of reinforcers, it is necessary to know what type of social reinforcers students typically respond to in the school setting. Certain reinforcers may embarrass students or make them feel uncomfortable. For example, some students may not want to be touched, even to the point of receiving a "high five." Older students may not want to receive words of praise in front of their peers. If unsure, ask the school administrator to define social reinforcers that are acceptable and meaningful to students.

Activity Reinforcers

Various types of enjoyable activities can be used as reinforcement. An effective way to determine activities that can be used as reinforcers is to observe children. Free time always ranks high among children's preferences. Some examples of activities that might be used to reinforce a class are free time to practice a skill, the opportunity to play a game, extra time in physical education class, the opportunity to help administer equipment, acting as a teacher's aide, being a teacher in a cross-aged tutoring situation, or being a team captain. Students might be given special privileges such as being "student of the day," getting to choose the game to play, or having lunch with the teacher.

Token (Extrinsic) Reinforcers

Many educators feel a need to offer some type of token as a reinforcer. It may be points, gold stars, certificates, trophies, or the like. Physical education is closely related to athletic competition, where awards are often given to winners. This causes some to believe that tokens should be used to motivate children in physical education. The less favorable aspect of giving tokens (ribbons or certificates) is that when they are given only to winners, losers become less likely to be motivated to perform in the future. Some teachers give participation certificates or ribbons to all students; however, such tokens have little reinforcement value. In addition, there is evidence to show that extrinsic rewards may decrease a child's intrinsic desire to participate (Greene & Lepper, 1975; Whitehead & Corbin, 1991). When token reinforcers are used, they work best with primary-grade children. However, after the age of 9 or so, many students see the tokens as bribery to behave in a certain manner. As a rule of thumb, it is best to use token reinforcers only if it appears that social reinforcers are ineffective.

Identifying Reinforcers That Are Meaningful to Learners

A common question is: How do I know what will be reinforcing to my students? It is impossible to know what will reinforce a student until it is administered. On the other hand, there are many reinforcers to which most children respond (e.g., praise, attention, smiles, games, free time, and privileges). A practical way to identify meaningful reinforcers is to observe children during free time and analyze things they enjoy doing. Another simple solution is to ask them what they would like to do. Most youngsters value more recess, free time, or other enjoyable activity.

Delivering Social Reinforcers

Effective use of social reinforcers requires teachers to praise and make positive statements. Some teachers feel uncomfortable when learning to administer positive reinforcement because it makes them feel insincere. A common complaint of teachers learning how to reinforce is, "I do not feel real and the children think I'm a fake." Any change in communication patterns makes people uncomfortable. New ways of communicating with a class require a period of adjustment. When you are learning new patterns of praise and reinforcement, you may feel as though your behavior is contrived and insincere (fortunately, most students will not know the difference). If you choose to avoid the discomfort, you choose to stay the same. The assumption that patterns of speech learned as a child are effective in an instructional setting is false. Teachers are made, not born, and effective communicators find success through hard work and dedication. If practiced regularly, new behavioral patterns will become a natural part of your repertoire after a period of time.

Praise is effective when it refers to specific behavior exhibited by the youngster. This contrasts with general statements, such as "Good job" or "You are an excellent performer." General and nonspecific statements do not tell the youngster what was done well. It leaves it to the student to try to identify what the teacher has in mind. If the student's thoughts do not align with the teacher's intent, it is entirely possible that incorrect behavior will be reinforced. To improve the specificity of feedback, describe the behavior to be reinforced rather than offer a global opinion of it. For example, compare the following:

> *Describing*: "I saw your excellent forward roll, James; you tucked your head just right."
>
> *Global Judgment*: "I saw your forward roll; way to go."

In the first example, the youngster is identified and the specific behavior performed is reinforced. In the second situation, it is impossible to identify what is correct (or wrong) or to whom the feedback is directed. In most cases, if a question can be asked about delivered praise or criticism (e.g., What was good? Why was it a poor performance?), the feedback is nonspecific and open to misinterpretation. To increase desired behavior, verbally or physically describe what makes the performance effective, incorrect, or noteworthy. This reinforces the student and communicates to the rest of the class the behavior expected by the instructor.

The Premack Principle

The Premack principle (Premack, 1965) is often used unknowingly to motivate students. This principle states that a highly desirable activity can be used to motivate students to learn an activity they enjoy to a lesser degree. In practice, this principle allows students to participate in a favorite activity if they perform a less enjoyable one. The Premack principle is often referred to as the "Eat your peas before you get dessert" rule. In other words, an activity that children enjoy can be used to motivate youngsters to participate in activities they are reticent to perform. The following are examples of the Premack principle:

> "You may shoot baskets (preferred) after you complete the passing drill (less desirable)."

> "When everybody is quiet (less desirable), we will begin the game (preferred)."

> "Those who raise their hands (less desirable) will be selected to answer the question (preferred)."

Prompt Desirable Behavior to Encourage New Behavior

Prompts are used to remind students to perform desired behavior and to encourage the development of new patterns of behavior. There are a number of ways to prompt children in the physical education setting. The most common are the following:

1. *Modeling.* The teacher performs the behavior desired to encourage students to respond in a similar fashion. For example, the teacher places his or her equipment on the floor when stopping the class to remind the class to do likewise. Modeling is an effective prompt for desired behavior, as young students will emulate the teacher.

2. *Verbal Cues.* This is a common method of prompting—using words such as "Hustle" and "Keep going." The purpose is to remind students of desired behavior. Usually, verbal clues are used to maintain the pace of the lesson, increase the intensity of the performance, or motivate youngsters to stay on task.

3. *Nonverbal Cues.* Many physical cues utilize body language to communicate concepts such as "Hustle," "Move over here," "Great performance," "Quiet down," and so on. In addition, when teaching skills, physically prompt youngsters by moving them into proper position, helping them through the correct pattern, or placing body parts in proper alignment.

When using prompts, a few points should be considered. Prompts should not be used to the point where students will not perform without them. In fact, the goal is to remove the prompt so that behavior will be self-motivated. This process of gradually removing the prompt is called *fading*. All teachers use prompts from time to time; however, the major purpose of prompting is to implement new behavior patterns and increase the occurrence of desired behavior. The weakest (least intrusive) prompt possible should be used to stimulate the behavior. For example, after misbehavior, you could give students a lecture about the importance of staying on task. Such a talk is time consuming and overreactionary. It is not suited to multiple (repetitive) use and is ineffective in the long run. A better choice is to use one or two concise words that are closely identified with the desired skill.

In addition to these points, assure that the prompt identifies the task being prompted. For example, if the teacher prompts the class to "hustle" and has not tied the prompt to desired behavior, there may be confusion. Some children may think it means to perform the skill as fast as possible; others may see it meaning to stop what they are doing and hustle to the teacher. Tie the prompt to the desired behavior (demonstrate what "hustle" means) in a consistent manner and make sure students clearly understand the meaning of the prompt.

Shape Desirable Behavior

Shaping techniques can be used to build new and desired behavior. Shaping is used when desired behavior does not exist; it uses extinction and reinforcement to shape new behavior. Shaping is rather slow and inefficient and should be used when prompting is not possible. Two principles are followed when shaping behavior.

First, differential reinforcement is used to increase the incidence of desired behavior. Reinforcement is administered when responses reach a predetermined criterion. Behavior that does not meet the criterion is ignored (extinction). An example to illustrate this principle involves asking a class to put their equipment down quickly. You decide that students should put the equipment on the floor within 5 seconds. Using differential reinforcement, you reinforce students whenever they meet the 5-second criterion and ignore their performance when it takes longer than 5 seconds.

Second, the criterion that must be reached for reinforcement to occur is gradually increased as you shift the criterion standard toward the desired goal. For example, if the desired behavior is for the class to become quiet within 5 seconds after a signal has been given, it might be necessary to start with a 12-second interval. Why the longer interval? In all likelihood, it is not reasonable to expect that an inattentive class will quiet down quickly. In a poorly managed class, if a 5-second interval is selected, there is a strong possibility that both teacher and students will be frustrated by the lack of success. In addition, this stringent standard of behavior will not be achieved often, resulting in very few opportunities to praise (reinforce) the class. The result is a situation where both teacher and youngsters feel they have failed. To avoid this possibility of failure, gradually move toward the desired terminal behavior. In this case, start with 12 seconds until the class performs as desired. Next, reduce the time to a 10-second interval and ask the class to perform to this new standard. Gradually repeat the process until the terminal behavior is reached.

Decrease Undesirable Behavior

Most effective techniques for improving class behavior are designed to guide students away from behavior that is disrupting the class. The following section offers a number of approaches for dealing with undesirable behavior. Try different methods and see what works best.

Negative Consequences

Negative consequences can be an effective means for decreasing undesirable behavior. Figure 5.3 outlines a specific plan for reducing undesirable student behavior. When using negative consequences, consider the following points:

FIGURE 5.3 *Implementing a Plan for Changing Student Behavior*

Changing behavior can be done if teachers are willing to experiment and be patient. Teachers want to change behavior quickly and on the spot; at times, they make incorrect decisions because they do not have time to think of an effective solution. In-class misbehavior can be temporarily stopped but may often go unchanged for the future. Realize that change will require long-term action that must be planned ahead of time. The following steps can be used to develop a plan for changing behavior:

- Identify a single behavior that needs to be changed, improved, or strengthened. Do not select more than one behavior, as it will make it much more difficult to monitor change.
- Identify a behavior that will be substituted for the behavior to be changed.
- Determine what positively reinforces the student. Have a discussion with the student to see what is reinforcing.
- Decide whether a negative reinforcer is needed to give momentum to the change process.
- Develop a plan for getting the desired behavior to occur. This will generate a behavior that can be reinforced and used to replace the undesirable behavior.
- Put the plan into effect and set a time frame for evaluation of the plan. Decide what modifications are needed to make the plan more effective. This modification may demand a different set or schedule of reinforcers or negative consequences. If an entirely different plan is needed (because the behavior has not decreased or changed), make such changes and proceed.
- Continue evaluating and modifying the plan.

---

1. Consequences should be clear and specific. Students should know exactly what will occur if they misbehave.

2. Negative consequences have to be enforceable. You must be able to carry out such consequences. For example, keeping a bus student after school may not be possible. Kicking a student out of class may not be possible (or desirable). Make sure that the negative consequence can be used in the school setting and is approved by the appropriate administrator.

3. Apply a negative consequence as near to the misbehavior as possible. Just as positive reinforcement should be delivered immediately following the desired behavior, so should negative consequences.

4. Negative consequences can be anything the student finds undesirable as long as they do not violate the rights or dignity of the student. Just as teachers need to know what reinforces students, they need to know what negative consequences are for students who misbehave.

5. Use negative consequences to teach youngsters how to behave properly rather than to punish them.

Whenever possible, choose positive reinforcement to increase desired behavior with the hope that it will replace negative behavior. For example, if a skilled youngster criticizes less able youngsters, ask that student to help others and serve as a student assistant. The intent is to teach the youngster to deliver positive and constructive feedback rather than criticism. Before choosing to use negative consequences, reinforce desired behavior exhibited by other students twice. For example, a youngster is slow to stop on signal, but the majority of other students are stopping and listening properly. Positively reinforce the correctly behaving students. Practice moving and stopping; stop and reinforce the correct behavior again. Often, misbehaving students emulate students who are being reinforced in order to receive similar positive feedback. If not, it may be necessary to use negative consequences. Negative consequences include reprimanding, removal of positive consequences, and time out.

Reprimands
This is a common approach used to decrease undesirable behavior. If done in a caring and constructive manner, reprimands can serve as effective reminders to behave.

1. Identify the unacceptable behavior, state briefly why it is unacceptable, and communicate to students what behavior is desired. An example is: "You were talking while I was speaking. It bothers other students, so please listen to me."

2. Do not reprimand students in front of others. Not only does it embarrass students but it also diminishes their self-esteem. When students feel belittled, they may lash out and react in a manner more severe than the original behavior.

3. Reprimands should speak about behavior, not the person. Ask that the behavior stop rather than tell the student "You are always causing problems in this class." General statements related to the personality or worth of the student should be avoided.

4. After reprimanding and asking for an acceptable behavior, reinforce it when it occurs. Be vigilant in looking for the desired behavior, since reinforcing such behavior causes it to occur more often in the future.

Remove Positive Consequences

This is a common approach used by parents, so many students are familiar with it. It involves removing something positive from the student when misbehavior occurs. For example, students give up some of their free time due to misbehavior. They lose points related to a grade. They are not allowed to participate in an activity that is exciting to them. To make removal of positive consequences effective, teachers must be sure that the students really want to participate in the removal activity. It would not work to keep a student out of a game if the student did not like the game. A few principles should be followed when using this technique:

1. Make sure the magnitude of the removal fits the crime. In other words, children who commit a minor infraction should not have to miss recess for a week.

2. Be consistent among all students and with the same students. Students think teachers are unfair if they are more severe with one student than another. In addition, a student penalized for a specific misbehavior should receive the same penalty for a later repetition.

3. Make sure students understand the consequences of their misbehavior before the penalties are implemented. This avoids applying penalties in an emotional, unthinking manner. If students know what the consequences are, they choose to accept the consequences when they choose to misbehave.

4. It can be beneficial to chart a student's misbehavior to see if the frequency is decreasing. Regardless of the method used, if the behavior is not decreasing or is increasing, change methods until a decrease in frequency occurs.

Time Out

The time-out procedure is an equitable technique for dealing with youngsters in a manner consistent with society. Rules are clearly posted and consequences are clear and easy to comprehend. It is a consistent approach for dealing with undesirable behavior that occurs randomly on an individual basis. The time-out approach moves youngsters out of the class setting and places them into a predesignated area when they misbehave. Time out means *time out from reinforcement*. It does not imply the student is a "bad person," but rather that rules have not been followed and there is a need for time out from the activity. When placing students in time out, communicate to children that they are acceptable individuals, but their misbehavior is unacceptable.

Being placed in time out communicates to youngsters that they have disrupted the class and must be removed so the rest of the class can participate as desired. Children can also use the time-out area as a "cooling-off" spot where they can move voluntarily if they become angry, embarrassed, or frustrated. If two (or more) youngsters have been placed in the time-out area for fighting or arguing, they should be placed at opposite ends of the area so that the behavior does not escalate. In addition, it can be mandated they stay in their half (or quadrant) of the teaching area until the next meeting of the class. This prevents recurring agitation between the combatants and the possibility of continued animosity.

The implementation of this plan should be discussed with students, so they know exactly what is acceptable and unacceptable behavior and what actions will be taken if they exhibit undesirable behavior. A list of desired behaviors, as well as consequences for unacceptable behavior, should be posted in the teaching area. Examples of desirable behavior might be listening when the teacher is instructing, keeping one's hands off others, and promptly performing the activities presented. In most cases, the list of desired behaviors should number between three and five items. A larger number of behaviors will confuse the class and make it difficult for them to comprehend the focus of the approach.

A key concept to remember is that time out does not serve as a deterrent if the youngster is reinforced. Time out means receiving no reinforcement. If class is a negative experience for students, taking them out of class will be rewarding rather than a negative consequence. Caution must be used in placing students in the time-out area. Too often, sitting a student out results in a reinforcing experience. For example, a student who is sent to the office gets to avoid schoolwork while visiting with friends who come into the office. Notoriety can be achieved among peers for surviving the office experience and being able to tell others, "I wasn't scared at all." Sitting on the side of the teaching area and making faces at peers may be a more reinforcing experience than participating in class activities. Remember: If students do not enjoy being in class, time out does not work.

As stated, establish consequences and post them in the area. A possible set of consequences for unacceptable behavior follows:

- *First Misbehavior.* The student is warned quietly on a personal basis to avoid embarrassment. At times, students are not aware that they are bothering others and a gentle reminder by the teacher will refocus these youngsters.
- *Second Misbehavior.* The student is told to go to a predesignated time-out spot. This might be a chair in the corner of the activity area. The student stays there until he or she is ready to reenter the activity and can demonstrate the desired behavior. It is acceptable for the student to go to the area and return to the activity, since the assumption is an agreement to terminate the misbehavior.

- *Third Misbehavior.* The student goes to time out for the remainder of the period. If the misbehavior continues each time the class meets, most schools will use an in-school suspension program. In-school suspension requires the student to leave his or her class of students, move into another room of students (different grade level), and receive little, if any, reinforcement.

The foregoing steps assume communication with the student about the misbehavior and the desired behavior. If these consequences are ineffective, the last alternative is to call the parents in for a conference with the principal and teacher. Students and parents need to understand that participating in educational endeavors is a privilege and people who choose to disrupt society ultimately lose their privileges (e.g., incarceration in reform school, prison, etc.).

Behavior Contracts

A *behavior contract* is a written statement specifying certain student behaviors that must occur to earn certain rewards or privileges. The contract is usually signed by the student and teacher, and is drawn up after a private conference to decide on the appropriate behaviors and rewards. This approach allows students to make decisions that will improve their own behavior.

The behavior contract can be a successful strategy for intermediate-grade students with severe behavior problems. Every attempt should be made to find rewards that occur naturally in physical education class (e.g., Frisbee play, jump rope games, aerobics, basketball, etc.). If not possible, different types of rewards may have to be used. For example, a student who is interested in music could be allowed to spend some time selecting records to be used for class during the next week. As behavior improves and the student's attitude becomes more positive, rewards should be switched to physical education activities. The contract is gradually phased out over a period of time as the youngster gains control of his or her behavior and is able to participate in normal class environments.

Contracts can be written for a small group of students or for an entire class with similar problems, but be careful about setting up a reward system for too many students. The system can become too complex or time consuming to supervise properly. The contract is best used with a limited number of students in several problem situations. An example of a behavior contract is shown in Figure 5.4.

Minimize Criticism

When criticism and punishment are used, it must be with caution and good judgment. Criticism is often used by teachers with the belief that it will improve the performance of students. Teachers find scolding and criticism to be their behavior control tools of choice because they give the impression

FIGURE 5.4   *Individual Behavior Contract*

I, _____, agree to follow the rules as listed below:

1. Listen when the teacher is talking.
2. Do not touch others during class.

If all the rules are followed during physical education class, I will earn 10 minutes of basketball activity for myself and a friend after school on Thursday between 3:00 and 3:45.

Signed: _____, Student

Signed: _____, Teacher

---

that the results are effective and immediate. Usually, the misbehavior stops and the teacher assumes that the situation has been rectified. Unfortunately, this is not always the case. Criticism and punishment lend a negative air to the instructional environment and have a negative impact on both student and teacher. The old saying "It hurts me more than you" is often the case. The majority of teachers feel uncomfortable when they criticize or punish students. It makes them feel as though they cannot handle students and that the class is incorrigible. This feeling of incompetence leads to a destructive cycle where students feel negative about the instructor and the instructor feels negative about the class. In the long run, this is a debilitating effect of criticism and punishment.

Another negative aspect of criticism is that it does not offer a solution. In a study by Thomas, Becker, and Armstrong (1968), a teacher was asked to stop praising a class. Off-task behavior increased from 8.7 percent to nearly 26 percent. When the teacher was asked to increase criticism from 5 times in 20 minutes to 16 times in 20 minutes, more off-task behavior was demonstrated. On some days, the percentage of off-task behavior increased to more than 50 percent. The point is that when attention is given to off-task behavior and no praise is offered for on-task accomplishment, the amount of off-task behavior increases dramatically. The teacher who primarily criticizes is reinforced by the students (they respond to the request of the criticism), but the students do not change. In fact, the students are reinforced (they receive attention from the teacher) for their off-task behavior. In addition, since their on-task behavior is not praised, it decreases. The net result is exactly the opposite of what is desired.

Use Punishment Judiciously

The question of whether punishment should be used in an educational setting is a difficult one. Punishment can have negative side effects because fear is the primary motivator. Teachers must consider the long-term need for punishment. If the long-term effects of using punishment are more beneficial than not using it, it would be unethical not to use punishment. In other words, if the child is going to be in a worse situation because punishment was not used to deter self-destructive behavior, then punishment should be used. It may be necessary to punish a child for protection from self-inflicted harm (e.g., using certain apparatus without supervision) or so that a child learns not to hurt others. Punishment in these situations will cause discomfort to the teacher and the child in the short run, but may allow the student to participate successfully in society later.

Most situations in the educational setting do not require punishment because they are not as severe as those just described. A major reason for avoiding punishment is that it can have undesirable side effects. When children are punished, they learn to avoid the source of the punishment. It forces them to be more covert in their actions. They spend time finding ways to be devious without being caught. Instead of encouraging students to discuss problems with teachers and parents, punishment teaches them to avoid these individuals for fear of being punished. Another side effect is that punishment teaches children how to be aggressive toward others. Children who have been physically or emotionally punished by parents act in similar fashion to others. The result is children who are secretive and aggressive with others—certainly an undesirable trait. Finally, if punishment is used to stop certain behavior, as soon as the punishment stops, the behavior returns. Thus, little has been learned; the punishment has just caused short-term change.

If it is necessary to use punishment, consider the following points:

1. *Be consistent and make the "punishment fit the crime."* Students quickly lose respect for a teacher who treats others with favoritism. They view the teacher as unfair if punishment is extreme or inequitable. Peers will quickly side with the student who is treated unfairly, causing a class morale problem for the instructor.

2. *Offer a warning signal.* This may prevent excessive use of punishment, as students will often behave after receiving a warning. In addition, they will probably view the teacher as caring and fair.

3. *Do not threaten students.* Offer only one warning. Threats have little impact on students and make them feel you cannot handle the class. One warning gives students the feeling that the teacher is not looking to punish them and is fair. Follow through; do not challenge or threaten students and then fail to deal with the behavior.

4. *The punishment should follow the misbehavior as soon as possible.* When punishment is delayed, it is much less effective and more often viewed as unfair.

5. *Punish softly and calmly.* Do not seek revenge or be vindictive. If responsible behavior is expected from students, teachers must reprimand and punish in a responsible manner. Studies (O'Leary & Becker, 1968) have demonstrated that soft reprimands are more effective than loud ones.

Try to avoid having negative feelings about a student and internalizing student misbehavior. Teachers who are punitive when handling deviant behavior destroy any chance for a worthwhile relationship. Misbehavior should be handled in a manner that contributes to the development of responsible, confident students who understand that people who function effectively in society must adjust to certain limits. Try to forget about past bouts of deviant behavior and approach the student in a positive fashion (with a clean slate) at the start of each class. If this is not done, students soon become labeled, which makes it much more difficult to make behavioral change. Students may also learn to live up to the teacher's negative expectations.

If punishment is used, make sure only those youngsters who misbehave are punished. Punishing an entire class for the deviant behavior of a few youngsters is not only unfair but it may also trigger undesirable side effects. Students become hostile toward those who caused the loss of privileges, and this peer hostility lowers the level of positive social interaction. If the group as a whole is misbehaving, punishing the entire group is appropriate.

Expulsion: Legal Considerations

If serious problems occur, consult with the principal. Many times, deviant behavior is part of a larger, more severe problem that is troubling a child. A cooperative approach may provide an effective solution. A group meeting involving parents, principal, and counselor may open avenues that encourage understanding and increase productive behavior.

Legal concerns involving a student's rights in disciplinary areas are an essential consideration. Although minor infractions may be handled routinely, expulsion and other substantial punishments can be imposed on students only after due process. The issue of student rights is complicated, and most school systems have established guidelines and procedures for dealing with students who have been removed from the class or school setting. Youngsters should be removed from class only if they are disruptive to the point of interfering with the learning experiences of other children and when all other means of altering behavior have not worked. Sending a child out of class is a last resort and means that both teacher and student have failed.

References and Suggested Readings

AAHPERD. (1976). *Personalized learning in physical education.* Reston, VA: AAHPERD.

Canter, L., & Canter, M. (1976). *Assertive discipline.* Santa Monica, CA: Canter and Associates.

Canter, L., & Canter, M. (1984). *Assertive discipline elementary resource materials workbook grades K–6.* Santa Monica, CA: Canter and Associates.

Charles, C. M. (1989). *Building classroom discipline* (3rd ed.). New York: Longman.

Cruickshank, D. R. (1980). *Teaching is tough.* Englewood Cliffs, NJ: Prentice-Hall.

Curwin, R. L., & Mendler, A. N. (1988). *Discipline with dignity.* Washington, DC: Association for Supervision and Curriculum Development.

Darst, P. W., & Whitehead, S. (1975). Developing a contingency management system for controlling student behavior. *Pennsylvania JOPER, 46*(3), 11–12.

Glasser, W. (1986). *Control theory in the classroom.* New York: Harper & Row.

Greene, D., & Lepper, M. R. (1975). Turning play into work: Effects of adult surveillance and extrinsic rewards on children's internal motivation. *Journal of Personality and Social Psychology, 31,* 479–486.

McKenzie, T., & Rushall, B. (1973). *Effects of various reinforcing contingencies on improving performance in a competitive swimming environment.* Unpublished paper. Halifax, Nova Scotia: Dalhousie University.

Nelson, J. (1987). *Positive discipline.* New York: Ballantine.

O'Leary, K. D., & Becker, W. C. (1968). The effects of intensity of a teacher's reprimands on children's behavior. *Journal of School Psychology, 7,* 8–11.

Paese, P. (1982). Effects of interdependent group contingencies in a secondary physical education setting. *Journal of Teaching in Physical Education, 2*(1), 29–37.

Premack, D. (1965). Reinforcement theory. In D. Levine (Ed.), *Nebraska symposium on motivation.* Lincoln: University of Nebraska Press.

Siedentop, D. (1991). *Developing teaching skills in physical education* (3rd ed.). Palo Alto, CA: Mayfield.

Thomas, D. R., Becker, W. C., & Armstrong, M. (1968). Production and elimination of disruptive classroom behavior by systematically varying teachers' behavior. *Journal of Applied Behavior Analysis, 1,* 35–45.

Whitehead, J. R., & Corbin, C. B. (1991). Effects of fitness test type, teacher, and gender on exercise intrinsic motivation and physical self-worth. *Journal of School Health, 61,* 11–16.

Wolfgang, C. H., & Glickman, C. D. (1980). *Solving discipline problems.* Boston: Allyn and Bacon.

Chapter SIX

Children with Disabilities

In this chapter, you will learn...

◆ *Why it is necessary and important to include children with disabilities in physical education experiences*

◆ *The mechanics of screening and assessing students for physical education participation*

◆ *How to develop an Individualized Education Program (IEP) for students*

◆ *Why the least restrictive environment should be used to place children with disabilities*

◆ *The definition of mainstreaming and the different methods of integrating students with disabilities into physical education*

◆ *About the importance of utilizing parental support to enhance physical education programs for students with disabilities*

◆ *Many ways to modify activities so children with disabilities can participate*

◆ *About specific disabilities and instructional procedures that assure effective instruction*

The Education for All Handicapped Children Act (Public Law 94-142) was passed by the Congress of the United States in 1975. The purpose of the law is clear and concise:

> It is the purpose of this act to assure that all handicapped children have available to them…a free appropriate public education which emphasizes special education and related services designed to meet their unique needs, to assure that the rights of handicapped children and their parents or guardians are protected, to assist States and localities to provide for the education of all handicapped children, and to assess and assure the effectiveness of efforts to educate handicapped children.*

In short, the law requires that all children with disabilities, ages 3 to 21, receive a free and appropriate education in the least restrictive environment. The law includes youngsters in public and private care facilities and schools. Children with disabilities who can learn in regular classes with the use of supplementary aides and services must be educated with youngsters who are able. Physical education is the only specific area mentioned in PL 94-142. The law indicates that the term *special education* "means specially designed instruction, instruction in physical education, home instruction, and instruction in hospitals and institutions."

To comply with PL 94-142, public schools must locate, identify, and evaluate all students who might have a disability. This screening process must be followed by a formal assessment procedure. Assessment must be made and an Individualized Education Program (IEP) developed for each youngster before placement into a special program can be made. The law states who will be responsible for developing the IEP and what the contents of the IEP will include. The passage of PL 94-142 offered a giant step forward in assuring equality and education for all Americans. The government also assured that funding would be made available to provide quality instruction. The law authorizes a payment to each state of 40 percent of the average per-pupil expenditure in U.S. elementary and secondary schools, multiplied by the number of children who are receiving special education and related services. The federal mandate reveals the concern of the public for comprehensive educational programs for all youngsters regardless of disability.

Screening and Assessment

An important component of the IEP process is screening and assessment of students. Every state is required by PL 94-142 to develop a plan for locating, identifying, and evaluating all children with disabilities.

---

* The term *handicapped* is used in PL 94-142 to include youngsters who are mentally retarded, hard of hearing, deaf, speech impaired, visually handicapped, seriously emotionally disturbed, orthopedically impaired, other health impaired, deaf-blind, multihandicapped, or specific learning disabled. Currently, *disabilities* is the term used to identify youngsters with handicapping conditions. This term is used throughout this chapter.

Screening

Generally, screening is a process that involves all students in a school setting and in a "child find" process. It is often conducted at the start of the school year and is performed districtwide. In most situations, screening tests may be administered without parental permission and are used to make initial identification of students who may need special services.

Assessment

Assessment is usually conducted after a "child find" screening by referring identified students to special education directors. A team of experts, which may include a physical education specialist, conducts the assessment. Due process for students and parents is an important requisite when conducting formal assessment procedures. Due process assures parents and children will be informed of their rights and have the opportunity to challenge educational decisions they feel are unfair or incorrect.

Due Process Guidelines

To assure due process is offered to parents and students, these guidelines must be followed:

- *Written Permission.* A written notice must be sent to parents stating that their child has been referred for assessment. The notice must explain that the district requests permission to conduct an evaluation to determine if special education services are required for their child. Also included in the permission letter are reasons for testing and the tests to be used. Before assessment can begin, the letter must be signed by the parents and returned to the district.

- *Interpretation of the Assessment.* The results of the assessment must be interpreted in a meeting with parents. Persons who are knowledgeable about the test procedures must be present to answer questions parents may ask. At the meeting, parents are told whether their child has any disabilities and what services will be provided for the child.

- *External Evaluation.* If parents are not satisfied with the results of the assessment, they may request an evaluation outside the school setting. The district must provide a list of agencies that can perform such assessment. If the results differ from the school district evaluation, the district pays for the external evaluation. However, if the results are similar, parents pay for the external testing.

- *Negotiation and Hearings.* If parents and the school district disagree on the results of the assessment, the district is required to negotiate the differences. When negotiations fail, an impartial hearing officer listens to both parties and renders an official decision. This is usually the final review; however, both parties do have the right to appeal to the state department of education, which renders a binding and final decision. Civil action through the legal system can be pursued should the district or parents still disagree with this action. However, few cases ever reach this level of long-term disagreement, and educators should not be hesitant to serve the needs of children with disabilities based on this concern.

- *Confidentiality.* As is the case with other student records, only parents of the child or authorized school personnel can review the student's records. Review by other parties can be done only after written permission has been given by the parents of the child under review.

Procedures for Assuring Assessment Standards

PL 94-142 requires that assessment will be held to certain standards to assure fair and objective results. The following areas are specifically delineated.

Selection of Test Instruments

Test instruments must be valid examinations that measure what they purport to measure. When selecting instruments, it must be clear to all parties how the tests were developed and how they will correctly measure the area of possible disability. More than one test procedure must be used to determine the student's status. Both formal and informal assessment techniques can be used to assure that the results measure the student's impairment rather than simply reflect the student's shortcomings.

It is an unfortunate situation that children must be labeled as disabled in order to reap the benefits of a special education program. The stigmatizing effect of labels and the fallibility of various means of testing students is a dilemma that must be faced. Although current pedagogical practices discourage labeling, it does occur because school districts have to certify the disability (to receive funding) through which the child is classified.

Administration Procedures

Disabilities often interfere with standard test procedures. For example, students have communication problems and need to be tested in a manner that assures their motor ability is measured rather than their lack of communication skills. Some students have visual and hearing disabilities that prevent using tests that rely on these faculties.

A probability of misdiagnosis and incorrectly classifying children as mentally retarded can occur with certain ethnic groups, such as Native Americans, African Americans, and Spanish-speaking children. These youngsters, often victims of poor and impoverished living, may be only environmentally disabled and in need of cultural enrichment. It is subtle discrimination that should be replaced with an understanding that children differ because of culture, poverty, migrancy, and language. Many of the tests are based on white, middle-class standards. Minority children should be carefully assessed to determine the validity of the testing procedure.

Team Evaluation

A number of experts should be used for assessment. A multidisciplinary team is assembled to assure that all facets of the child will be reviewed and evaluated. It is the responsibility of the school district to assure this occurs.

Development of the IEP

PL 94-142 requires that an IEP be developed for each child with a disability who receives special education and related services. The IEP is developed by a committee as stipulated by the law. Included on the committee are the following members: a local education association representative who is qualified to provide and supervise the administration of special education, the child's parents, the teachers who have direct responsibility for implementing the IEP, and, when appropriate, the student. Other individuals may be included at the discretion of the parents or the school district. This program identifies the child's unique qualities and determines educationally relevant strengths and weaknesses. A plan is then devised based on the diagnosed strengths and weaknesses. Figure 6.1 is an example of a comprehensive IEP form. The IEP must contain the following material:

1. Current status of the child's level of educational performance
2. A statement of long-term goals and short-term instructional objectives
3. A statement of special education and related services that will be provided to the youngster (as well as a report as to the extent the youngster will be able to participate in regular educational programs)
4. The dates for initiation of services and anticipated duration of the services
5. Appropriate objective criteria for determining on an annual basis whether the short-term objectives are being reached

Developing and sequencing objectives for the student is the first step in formulating the IEP. Short-range and long-range goals are delineated and data collection procedures and testing schedules are established to monitor the child's progress. Materials and strategies to be used in implementing the IEP must also be established. Finally, methods of evaluation to be used are determined in order to monitor the student's progress and the effectiveness of the program. (Computer assistance is helpful in relieving laborious hand recording.) Movement to a less restrictive environment should be based on achievement of specified competencies that are necessary in the new environment.

The IEP must contain a section determining whether specially designed physical education is needed. If not, the child should be held to the same expectations as the peer group. A child who needs special physical education could have an IEP with specified goals and objectives and be mainstreamed in regular physical education with goals that do not resemble those of classmates.

Continued and periodic follow-up of the child is necessary. Effective communication between special and regular teachers is essential because the child's progress needs careful monitoring. At the completion of the designated time period or school year, a written progress report is filed along with recommendations for action during the coming year or time period. Here,

FIGURE 6.1 Example of an Individualized Educational Plan

☐ Initial Placement
☐ Re-evaluation
INDIVIDUALIZED EDUCATION PROGRAM   ☐ Change of Placement
☐ Review

A. STUDENT INFORMATION:
Student Name _____ Student No. _____ Home School _____
              Last   First   Middle
Date of Birth _____ Chronological Age ___ (M___ or F___) Present Placement/Grade _____
Parent/Guardian Name(s)_____ Receiving School _____
Home Address _____ Program Recommended _____
              Street   City/State   Zip
Home Phone _____ Work Phone _____ Starting Date _____
Emergency Phone _____ Three (3) Year Re-evaluation Due Date ____/____/____
Primary Language (Home) _____ (Child)_____ Interpreter Needed: Yes ____ No ____

B. VISION SCREENING RESULTS: Pass ____ Fail ____   **HEARING SCREENING RESULTS:** Pass ____ Fail ____
Date: _____ Comments: _____   Date: _____ Comments: _____
_____   _____

C. REQUIRED OBSERVATION(S): (All categories other than regular teacher)
_____ By: _____ _____ By: _____ _____ By: _____
  Date(s)   Name(s)   Date(s)   Name(s)   Date(s)   Name(s)

D. SUMMARY OF PRESENT LEVELS OF PERFORMANCE:
Educational: _____
_____
_____
_____
_____
_____
_____
_____
_____
_____
_____
_____
_____

Behavioral: _____
_____
_____
_____
_____
_____
_____
_____
_____
_____
_____
_____

E. Additional justification. See comments_____ See addendum_____
                                    Initial   Initial

F. PLACEMENT RECOMMENDATION INDICATING LEAST RESTRICTIVE ENVIRONMENT:
Related services needed: Yes _____ No _____ (*List below.)

Placement Recommendation	Person Responsible	Amount of Time (Range)	Entry Date On/About	Review Reports On/About	Projected Ending Date	IEP Review Date
Primary:						
*Related Services:						

Transportation Needed? Yes _____ No _____ (If Yes, submit MPS Special Education Transportation Request Form.)

Describe extent student will participate in regular program: _____
_____

Page 1 of _____

(continued)

FIGURE 6.1 *(Continued)*

INDIVIDUALIZED EDUCATION PROGRAM

REPORT OF MULTIDISCIPLINARY CONFERENCE
Date Held _____

Student Name _____   Student No. _____

G. **PROGRAM PLANNING:**
Long-Term Goals: Short-Term Objectives (Goals):

H. **EVALUATION:**
Evaluation criteria are described in the Individual Implementation Plan (IIP) which is available in the classroom file.

I. **PLACEMENT COMMITTEE:**
The following have been consulted or have participated in the placement and IEP decisions:

Names of Members	Position	Present (Initial)	Oral Report	Written Report	Signatures
	Parents/Guardian				
	Parents/Guardian				
	School Administrator				
	Special Ed Administrator				
	School Psychologist				
	Nurse				
	Teacher(s) Receiving				
	Teacher(s) Referring				
	Interpreter				

Dissenting Opinion: Yes _____ No _____ If Yes, see comments _____ (Initial)   See addendum _____ (Initial)

J. **PARENT (OR GUARDIAN) STATEMENT:**
We agree to the placement recommended in this IEP. Yes _____ No _____

We give our permission to have our child counseled by the professional staff, if necessary. Yes _____ No _____

We understand that placement will be on a continuing trial basis and we will be contacted if any placement changes are contemplated. We are aware that such placement does not guarantee success; however, in order to help our child, we accept the responsibility to cooperate in every way with the school program. We acknowledge that we have been notified of and have received a copy of our due process rights pertaining to Special Education placement and have a basic understanding of these rights. We acknowledge that we have received a copy of the completed IEP Form.

_____   _____
Parent or Guardian Signature   Date

COMMENTS: _____

Page 2 of _____

again, the computer is of valuable assistance. A program for the summer months is often an excellent prescription to ensure improvement is maintained. Records should be complete so that information about the youngster's problem and the effects of long-term treatment are always available.

Criteria for Placement of Children

A difficult problem arises in determining what standards will be used for placing children into special programs. Several states have adopted criteria for determining eligibility of children for adapted physical education classes. State guidelines differ, but guidelines in your area should be followed closely if they are in place. These standards are based on the administration of standardized tests for which norms or percentiles have been developed. This procedure helps assure objective guidelines are used and avoids subjective judgment that may be open to disagreement and controversy. For example, criteria used by the state of Alabama are as follows:

1. Perform below the 30th percentile on standardized tests of
   a. motor development
   b. motor proficiency
   c. fundamental motor skills and patterns
   d. physical fitness
   e. game/sport skills
   f. perceptual motor functioning
   g. posture screening
2. Exhibit a developmental delay of two or more years based on appropriate assessment instruments.
3. Function within the severe or profound range as determined by special education eligibility standards.
4. Possess social/emotional or physical capabilities that would render it unlikely for the student to reach his or her physical education goals without significant modification or exclusion from the regular physical education class.

Creating the Least Restrictive Environment

PL 94-142 uses the term *least restrictive environment* to determine placement of children with disabilities. Focus should be on placing a child into a setting that offers the most opportunity for educational advancement. It is inappropriate to place a youngster in an environment where success is impossible. On the other hand, it is debilitating to put a child in a setting that is more restrictive than necessary. Special educators strongly support a physical education program that offers a variety of experiences, from participation in regular physical education classes to physical education in a full-time special school. Figure 6.2 shows a series of options that might be available for physical education.

The least restrictive environment also varies depending on the content of the instructional presentation. For example, for a student in a wheelchair, a soccer or football unit might be very restrictive, whereas in a swimming unit, the environment would not be restrictive. For a student who is emotionally challenged, the command style of presentation might be the least restrictive environment, while an exploration style of instruction would be more restrictive and would invite failure. Consistent and regular judgments need to be made, as curriculum content and teaching styles vary and change the type of environment the student enters. It is shortsighted to place students into a situation and then forget about them. Evaluation and modification of environments need to be ongoing.

Mainstreaming

Mainstreaming involves the practice of placing children who have disabilities into classes with able youngsters. Prudent placement in a least restricted educational environment means the setting must be as normal as possible (normalization), while ensuring the child can fit in and achieve success in that

FIGURE 6.2 *Physical Education Options, Least to Most Restrictive Environments*

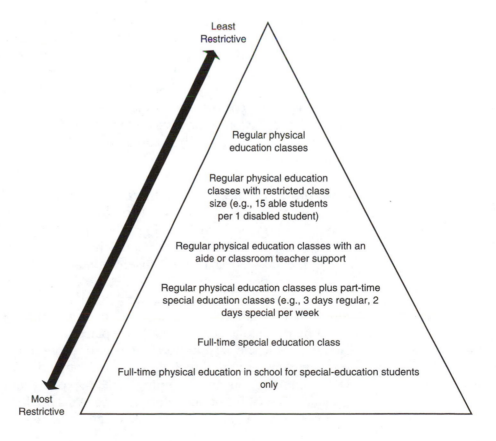

placement. The placement may be mainstreaming, but it is not confined to this approach. Several categories of placement can be defined relevant to physical education.

1. *Full Mainstreaming.* Children with disabilities function as full-time members of a regular classroom group. Within the limitations of their challenge, they participate in physical education with able peers. An example is students who have auditory impairments who are able to participate fully with a minimal amount of assistance.

2. *Mainstreaming for Physical Education Only.* Children with disabilities are not members of the regular classroom groups but participate in physical education with regular classes. Students in this setting might be youngsters with emotional disabilities who are grouped in the classroom and attend regular physical education classes.

3. *Partial Mainstreaming.* Students take part in selected physical education experiences but do not attend on a full-time basis because they can meet with success in only some of the offerings. Their developmental needs are usually met in special classes.

4. *Special Developmental Classes.* Students with disabilities are in segregated special education classes.

5. *Reverse Mainstreaming.* Able children are brought into a special physical education class to promote intergroup peer relationships.

Segregation can be maintained only if it is in the best interests of the child. The thrust of segregated programs should be to establish a level of skill and social proficiency that will eventually enable the special child to be transferred to a less restricted learning environment. The emphasis on placement in the least restrictive environment in which the child, as an individual, can profit most is the cornerstone of the educational process. Children with disabilities, working on their own, often have been denied opportunities to interact with peers and to become a part of the social and academic classroom network.

Guidelines for Successful Mainstreaming Experiences
The concern is not whether to mainstream, but how to mainstream effectively. An important consideration when planning the IEP is whether the child is ready for mainstreaming. Many children with disabilities have severe developmental lags that become insurmountable factors working against successful integration into normal classes. The child must be physically able to accomplish a portion of the program without much, if any, assistance. Placement should be limited to certain activities in which success can be achieved.

When a child is deemed ready for placement, consultation between the teacher and the special education supervisor is of prime importance. In a setting where emotions and feelings can run high, it is important to ensure regular communication and planning. The reception and acceptance of the special children must not be left to chance. A scheduled plan should be instituted before the youngster is mainstreamed. Discuss the needs of the child and develop realistic expected outcomes. It is quite possible the special education teacher may have to participate in the physical education class to assure a smooth transition. The thrust should center on what a child can do rather than on what he or she cannot do. Whether students have or do not have disabilities, they must have opportunities to make appropriate progress. The educational needs of children with disabilities must be met without jeopardizing the progress of other students. This does not rule out activity modifications so that those with disabilities can be included. Some adapted equipment may also be necessary.

Help all students understand the problems related to having disabilities. Make it a goal to have students understand, accept, and live comfortably with persons with disabilities. They should recognize that students with disabilities are functional and worthwhile individuals who can make significant contributions to society. The concept of understanding and appreciating individual differences is one that merits positive development and should concentrate on three aspects:

1. Recognize the similarities among all people: their hopes, rights, aspirations, and goals.

2. Understand human differences and center on the concept that all people have disabilities. For some, disabilities are of such nature and severity that they interfere with normal living.

3. Explore ways to deal with those who differ and stress the acceptance of all children as worthwhile individuals. People with disabilities deserve consideration and understanding based on empathy, not sympathy. Overcompensation should be avoided.

Children with disabilities should not be permitted to use their challenge as a crutch or as an excuse for substandard work. Youngsters should not be allowed to manipulate people into helping with tasks they are capable of doing. Coping skills need to be developed, because children with disabilities do encounter teasing, ignorance, and rejection at various times.

Once the mainstreamed child, able students, and teacher have undergone preliminary preparation, consideration can be given to integrating the youngster with a disability into the learning environment. Mainstreaming allows the child to make commendable educational progress, to achieve in those areas outlined in the IEP, to learn to accept limitations, to observe and model appropriate behavior, to become more socially accepted by others, and, in general, to become a part of the real world. Some guidelines for successful integration of children with disabilities into physical education follow.

1. In addition to participation in the regular program of activities, meeting the target goals as specified in the IEP is important. This often involves resources beyond the physical education class, including special work and homework.

2. Build ego strength by stressing abilities. Eliminate established practices that unwittingly contribute to embarrassment and failure.

3. Foster peer acceptance. This generally begins when the teacher accepts the child as a functioning, participating member of the class.

4. Concentrate on the child's physical education needs and not on the disability. Give strong attention to fundamental skills and physical fitness qualities.

5. Provide continual monitoring and assess periodically the child's target goals. Anecdotal and periodic recordkeeping are implicit in this guideline.

6. Be aware of the child's feelings and anxiety concerning progress and integration. Provide positive feedback as a basic practice.

7. Modify the regular program to meet the unique capacities, physical needs, and social needs of youngsters with disabilities.

8. Provide individual assistance and keep youngsters active. Peer or paraprofessional help may be needed. On-task time is important.

9. Consult regularly with the special education consultant.

10. Give consideration to more individualization within the program so that youngsters with disabilities are smoothly integrated.

Teacher Behavior and the Mainstreaming Process

The success or failure of the mainstreaming process rests largely on the interaction between the teacher and the child with a disability. There is no foolproof, teacher-proof system. Purposes and derived goals are perhaps more important to children with disabilities than to so-called normal peers. Proper levels of organic fitness and skill are vital for healthful living. Such levels enable them to compete with peers. All teachers have to accept responsibility for meeting the needs of children, including those children with disabilities.

Couch explanations and directions in terms that all students, including those with mental retardation, can understand. Be sure students with disabilities understand what is to be accomplished before the learning experiences begin, especially when working with the hearing impaired. Try to find some activity through which they can achieve peer regard. Avoid placing children with disabilities in situations where success is not likely. Conversely, give them opportunities that make the best use of their talents. Obvious increments of improvement toward terminal objectives are excellent motivators for both children and teachers. Let youngsters know that you are vitally interested in their progress.

Apply multisensory approaches when teaching children with disabilities. Visual and auditory modes of learning may not reach slow learners. Manipulate the child through a given movement to communicate the correct "feel." Touch or rub the involved part of the body to provide tactile stimulation. Emphasis should be on helping children perform the skill, not doing it for them.

Seek sources of information to aid in dealing effectively with children with disabilities. Books about disabilities and suggested guidelines for dealing with special children are available. Attend (or organize) workshops that feature knowledgeable individuals who have successful programs and who can help solve specific problems.

Utilizing Parental Support

Having parents on the IEP committee establishes a line of communication between home and school and involves parents. Some kind of home training or homework may be recommended, particularly with younger children. If home training is indicated, two factors are important. First, parents must be committed in terms of time and effort. Their work need not be burdensome but must be done regularly in accordance with the sequenced learning patterns. Second, the school must supply printed and sequenced learning activities for a systematic approach to the homework. Materials should be understandable so that what is to be accomplished is not in doubt. Parents should see obvious progress in their child as assignments unfold.

Older children with disabilities may accept some responsibility for home training, relegating the parent to the role of an interested spectator who provides encouragement. Even if homework is not feasible, parental interest and support are positive factors. Parents can help their youngster realize what skills have been learned and what progress has been made.

Recruiting and Training Aides

The use of aides can be an effective way of increasing the amount of instruction and practice for youngsters with disabilites. Volunteers are usually easy to find among various community organizations, such as parent-teacher groups, foster grandparents, and community colleges. Also, high school students can serve as volunteers and have been shown to work effectively with elementary school youngsters. An initial meeting with volunteer aides to explain the type of youngsters they will be working with and what their responsibilities will involve is useful. Aides must receive training to learn how to be most effective in assisting the instructor. Training should include learning how to work effectively with individuals, record data, and develop special materials and instructional supplies. In addition, aides in training should receive experience in working with youngsters, to see if they are capable and enjoy such work.

There are many roles aides can assume that increase the effectiveness of the instructional situation. Aides may gather and locate equipment and supplies prior to the lesson, officiate games and assure that they run smoothly, and similar activites. Seasoned aides enjoy and are capable of offering one-on-one or small-group instruction to youngsters. Aides should not reduce the need for involvement of the instructor—they should only implement instructional strategies that have been organized and developed by the educator.

Modifying Participation for Children with Disabilities

Children with disabilities need additional consideration when participating in group activities, particularly when the activity is competitive. Much depends on the physical condition of the child and the type of impairment. Children like to win in a competitive situation, and resentment can be created if a team loss is attributed to the presence of a child with a disability. Equalization is the key. Rules can be changed for everyone so that the child who is disabled has a chance to contribute to group success (see Figure 6.3). On the other hand, children need to recognize that everyone, including the disabled and the inept, has a right to play.

Be aware of situations that might devalue the child socially. Never use the degrading method of having captains choose from a group of waiting children. Elimination games should be changed so that points are scored instead of players being eliminated. (This is an important consideration for all youngsters.) Determine the most desirable involvement for children with disabilities by analyzing participants' roles in game and sport activities. Assign a role or position that will make the experience as natural or normal as possible.

Offer a variety of individual and dual activities. Youngsters who have disabilities need to build confidence in their skills before they want to participate with others. Individual activities give children a greater amount of

FIGURE 6.3   *Modifying an Activity for Successful Participation*

practice time without the pressure of failing in front of peers. The aim of these techniques is to make the children with disabilities less visible so that they are not set apart from able classmates. Using youngsters with disabilities as umpires or scorekeepers should be a last resort. Overprotectiveness benefits no one and prevents the special student from experiencing challenge and personal accomplishment. The tendency to underestimate abilities of students must be avoided. The following lists offer ideas for modifying activities to facilitate integration of youngsters with disabilities.

Modifications for Youngsters Lacking Strength and Endurance

1. Lower or enlarge the size of the goal. In basketball, the goal can be lowered; in soccer, the goal might be enlarged.

2. Modify the tempo of the game. For example, games might be performed using a brisk walk rather than running. Another way to modify tempo is to stop the game regularly for substitution. Auto-substitutions can be an excellent method for allowing students to determine when they are fatigued. They ask a predetermined substitute to take their place.

3. Reduce the weight and/or modify the size of the projectile. A lighter object will move more slowly and inflict less damage upon impact. A larger object will move more slowly and be easier for youngsters to track visually and to catch.

4. Reduce the distance that a ball must be thrown or served. Options are to reduce the dimensions of the playing area or add more players to the game. In serving, others can help make the serve playable. For example, in volleyball, other teammates can bat the serve over the net as long as it does not touch the floor.

5. In games that are played to a certain number of points, reduce the number required for a win. For example, volleyball games can be played to 7 or 11, depending on the skill and intensity of the players.

6. Modify striking implements by shortening and reducing their weight. Rackets are much easier to control when they are shortened. Softball bats are easier to control when the player "chokes up" or selects a lighter bat.

7. In some games, it is possible to slow the ball down by letting some of the air out of it. This will reduce the speed of rebound and make the ball easier to control in a restricted area. It will also keep the ball from rolling away from players when it is not under control.

8. Play a game in a different position. Some games may be played in a sitting or lying position, which is easier and less demanding than standing or running.

9. Provide matching or substitution. Match another child on borrowed crutches with a child on braces. Two players can be combined to play one position. A student in a desk chair with wheels can be matched against a child in a wheelchair.

10. Youngsters can substitute skills for each other. For example, a child can strike an object but may lack the mobility to run. Permit substitute courtesy runners.

Modifications for Youngsters Lacking Coordination

1. Increase the size of the goal or target. Enlarging the size of a basketball goal increases the opportunity for success. Another alternative is to offer points for hitting the backboard instead of making a goal. Since scoring is self-motivating, modification should occur until success is assured.

2. Lack of coordination will make uncoordinated youngsters more susceptible to injury from a projectile. Offer protection by using various types of protectors (glasses, chest protectors, face masks, etc.).

3. When teaching throwing, allow the opportunity to throw at maximum velocity without concern for accuracy. Use small balls that can be grasped easily. Fleece balls and beanbags are easy to hold and release.

4. When learning to strike an object, begin with one that is held stationary. The use of a batting tee or tennis ball fastened to a string can offer the child an opportunity for success. In addition, a larger racket or bat can be used and the youngster can choke up on the grip.

5. If a great deal of time is spent recovering a projectile, children receive few practice trials and feel frustrated. Place them near a backstop or use a goal that rebounds the projectile to the shooter.

6. When learning to catch, use a soft, lightweight, and slow-moving object. Beach balls and balloons are excellent for beginning catching skills because they allow youngsters to track their movement visually. In addition, foam rubber balls eliminate the fear of being hurt by a thrown or batted projectile.

Modifications for Youngsters Lacking Balance and Agility

1. Increase the width of rails, lines, and beams when practicing balance. Carrying a long pole will help minimize rapid shifts of balance and is a useful lead-up activity.

2. Increase the width of the base of support. Youngsters should be taught to keep their feet spread at least to shoulder width.

3. The more body parts in contact with the floor, the easier it is to balance the body. Beginning balance practice should emphasize controlled movement using as many body parts as possible.

4. Increase the surface area of the body parts in contact with the floor or beam. For example, walking flatfooted is easier than walking on tiptoes.

5. Lower the center of gravity. This offers more stability and greater balance to the child. Place emphasis on bending the knees and leaning slightly forward.

6. Assure that surfaces offer good friction. Floors and shoes should not be slick or children will fall. Carpets or tumbling mats increase a child's traction.

7. Some children require balance assistance. A barre, cane, or chair can be used to keep the youngster from falling.

8. Children with balance problems inevitably fall. Offer practice in learning how to fall so that children will know how to absorb the force of the fall.

Understanding Specific Disabilities

To assist a child with a challenge, an understanding of the disability and what it means to the child is essential. Basic information is provided here, and additional materials may be secured from special education consultants. National associations offer information about various disabilities and suggest ways of helping special children.

Mental Retardation

The capacity of the child who is mentally retarded does not allow the child to be served by the standard program. Mental retardation is a question of degree, usually measured in terms of intelligence quotient (IQ). Children with mild retardation (with IQs ranging roughly from 50 to 75 or 80) are most often mainstreamed in both physical education and the regular classroom. Children with IQs below 50 usually cannot function in a regular classroom environment; they need special classes. These children are generally not mainstreamed and so are excluded from the following discussion.

Academically, children with mild retardation (also termed educable mentally retarded) are slower to understand directions, follow instructions, complete tasks, and make progress. Conceptually, they have difficulty pulling facts together and drawing conclusions. Their motivation to stay on task is generally lower. Academic success may have eluded them. These realities must be considered in the physical education setting. Improvement in these areas is a goal to be achieved.

Do children who are retarded differ physically from other students? In a study comparing 71 boys who are educable mentally retarded boys with 71 boys who are not, aged 6 to 10 years, the following was noted. Differences between the two groups, in respect to opportunities to be physically active, tend to be substantial. Similarly, the motivation to be physically active may be less in the retarded—a reflection of their general motor ineptness. The relatively large proportion of subcutaneous tissue in the retarded is more than suggestive of a physically inactive life resulting in a corresponding low level of motor performance (Dobbins, Garron, & Rarick, 1981).

In another study (Ulrich, 1983), a comparison was made of the developmental levels of 117 disabled and 96 educable mentally retarded children with respect to criterion-referenced testing of 12 fundamental motor skills and 4 physical fitness skills. The investigation supports the findings of the previous study in that the students who are educable mentally retarded lagged 3.5 years behind the other children in motor skill development, as based on the researcher's selected criterion reference point. The investigator attributes this lag to a lack of opportunity for movement experiences at an early age. The children with disabilities were from special education classes, not from a mainstreaming situation.

Instructional Procedures

Studies of students with mild retardation support the assumption that they can learn, but do so at a slower rate and not to the depth of children with normal mental functioning. To help the mildly retarded develop their capacities so that they can become participating members of society, the learning process should concentrate on fundamental skills and fitness qualities. Unless this base is established, the child who is retarded faces considerable difficulty later in learning specialized skills. Minimizing skill and fitness lags can help ease the child into mainstream living.

The fitness approach involves motivation, acquisition of developmental techniques, and application of these to a personalized fitness program. The child who is retarded reacts well to goal setting, provided that the goals are challenging yet attainable. The pace of learning depends on the degree of retardation. Before children with mental retardation can learn, they need to know what is expected and how it is to be accomplished. Common sense must govern the determination of progress increments. These should be challenging but within the performer's grasp. Often, past experiences have made children who are retarded the victims of a failure syndrome. The satisfaction of accomplishment must supplant this poor self-image.

Place emphasis on gross motor movement that is progressive in nature. Teach activities that are presented through demonstration rather than verbalization. Many of the skills may have to be accompanied by manual assistance to help children get the "feel" of the skill. To avoid boredom and frustration, practice periods should be short. Allow ample opportunity for youngsters to show off skills they can perform so that they can enjoy the feeling of accomplishment. Shaping behavior by accepting approximation of the skill will encourage the children to keep trying. Progress arrives in small increments; be sensitive to improvement and accomplishment, no matter how small.

Trying should be rewarded. Many youngsters are reticent to try a new activity. Instructions should be repeated a number of times. Safety rules must be followed, as these youngsters may not understand the risk of injury involved.

Epilepsy

Epilepsy is a dysfunction of the electrical impulses emitted by the brain. It is not an organic disease. It can happen at any period of life but generally shows up during early childhood. With proper care and medication, many children overcome this condition and live normal lives.

Epilepsy is a hidden problem. A child with epilepsy looks, acts, and is like other children except for unpredictable seizures. Unfortunately, epilepsy carries an unwarranted social stigma. A child with epilepsy meets with a lack of acceptance, even when adequate explanations are made to those sharing the child's environment. A major seizure can be frightening to others. Revulsion is another possible reaction of observers.

Gaining control of seizures is often a long procedure, involving experimentation with appropriate anticonvulsive medication in proper doses. Fortunately, most epilepsy can be controlled or minimized with proper medication. One factor in control is to be sure that the child is taking the medication as prescribed.

Sometimes a child can recognize signs of seizure onset. If this occurs in a physical education class, the child should have the privilege of moving to the sideline without permission. A seizure may, however, occur without warning. The instructor should know the signs of a seizure and react accordingly. The teacher may be the first (even before the child) to recognize that a seizure is imminent.

Three kinds of seizure are identified. A *petit mal* seizure involves a brief period (a few seconds) of blackout. No one is aware of the problem, including the child. Sometimes it is labeled inattention and thus is difficult to identify. A *psychomotor epileptic* seizure is longer lasting (perhaps a few minutes) and is characterized by involuntary movements and twitching. The child acts like a sleepwalker and cannot be stopped or helped. The affected youngster does not respond when addressed and is unaware of the seizure. A *grand mal* seizure is a total seizure with complete neurological involvement. The child may become unconscious and lose control of the bladder or bowels, resulting in loss of urine, stool, or both. Rigidity and tremors can appear. The seizure must run its course.

Two points are important. First, throughout any seizure or incident, preserve a matter-of-fact attitude and try not to exhibit pity. Second, educate the other children to understand and empathize with the problem. Stress what the condition is and, later, what it is not. Explain that the behavior during a seizure is a response to an unusual output of electrical discharges from the brain. Everyone needs these discharges to function in normal living, but the person with epilepsy is subject to an unusual amount of the discharges, which results in unusual activity. The condition involves a natural phenomenon that gets out of control.

Children need to understand that the seizure must run its course. When the seizure is over, everyone can resume normal activity, including the involved child, although the child may be disoriented and uncoordinated for a brief period of time. Offer the child the option of resting or returning to activity. Proper emotional climate of the class is established when you maintain an accepting and relaxed attitude.

Information about epilepsy should be a part of the standard health curriculum in the school, rather than a reaction to an epileptic seizure or to the presence of a student who may have seizures. Epilepsy can be discussed as a topic relevant to understanding the central nervous system. Certain risks are involved if the lessons have as their focus the problems of a particular child, because this may heighten the child's feelings of exclusion and place disproportionate attention on what might have been a relatively inconsequential aspect of the student's life. (This caution does not rule out helpful information being given to peers when a seizure has taken place.)

In the event of a grand mal seizure, some routine procedures should be followed. Have available a blanket, a pillow, and towels to clean up any mess that might occur. Make the child comfortable if there is time. Do not try to restrain the child. Put nothing in the mouth. Support the child's head on the pillow, turning it to one side to allow the saliva to drain. Remove from the area any hard or sharp objects that might cause harm. Secure help from a doctor or nurse if the seizure continues more than three or four minutes or if seizures occur three or more times during a school day. Always notify the school nurse and the parents that a seizure has occurred. Assure the class that the seizure will pass and that the involved child will not be harmed or affected.

Instructional Procedures

Recommendations regarding special modes of conduct and guidelines governing participation in school activities must come from the child's physician, since most epileptic children are under medical supervision. The instructor should stay within these guidelines while avoiding being overprotective.

Today's approach is to bring epilepsy into the open. A concerted effort should be made to educate today's children so that traditional attitudes toward the condition can be altered. Emphasize inclusion of the child rather than exclusion. If there is some doubt about control of the seizures, climbing and elevated activities should be eliminated.

Perhaps tomorrow's adults will possess a better understanding. The child with epilepsy is a normal, functioning person except at the time of a seizure. Epilepsy is not a form of mental illness, and most people with epilepsy are not mentally retarded.

Visual Impairment

Mainstreaming for the visually impaired must be handled carefully and with common sense. The visually impaired designation includes those who are partially sighted as well as those who are legally blind. One has only to move about in a dark room to realize the mobility problems faced by a visually impaired child. This disability poses movement problems and puts limits on participation in certain types of physical activity. Total mainstreaming may not be a feasible solution.

There is a need to bring the child into contact with other children, however, and to focus on the child's unique qualities and strengths. Empathy for and acceptance of the visually impaired child are most important. The task of monitoring movement and helping this child should be considered a privilege to be rotated among class members. If participation in the class activity selected is contraindicated, the monitor can help provide an alternate activity.

Instructional Procedures

A child who has visual impairments has to develop confidence in his or her ability to move freely and surely within the limits of the disability. Since limited mobility often leads to reduced activity, this inclination can be countered with a specialized physical fitness and movement program in which the lack of sight does not prove insurmountable. The child can take part in group fitness activities with assistance as needed. Exercises should pose few problems. Rope jumping is an excellent activity. Individual movement activities, stunts and tumbling, rhythms and dances (particularly partner dances), and selected apparatus activities can be appropriate. Low balance beams, bench activities, climbing apparatus, and climbing ropes may be within the child's capacity. Manipulative activities, involving tactile senses, are not always appropriate. If the child has some vision, however, brightly colored balls against a contrasting background in good light can permit controlled throwing, tracking, and catching. Through the selection of activities, the sense of balance should be challenged regularly to contribute to sureness of movement. Because vision is limited, other balance controls also need to be developed.

The child who is visually impaired ordinarily cannot take visual cues from other children or the teacher, so explanations must be precise and clear. Use a whistle or loud verbal cue to signal the class. For some situations, an assigned peer can monitor activity, helping as needed or requested. In running situations, the helper can hold hands with the child who is visually impaired. Another way to aid the child is with physical guidance until the feel of a movement pattern is established. This should be a last choice, however, occurring only after the child has had a chance to interpret the verbal instructions and still cannot meet the challenge. Touching a part of the child's body to establish correct sequencing in a movement pattern also can be of help.

Auditory Impairment

Children with auditory impairments are those who are deaf or who must wear hearing aids. In physical education classes, these children are capable of performing most, if not all, activities that other children can perform. Because most instruction is verbal, a child who is deaf is isolated and often frustrated in a mainstreaming situation unless other means of communication are established. Accomplishing this while keeping the class functioning normally constitutes a problem of considerable magnitude.

Some advocates for the deaf contend that implementing PL 94-142 with its emphasis on mainstreaming is not appropriate for children who are deaf and that it thwarts their development. Teaching the deaf is a challenging and specialized process, requiring different communication techniques. Many such children have poor or unintelligible speech and inevitably develop a language gap with the hearing world. Sign language, lip reading, and speech training are all important facets of communicative ability for the deaf. Integrating a child who is deaf into the regular physical education class setting is a process that must be handled with common sense. The experience should be satisfying to him or her or it is a failure.

Instructional Procedures
Certainly children who are hearing impaired can perform physically and at the same level as children with normal hearing when given the opportunity.

One successful approach to teaching both kinds of youngsters is to use contract or task card techniques. Written instructions can be read loudly by the teacher or monitor. Pairing children with severe hearing loss with other children can be a frustrating experience for both, but meaningful possibilities also exist. Such a pairing necessitates lip reading, the use of verbal cues, or strong amplification on a hearing aid. Visual cues, featuring a "do as I do" approach, can stimulate certain types of activity.

The child who is deaf should be near the teacher to increase the opportunities to read lips and receive facial cues. Keep the class physically active. Avoid long delays for explanations or question and answer periods. This becomes a blank time for the hearing impaired and leads to frustration and aggressive action. For rhythmic activities, some devices can be of benefit. Keep record player speakers on the floor to provide vibration. Use a metronome or blinking light. For controlling movement patterns, hand signals should be developed for starting, stopping, moving to an area, assembling near the teacher, sitting down, and so on.

Static and dynamic balance problems are prevalent among children who are hearing impaired. Focus on activities that challenge balance and insist on proper procedures. Have the child maintain the position or movement for 10 to 15 seconds and recover to the original position, all in good balance.

Orthopedic Disabilities

Orthopedic disabilities in children encompass a range of physical ailments, some of which may involve external support items such as splints, braces, crutches, and wheelchairs. A few postpolio cases may be encountered. Generalizing procedures for such a range of physical abnormalities is difficult. Children with orthopedic problems usually function on an academic level with other children and are regular members of a classroom.

Instructional Procedures

Instructional focus must be on what the child can do and on the physical needs that are to be met. Mobility is a problem for most, and modification is needed if the class activity demands running or agility. Individualized programs are made to order for this group, because the achievement goals can be set within the child's capacity to perform.

Although volleyball and basketball are popular team sports, there will be few leisure opportunities in which individuals with orthopedic disabilities may participate due to the difficulty of getting enough participants together for team play. Strong emphasis should be placed on individual and dual sports such as tennis, track and field, road racing, table tennis, badminton, and swimming. This allows students who are orthopedically impaired to play a dual sport with an opponent (abled or disabled) or to participate individually in activities such as road racing and swimming.

For children in wheelchairs, certain measures are implicit. Special work is needed to develop general musculature to improve conditions for coping with the disability and to prevent muscle atrophy. In particular, these children need strong arm and shoulder musculature to transfer in and out of the wheelchair without assistance. Flexibility training to prevent and relieve permanent muscle shortening (contracture) should be instituted. Cardiorespiratory training is needed to maintain or improve aerobic capacity, as immobility in the chair decreases activity. From these experiences, children in wheelchairs should derive a personal, functioning program of activity that can carry over into daily living (see Figure 6.4).

Time devoted to special health care after class must be considered for children with braces or in wheelchairs. Children with braces should inspect skin contact areas to look for irritation. If they have perspired, a washcloth and towel will help them freshen up and remove irritants. Children in wheelchairs can transfer to sturdy chairs that are rigid and stabilized to allow the wheelchairs to dry out. Adequate cushioning should be provided for any surface to which an orthopedically impaired person transfers, such as chairs, weight machines, and pool decks, for the prevention of pressure sores and skin abrasions. Schedules can be adjusted so that time for this care is available. Scheduling the class during the last period before lunch or recess or at the end of the day allows this time. Children with temporary conditions (fractures, sprains, strains) are handled on an individual basis, according to physician recommendations. Remedial work may be indicated.

FIGURE 6.4   Youngsters with Disabilities Can Experience the Joy of Participation

Emotional Disturbances

Public Law 94-142 refers to students with behavior disorders as "severely emotionally disturbed." Children who are emotionally disturbed represent an enigma for mainstreaming. They have been removed from the regular classroom situation because they may cause a disruption and because they need psychological services. Physical education seems to be one area in which they can find success. Each case is different, however, and generalization is difficult.

Instructional Procedures

An important key when working with youngsters who are emotionally disturbed is to establish a learning environment that is fair and consistent. The child needs to know exactly what is expected and accepted in the instructional setting. In addition, rules must be clearly defined and nonpunitive in nature. Explanation of reasons for rules should be a regular topic of discussion, as these youngsters often feel that someone is making rules that are meant to punish them personally.

Youngsters who are severely emotionally disturbed are in need of a stable and organized environment that focuses on individual progress. They will become easily frustrated and quit if the activities are too difficult or cause embarrassment. It is important to expect unexpected outbursts, even when instructional procedures have been correct. If the unexpected is anticipated, you will not feel as threatened or hurt by the student's behavior. Emphasis should be placed on development of the affective domain. These students need help building positive self-concepts, expressing their feelings appropriately, and learning to accept responsibility for their own behavior.

All youngsters need to know their limits of behavior, especially those who are emotionally disturbed. Set the limits and then enforce them consistently. Youngsters must know who is in charge and what will be accepted. It may take a long time to develop confidence in children who are emotionally disturbed, and vice versa. During this time, it is important to build a sense of trust. Plan on problems and be ready to deal with them before they occur. A teacher who is patient and understanding can have a positive effect on children with this disability; loving and forgiving teachers are highly effective.

Learning Disabilities

Learning disabilities encompass a range of problems that lack a clear definition. Examples of terms used to describe various learning disabilities are *perceptual handicaps*, *brain injury*, *minimal brain dysfunction*, *dyslexia*, and *developmental aphasia*. This definition used by the federal government is so broad that over 40 percent of school-aged youngsters can qualify as being learning disabled. More boys than girls (a 2:1 ratio) are identified as learning disabled in today's schools. Additionally, many more elementary than secondary school children are identified. Characteristics of youngsters with learning disabilities might include one or more of the following: hyperactivity, short attention span, perceptual-motor problems, poor self-concept, clumsiness, poor short- or long-term memory, and an unwillingness to persevere when learning motor tasks.

The causes of learning disabilities are poorly understood. Two major theories are currently popular for explaining these problems (Horvath, 1990). The first theory supposes that learning disabilities are organically based, with one of the major causal factors being an injury to the brain. Individuals who are brain injured are unable to efficiently receive and integrate sensory impulses. The second hypothesis is that learning disabilities are biochemically based. This theory supposes that several biochemical factors such as allergies, mineral and vitamin deficiencies, and glandular disorders cause learning disabilities. It is important to modify the physical education program on an individualized basis for these children, since their disabilities are unique.

Instructional Procedures

Working with youngsters who are learning disabled is similar to working with children who are emotionally disturbed. The program should be structured and conducted in similar fashion on a day-to-day basis. Youngsters should not be surprised with unexpected changes in the routines. The activity area should be arranged so distractions are kept to a minimum. Equipment should be distributed and collected using a similar routine. This unchanging structure allows the children to explore the environment with confidence. The teaching area should be restricted to the smallest possible size so that student/teacher distance is kept to a minimum. An environment without limits may cause some youngsters to feel threatened or out of control.

Students with learning disabilities often find it difficult to learn independently or wait for a turn. Lessons should demand active participation and require students to be on task a large share of the lesson time. It may be necessary to introduce cross-aged tutoring or invite parent volunteers in to work individually with students. Attention based on firmness and concern will help these students learn motor skills and deal with extraneous distractions in their environment. Instructions should be short and concise sentences, given one at a time.

Asthma, Cerebral Palsy, Cardiac Problems, and Diabetes

Children with asthma have restricted breathing capacity. In the past, doctors were quick to excuse these children from participating in physical education classes, but recent research is showing that physical activity is not contraindicated. A study by Varray, Mercier, Terral, and Prefaut (1991) showed that children with asthma were capable of participating in high-intensity exercise without complications. Children who were 11 years old participated in a swimming program and reached an intensity level within 5 percent of their maximal heart rate. These youngsters showed a significant increase in cardiovascular fitness. Parents of the children reported a decrease in the intensity of wheezing attacks and were often able to control asthmatic attacks through relaxation and breathing exercises. The researchers concluded that when workloads are individualized for asthmatic children, their cardiovascular fitness can be enhanced through aerobic training. A key to follow when working with children with asthma is to allow each youngster to be the judge of his or her workload capacity and to stop when rest is needed.

Cerebral palsy, like epilepsy, has strong negative social implications. Peer education and guidance are necessary. The signs of cerebral palsy are quite visible and, in severe cases, result in odd, uncoordinated movements and a characteristic gait. Medical supervision indicates the limits of the child's activities. Children with cerebral palsy are usually of normal intelligence; their chief problem is control of movement. An important goal is ensuring that they can achieve competency in performing simple movements. The excitability threshold is critical and must not be exceeded. Many need support services for special training in both neural and movement control.

Children with cardiac problems are generally under the guidance of a physician. Limitations and restrictions should be followed to the letter. The child should, however, be encouraged to work to the limits of the prescription.

Diabetes is an inability to metabolize carbohydrates that results from the body's failure to supply insulin. Insulin is taken either orally or by injection to control serious cases. If the child is overweight, a program of weight reduction and exercise prescription are partial solutions. Diabetics are usually under medical supervision. Knowing that a child with diabetes is in the physical education class is important, because the child must be monitored to detect the possibility of hypoglycemia (abnormally low blood sugar level). The condition can be accompanied by trembling, weakness, hunger, incoherence, and even coma or convulsions. The solution is to raise the blood sugar level immediately through oral consumption of simple sugar (e.g., skim milk, orange juice) or some other easily converted carbohydrate. The diabetic usually carries carbohydrates, but a supply should be available to the instructor. Immediate action is needed because low blood sugar level can be dangerous, even leading to loss of life. The diabetic probably has enough control to participate in almost any activity. This is evidenced by the number of diabetic professional athletes who meet the demands of high activity without difficulty.

References and Suggested Readings

Arnheim, D. D., & Sinclair, W. A. (1985). *Physical education for special populations: A developmental, adapted, and remedial approach.* Englewood Cliffs, NJ: Prentice-Hall.

Cooper Institute for Aerobics Research. (1992). *The Prudential Fitnessgram Test administration manual.* Dallas: Cooper Institute for Aerobics Research.

Dobbins, D. A., Garron, R., & Rarick, G. L. (1981). The motor performance of educable mentally retarded and intellectually normal boys after covariate control for differences in body size. *Research Quarterly, 52*(1), 6–7.

Epstein, L. H., et al. (1984). The modification of activity patterns and energy expenditure in obese young girls. *Behavior Therapy, 15*(1): 101–108.

Fait, H. F., & Dunn, J. M. (1984). *Special physical education: Adapted, individualized approach.* Philadelphia: W. B. Saunders.

Foster, G. D., Wadden, T. A., & Brownell, K. D. (1985). Peer-led program for the treatment and prevention of obesity in the schools. *Journal of Consulting and Clinical Psychology, 53*(4), 538–540.

Horvath, M. (1990). *Physical education and sport for exceptional students.* Dubuque, IA: Wm. C. Brown.

Seaman, J. A., & DePauw, K. P. (1982). *The new adapted physical education.* Palo Alto, CA: Mayfield.

Sherrill, C. (1986). *Adapted physical education and recreation.* Dubuque, IA: Wm. C. Brown.

Ulrich, D. A. (1983). A comparison of the qualitative motor performance of normal, educable, and trainable mentally retarded students. In R. L. Eason, T. L. Smith, & F. Caron (Eds.), *Adapted physical activity.* Champaign, IL: Human Kinetics.

Varray, A. L., Mercier, J. G., Terral, C. M., & Prefaut, C. G. (1991). Individualized aerobic and high intensity training for asthmatic children in an exercise readaption program. *Chest, 99,* 579–586.

Chapter SEVEN

Legal Liability and Proper Care of Students

In this chapter, you will learn...

◆ *About negligence and the four points courts use to judge whether a teacher is liable*

◆ *What the different categories of negligence are, including malfeasance, misfeasance, and nonfeasance*

◆ *The defenses used in court to show a teacher is not negligent in conducting his or her duties*

◆ *To safely supervise students and what minimum standards of conduct must be followed*

◆ *How to make sure equipment and facilities are safe for students to use*

◆ *How to establish procedures to assure a safe environment*

◆ *What steps to follow in establishing an emergency care plan*

◆ *How to minimize the effects of a lawsuit*

◆ *To effectively use a safety and liability checklist*

School district personnel, including teaching and nonteaching members, are obligated to exercise ordinary care for the safety of students. This duty is manifested as the ability to anticipate reasonably foreseeable dangers and the responsibility to take necessary precautions to prevent problems from occurring. Failure to do so may cause the district to be the target of lawsuits.

Compared with other subject matter areas, physical education is particularly vulnerable to accidents and resultant injuries. More than 50 percent of all accidents in the school setting occur on the playground and in the gymnasium. Even though schools cannot be held financially accountable for costs associated with treatment of injuries, they can be forced to pay these expenses if the injured party sues and wins judgment. Legal suits are conducted under respective state statutes. Principles underlying legal action are similar, but certain regulations and procedures vary among states. Acquire a copy of the legal liability policy in your district. Districts usually have a written definition of situations in which teachers can be held liable.

All students have the right to freedom from injury caused by others or due to participation in a program. Courts have ruled that teachers owe their students a duty of care to protect them from harm. You must offer a standard of care that any reasonable and prudent professional with similar training would apply under the given circumstances. A teacher is required to exercise the teaching skill, discretion, and knowledge that members of the profession in good standing normally possess in similar situations. Lawsuits usually occur when citizens believe that this standard of care was not exercised.

Liability is the responsibility to perform a duty to a particular group. It is an obligation to perform in a particular way that is required by law and enforced by court action. You are bound by contract to carry out duties in a reasonable and prudent manner. Liability is always a legal matter. It must be proved in a court of law that negligence occurred before one can be held liable.

Torts

In education, a tort is concerned with the teacher/student relationship and is a legal wrong that results in direct or indirect injury to another individual or to property. The following legal definition is from *Black's Law Dictionary* (1990): "[A tort is] a private or civil wrong or injury, other than breach of contract, for which the court will provide a remedy in the form of an action for damages. Three elements of every tort action are: existence of legal duty from defendant to plaintiff, breach of duty, and damage as proximate result."

As the result of a tort, the court can give a monetary reward for damages that occurred. The court can also give a monetary reward for punitive damages if a breach of duty can be established. Usually, the court rewards the offended individual for damages that occurred due to the negligence of the instructor or other responsible individual. Punitive damages are much less common.

Negligence and Liability

Liability is usually concerned with a breach of duty through negligence. Lawyers examine the situation that gave rise to the injury to establish if liability can be determined. Four major points must be established to determine if a teacher was negligent.

1. *Duty.* The first point considered is that of duty owed to the participants. Did the school or teacher owe students a duty of care that implies conforming to certain standards of conduct? When examining duty or breach of duty, the court looks at reasonable care that a member of the profession in good standing would provide. In other words, to determine a reasonable standard, the court uses the conduct of other teachers as a standard for comparison.

2. *Breach of Duty.* The teacher must commit a breach of duty by failing to conform to the required duty. After it is established that a duty was required, it must be proved that the teacher did not perform that duty. Two situations are possible: (a) the teacher did something that was not supposed to be done (e.g., put boxing gloves on students to resolve their differences) or (b) the teacher did not do something that should have been done (e.g., failed to teach an activity using proper progressions).

3. *Injury.* An injury must occur if liability is to be established. If no injury or harm occurs, there is no liability. Further, it must be proved that the injured party is entitled to compensatory damages for financial loss or physical discomfort.

4. *Proximate Cause.* The failure of the teacher to conform to the required standard must be the proximate cause of the resulting injury. It must be proved that the injury was caused by the teacher's breach of duty. It is not enough to prove simply that a breach of duty occurred. It must simultaneously be shown that the injury was a direct result of the teacher's failure to provide a reasonable standard of care.

Foreseeability

A key to the issue of negligence is foreseeability. Courts expect that a trained professional is able to foresee potentially harmful situations. Was it possible for the teacher to predict and anticipate the danger of the harmful act or situation and to take appropriate measures to prevent it from occurring? If the injured party can prove that the teacher should have foreseen the danger involved in an activity or situation (even in part), the teacher will be found negligent for failing to act in a reasonable and prudent manner.

This points out the necessity of examining all activities, equipment, and facilities for possible hazards and sources of accident. As an example, a common game (unfortunately) in many school settings is bombardment, or dodge ball. During the game, a student is hit in the eye by a ball and loses vision in that eye. Was this a foreseeable accident that could have been prevented? Were the balls being used capable of inflicting severe injury? Were students aware of rules that might have prevented this injury? Were the abilities of the students somewhat equal, or were some capable of throwing with such velocity that injury was predictable? Were all students forced to play the game? These questions would likely be considered in court in an attempt to prove that the teacher should have been able to predict the overly dangerous situation.

Types of Negligence

Negligence is defined by the court as conduct that falls below a standard of care established to protect others from unreasonable risk or harm. Several types of negligence can be categorized.

Malfeasance

Malfeasance occurs when the teacher does something improper by committing an act that is unlawful and wrongful, with no legal basis (often referred to as an act of commission). Malfeasance can be illustrated by the following incident. A male student misbehaved on numerous occasions. In desperation, the teacher gave the student a choice of punishment—a severe spanking in front of the class or running many laps around the field. The student chose the former and suffered physical and emotional damage. Even though the teacher gave the student a choice whereby he could have avoided the paddling, the teacher is still liable for any physical or emotional harm caused.

Misfeasance

Misfeasance occurs when the teacher follows the proper procedures but does not perform according to the required standard of conduct. Misfeasance is based on performance of the proper action, but not up to the required standard. It is usually the subpar performance of an act that might have been otherwise lawfully done. An example would be a teacher offering to spot a student during a tumbling routine and then not doing the spotting properly. If the student is injured due to a faulty spot, the teacher can be held liable.

Nonfeasance

Nonfeasance is based on lack of action in carrying out a duty. This is usually an act of omission: The teacher knew the proper procedures but failed to follow them. Teachers can be found negligent if they act or fail to act. Understanding and carrying out proper procedures and duties in a manner befitting members of the profession is essential. In contrast to the misfeasance example, nonfeasance occurs when a teacher knows that it is necessary to spot certain gymnastic routines but fails to do so. Courts expect teachers to behave with more skill and insight than parents (Strickland, Phillip, & Phillips, 1976). Teachers are expected to behave with greater competency because they have been educated to give students a higher standard of professional care than parents.

Contributory Negligence

The situation is different when the injured student is partially or wholly at fault. Students are expected to exercise sensible care and to follow directions or regulations designed to protect them from injury. Improper behavior by the injured party that causes the accident is usually ruled to be contributory negligence, because the injured party contributed to the resulting harm. This responsibility is directly related to the maturity, ability, and experience of the child. For example, most states have laws specifying that a child under 7 years of age is incapable of contributory negligence (Baley & Matthews, 1984). To illustrate contributory negligence, assume that a teacher has thoroughly explained safety rules to be followed while hitting softballs. As students begin to practice, one of them runs through a restricted area that is well marked and is hit by a bat. Depending on the age and maturity of the child, the possibility is strong that the student will be held liable for such action.

Comparative or Shared Negligence

Under the doctrine of comparative negligence, the injured party can recover only if he or she is found to be less negligent than the defendant (the teacher). Where statutes apply, the amount of recovery is generally reduced in proportion to the injured party's participation in the circumstances leading to the injury.

Common Defenses against Negligence

Negligence must be proved in a court of law. Many times, teachers are negligent in carrying out their duties, yet the injured party does not take the case to court. If a teacher is sued, some of the following defenses are used in an attempt to show that the teacher's action was not the primary cause of the accident.

Act of God

The act of God defense places the cause of injury on forces beyond the control of the teacher or the school. The defense is made that it was impossible to predict an unsafe condition, but through an act of God, the injury occurred. Typical acts would be a gust of wind that blew over a volleyball standard or a cloudburst of rain that made a surface slick. The act of God defense can be used only in cases in which the injury still would have occurred even though reasonable and prudent action had been taken.

Proximate Cause

This defense attempts to prove that the accident was not caused by the negligence of the teacher. There must be a close relationship between the breach of duty by the teacher and the injury. This is a common defense in cases dealing with proper supervision. For example, a student is participating in an activity supervised by the teacher. When the teacher leaves the playing area to get a cup of coffee, the student is injured. The defense lawyer will try to show that the accident would have occurred regardless of whether or not the teacher was there.

Assumption of Risk

Clearly, physical education is a high-risk activity when compared with most other curriculum areas. The participant assumes the risk of an activity when choosing to be part of that activity. The assumption of risk defense is seldom used in physical education because students are not often allowed to choose to participate or not participate. An instructor for an elective program that allows students to choose desired units of instruction might find this a better defense than one who teaches a totally required program. Athletic and sport club participation is by choice, and players must assume a greater risk in activities such as football and gymnastics.

Contributory Negligence

Contributory negligence is often used by the defense in an attempt to convince the court that the injured party acted in a manner that was abnormal. In other words, the injured individual did not act in a manner that was typical of students of similar age and maturity. The defense attempts to demonstrate that the activity or equipment in question was used for years with no record of accident. A case is made based on the manner of presentation—how students were taught to act in a safe manner—and that the injured student acted outside the parameters of safe conduct. A key point in this defense is whether the activity was suitable for the age and maturity level of the participants.

Areas of Responsibility

A two-tiered approach for analyzing injuries is useful for determining responsibility. The first tier includes the duties that the administration must assume in support of the program. The second tier defines the duties of the instructor or staff member charged with teaching or supervising students. Each party has a role to fill, but some overlap occurs. The following example illustrates the differences.

A student is hurt while performing a tumbling stunt. A lawsuit ensues, charging the teacher with negligence for not following safe procedures. The administration could also be included in the suit, being charged with negligence for hiring an incompetent (not qualified) instructor. The two levels of responsibility should be considered when delegating responsibility because:

1. They identify different functions and responsibilities of the teaching staff and administration.

2. They provide a framework for reducing injuries and improving safety procedures.

3. They provide perspective for following legal precedents.

4. In the described responsibilities that follow, both administrative and instructional duties are presented.

Supervision

All activities in a school setting must be supervised, including recess, lunch times, and field trips. The responsibilities of the school are critical if supervision is to function properly.

Administration

Two levels are identified in supervision: general and specific. *General supervision* (e.g., playground duty) refers to broad coverage, when students are not under direct control of a teacher or a designated individual. A plan of supervision should be made, designating the areas to be covered and including where and how the supervisor should rotate. This plan, kept in the principal's office, should cover rules of conduct governing student behavior. Rules should be posted prominently on bulletin boards, especially in classrooms. In addition to the plan, administrators must select qualified personnel, provide necessary training, and monitor the plan properly.

The general supervisor must be concerned primarily with student behavior, focusing on the student's right to a relaxing recreational experience. Supervisors should observe the area, looking for breaches of discipline, particularly when an individual or group "picks on" another youngster. The supervisor needs to look for protruding sprinkler heads, broken glass, and debris on the play area. If it becomes necessary to leave the area, a qualified substitute must be found to prevent the area from going unsupervised.

Staff

General supervision is necessary during recess, before and after school, during lunch break, and during certain other sessions where instruction is not offered. The supervisor should know the school's plan for supervision as well as the emergency care procedures to follow in case of an accident. Supervision is a positive act that requires the supervisor to be actively involved and moving throughout the area. The number of supervisors should be determined by the type of activity, the size of the area, and the number and age of the students.

Specific supervision requires that the instructor be with a certain group of students (e.g., a class). An example is spotting students who are performing challenging gymnastic activities. If certain pieces of apparatus require special care and proper use, the rules and regulations should be posted near the apparatus (for upper-grade children). Students should be made aware of the rules and should receive appropriate instruction and guidance in applying the rules. When rules are modified, they should be rewritten in proper form. There is no substitute for documentation when the need to defend policies and approaches arises.

When teaching, arrange and teach the class so that all students are always in view. This implies supervising from the perimeter of the area. Teachers who are at the center of the student group with many students behind them will find it impossible to supervise a class safely and effectively. Equipment and apparatus should not go unsupervised at any time when left accessible to students in the area. An example would be equipment that is left on the playing field between classes. If other students in the area have easy access to the equipment, they may use it in an unsafe manner, and the teacher can be found liable if an injury occurs.

Do not agree to supervise activities in which you are unqualified to anticipate possible hazards. If this situation arises, a written memo should be sent to the department head or principal stating such lack of insight and qualification. Maintain a copy for your files.

Merriman (1993) offers five recommendations to assure that adequate supervision occurs:

1. The supervisor must be in the immediate vicinity (within sight and hearing).

2. If required to leave, the supervisor must have an adequate replacement in place before departing. Adequate replacements do not include paraprofessionals, student teachers, custodial help, or untrained teachers.

3. Supervision procedures must be preplanned and incorporated into daily lessons.

4. Supervision procedures should include what to observe, what to listen for, where to stand for the most effective view, and what to do if a problem arises.

5. Supervision requires that age, maturity, and skill ability of participants must always be considered, as must be the inherent risk of the activity.

Instruction

Instructional responsibility rests primarily with the teacher, but administrative personnel have certain defined functions.

Administration

The administration should review and approve the curricular plan. The curriculum should be reviewed regularly to assure that it is current and updated. Activities included in the curriculum should be based on contributions they make to the growth and development of youngsters. It makes little sense in a court of law to say that an activity was included "for the fun of it" or "because students liked it." Instead, make sure activities in the curriculum are included because they meet program objectives.

Administrators are obligated to support the program with adequate finances. The principal and higher administrators should visit the program periodically. Familiarity with program content and operation obviates the possibility that practices were occurring without adequate administrative supervision.

Instructional Staff

With regard to instruction, the teacher has a duty to protect students from unreasonable physical or mental harm. This includes avoiding any acts or omissions that might cause such harm. The teacher is educated and experienced and must be able to foresee situations that could be harmful.

The major area of concern involving instruction is whether the student received adequate instruction before or during activity participation. Adequate instruction means (1) teaching children how to perform activities correctly and use equipment and apparatus properly and (2) teaching youngsters necessary safety precautions. If instructions are given, they must be correct, understandable, and include proper technique, or the instructor can be held liable. The risk involved in an activity must be communicated to the learner.

The age and maturity level of students play an important role in the selection of activities. Younger students require more care, instructions that are easy to comprehend, and clear restrictions in the name of safety. Some students have a lack of appropriate fear in activities, and the teacher must be aware of this when discussing safety factors. A very young child may have little concern about performing a high-risk activity if an instructor is nearby. This places much responsibility on the instructor to give adequate instruction and supervision.

Careful planning is a necessity. Written curriculum guides and lesson plans offer a well-prepared approach that can withstand scrutiny and examination by other teachers and administrators. Written lesson plans should include proper sequence and progression of skill. Teachers are on defensible grounds if they can show that the progression of activities was based on presentations designed by experts and was followed carefully during the teaching act. District and state guidelines enforcing instructional sequences and restricted activities should be checked closely.

Proper instruction demands that students not be forced to participate. If a youngster is required to perform an activity unwillingly, the teacher may be open to a lawsuit. In a lawsuit dealing with stunts and tumbling (Appenzeller, 1970), the court held the teacher liable when a student claimed that she was not given adequate instruction in how to perform a stunt called "roll over two." The teacher was held liable because the student claimed she was forced to try the stunt before adequate instruction was offered. Gymnastics and tumbling are areas in which lawsuits are prevalent due to a lack of adequate instruction. Posting the proper sequence of skills and lead-up activities may be useful to ensure that they have been presented properly. Teachers need to tread the line carefully between helpful encouragement and forcing students to try new activities.

For teachers who incorporate punishment as a part of the instructional process, the consequences of its use should be examined carefully before implementation. Physical punishment that brings about permanent or long-lasting damage is certainly indefensible. The punishment used must be in line with the physical maturity and health of the student involved. Having students perform laps when they have misbehaved might go unchallenged for years. However, what if a student with congenital heart disease or asthma is asked to run and suffers injury or illness? What if the student is running unsupervised and is injured from a fall or suffers heat exhaustion? In these examples, defending such punitive practices would be difficult. Making students perform physical activity for misbehavior is indefensible under any circumstance. If a child is injured while performing physical punishment, teachers are usually found liable and held responsible for the injury.

The following points can help teachers plan for meaningful and safe instruction:

1. Sequence all activities in units of instruction and develop written lesson plans. Many problems occur when snap judgments are made under the daily pressure and strain of teaching.

2. Scrutinize high-risk activities to assure that all safety procedures have been implemented. If in doubt, discuss the activities with other experienced teachers and administrators.

3. Activities used in the curriculum must be within the developmental limits of the students. Since the range of maturity and development of youngsters in a class is usually wide, activities may be beyond the ability level of some students.

4. If students' grades are based on the number of activities in which they participate, some students may feel forced to try all activities. Teachers should make it clear to students that the choice to participate belongs to them. When they are afraid of getting hurt, they can elect not to perform an activity.

5. Include in written lesson plans the necessary safety equipment. The lesson plan should detail how equipment should be arranged, the placement of mats, and where the instructor will carry out supervision.

6. If a student claims injury or brings a note from parents requesting that the student not participate in physical activity, the teacher must honor the communication. Excuses are almost always given at the start of the period when the teacher is busy with many other duties (e.g., getting equipment ready, taking roll, and opening lockers). It is difficult to make a thoughtful judgment at this time. The school nurse is qualified to make these judgments when they relate to health and should be used in that capacity. If the excuses continue over a long period of time, the teacher or nurse should have a conference with the parents to rectify the situation.

7. Make sure activities included in the instructional process are in line with the available equipment and facilities. An example is the amount of space available. If a soccer lead-up activity is brought indoors because of inclement weather, it may no longer be a safe and appropriate activity.

8. If spotting is required for safe completion of activities, it should always be done by the instructor or by trained students. Teaching students how to spot is as important as teaching them physical skills. Safe conduct must be learned.

9. If students are working independently at stations, carefully constructed and written task cards can help eliminate unsafe practices.

10. Have a written emergency care plan posted in the gymnasium. This plan should be approved by health care professionals and should be followed to the letter when an injury occurs.

Equipment and Facilities

School responsibility for equipment and facilities is required for both noninstructional and class use.

Administration

The principal and the custodian should oversee the fields and playground equipment that are used for recess and outside activities. Students should be instructed to report broken and unsafe equipment, as well as hazards (glass, cans, rocks), to the principal's office. If equipment is faulty, it should be removed from the area. A regular inspection of equipment and facilities should be instituted, perhaps weekly, by the principal or the custodian. Results of the inspection should be filed with the school district safety committee. Replacement of sawdust, sand, or other shock-absorbing material must be done regularly.

Administrators should develop a written checklist of equipment and apparatus for the purpose of recording scheduled safety inspections. The date of inspection should be noted to show that inspection occurs at regular intervals. If a potentially dangerous situation exists, rules or warnings should be posted so that students and teachers are made aware of the risk before participation is allowed.

Proper installation of equipment is critical. Climbing equipment and other equipment that must be anchored should be installed by a reputable firm that guarantees its work. When examining apparatus, inspection of the installation is important. Maintenance of facilities is also important. Grass should be kept short and the grounds inspected for debris. Holes in the ground should be filled and loose gravel removed. A proper finish that prevents excessive slipping should be used on indoor floors. Shower rooms should have a roughened floor finish applied to prevent falls when the floors are wet.

Equipment and facilities used in the physical education program must allow safe participation in activity. The choice of apparatus and equipment should be based on the growth and developmental levels of the students. For example, allowing elementary school children to use a horizontal ladder that was designed for high school students may result in a fall that causes injury. Hazards found on playing fields need to be repaired and eliminated. The legal concept of an attractive nuisance should be understood. This implies that some piece of equipment or apparatus, usually left unsupervised, was so attractive to children that they could not be expected to avoid it. When an injury occurs, even though students may have been using the apparatus incorrectly, the teachers and the school are often held liable because the attractive nuisance should have been removed from the area when unsupervised.

Instructional Staff

Indoor facilities are of primary concern for physical education instruction. While the administration is charged with overall responsibility for facilities and equipment, including periodic inspection, the instructor should make a regular safety inspection of the instructional area. If corrective action is needed, the principal or other designated administrator should be notified in writing. Verbal notification is not enough, since it offers little legal protection to the instructor.

Facilities should be used in a safe manner. Often, the side and end lines of playing fields for sports such as football, soccer, and field hockey are placed too close to walls, curbings, or fences. The boundaries should be moved to allow adequate room for deceleration, even though the size of the playing area may be reduced. In the gymnasium, students should not be asked to run to a line that is close to a wall. Another common hazard is baskets positioned too close to the playing area. The poles that support the baskets must be padded.

Proper use of equipment and apparatus is important. Regardless of the state of equipment repair, if it is misused, it may result in an injury. Students must receive instruction in the proper use of equipment and apparatus before they are issued to the students and used. All safety instruction should be included in the written lesson plan to ensure that all points are covered.

Equipment should be purchased on the basis of quality and safety as well as potential use. Many lawsuits occur because of unsafe equipment and apparatus. The liability for such equipment may rest with the manufacturer, but this has to be proved, which means that the teacher must state, in writing, the exact specifications of the desired equipment. The process of bidding for lower-priced items may result in the purchase of less safe equipment. If teachers have specified proper equipment in writing, however, the possibility of their being held liable for injury is reduced.

The Sports Program

A common problem for school administrators with elementary school sports programs is providing qualified coaches. The administration should set minimum requirements for coaches and assure that incompetent individuals are removed from coaching duties. When students are involved in extracurricular activity, teachers (coaches) are responsible for the safe conduct of activities. The following areas often give rise to lawsuits if they are not handled carefully.

Mismatching Opponents

A common error that gives rise to lawsuits is the mismatching of students on the basis of size and ability. Just because competitors are the same sex and choose to participate does not absolve the instructor of liability if an injury occurs. The question that courts examine is whether an effort was made to match students according to height, weight, and ability. Courts are less understanding about mismatching in the physical education setting compared with an athletic contest, but mismatching is a factor that should be avoided in any situation.

Waiver Forms

Participants in extracurricular activities should be required to sign a responsibility waiver form. The form should explain the risks involved in voluntary participation and discuss briefly the types of injuries that have occurred in the past during practice and competition. Supervisors should remember that waiver slips do not waive the rights of participants, and that teachers and coaches still can be found liable if injuries occur. The waiver form does communicate clearly, however, the risks involved and may be a strong "assumption of risk" defense.

Medical Examinations

Participants must have a medical examination before participating. Records of the examination should be kept on file and should be identified prominently when physical restrictions or limitations exist. It is common to "red dot" the folders of students who have a history of medical problems. Students must not be allowed to participate unless they purchase medical insurance; evidence of such coverage should be kept in the folders of athletic participants.

Preseason Conditioning

Preseason conditioning should be undertaken in a systematic and progressive fashion. Starting the season with a mile run for time makes little sense if students have not been preconditioned. Coaches should be aware of guidelines dealing with heat and humidity (see Chapter 2).

Transportation of Students

Whenever students are transported, teachers are responsible for their safety both en route and during the activity. Transportation liability can be avoided by not providing transportation, but instead requiring participants to meet at the site of the event (Pittman, 1993). If the school must provide transportation, licensed drivers and school-approved vehicles should always be used. Travel plans should include official approval from the appropriate school administrator. One special note: If the driver receives pay or reimbursement for the trip, the possibility of being held liable for injury increases dramatically. To make the matter worse, many insurance policies do not cover drivers who receive compensation for transporting students. If you are transporting students and receiving reimbursement, a special insurance rider that provides liability coverage for this situation should be purchased.

Safety

The major thrust of safety should be to prevent situations that cause accidents. It is estimated that over 70 percent of injuries that occur in sport and related activities could be prevented through proper safety procedures. On the other hand, some accidents occur despite precautions, and proper emergency procedures should be established to cope with any situation. A comprehensive study of injuries received in sport and related activities was conducted by the U.S. Consumer Product Safety Commission (1992). This study involved a network of computers in 119 hospital emergency rooms that channeled injury data to a central point. The sports and activities that produced the most injuries were, in order, football, touch football, baseball, basketball, gymnastics, and skiing. The facility that produced the most disabling injuries was the swimming pool.

Learning to recognize potential high-risk situations is an important factor in preventing accidents. Teachers must possess a clear understanding of the hazards and potential dangers of an activity before they can establish controls. Instructors must not assume that participants are aware of the dangers and risks involved in various activities. Students must be told of all dangers and risks before participation.

Guidelines for Safety

1. Inservice sessions in safety should be administered by experienced and knowledgeable teachers. Department heads may be responsible for the training, or outside experts can be employed to undertake the responsibility. Giving in-district credit to participating teachers offers strong indication that the district is concerned about using proper safety techniques.

2. Medical records should be reviewed at the start of the school year. Atypical students should be identified and noted within each class listing before the first instructional day. If necessary, the teacher or school nurse can call the doctor of a student who is disabled or restricted in activity to inquire about the situation and discuss special needs. Teachers should be notified by the school nurse about youngsters who have special (e.g., epilepsy) or temporary problems (e.g., medication).

3. Throughout the school year, safety orientations should be conducted with students. Discussions should include potentially dangerous situations, class conduct, and rules for proper use of equipment and apparatus. Teachers should urge students to report any conditions that might cause an accident.

4. Safety rules for specific units of instruction should be discussed at the onset of each unit. Rules should be posted and regularly brought to the attention of students. Posters and bulletin boards can promote safety in an enjoyable and stimulating manner.

5. If students are to serve as instructional aides, they should be trained. Aides must understand the techniques of spotting, for example, and must receive proper instruction if they are to be a part of the educational process. Caution must be used when using student aides because teachers are still responsible even if an aide performed a duty incorrectly.

6. Instructional practices need to be monitored for possible hazards. For example, students in competitive situations should be matched by size, maturity, and ability. Proper instruction necessary for safe participation should occur prior to activity. Instructors should receive a competence check to ensure that they are adequately trained to give instruction in various activities. The instructional area should be properly prepared for safe participation; if the area is lacking necessary apparatus and safety devices, instruction should be modified to meet safety standards.

7. An inventory of equipment and apparatus should include a safety checklist. Whenever necessary, equipment in need of repair should be sent to proper agents. If the cost of repair is greater than 40 percent of the replacement cost, discarding the equipment or apparatus is usually a more economical choice.

8. When an injury occurs, it should be recorded and a report placed in the student's file. An injury should also be filed by type of injury, such as ankle sprain or broken arm. The report should list the activity and the conditions to facilitate analysis at regular intervals. The analysis may show that injuries are occurring regularly during a specific activity or on a certain piece of equipment. This process can give direction for creating a safer environment or for defending the safety record of a sport, activity, or piece of equipment.

9. Maintain up-to-date first-aid and CPR certification. Administrators should ensure that teachers meet these standards and should provide training sessions when necessary.

The Safety Committee

Safety should be publicized regularly throughout the school, and a mechanism should exist that allows students, parents, and teachers to voice concerns about unsafe conditions. A safety committee can meet at regular intervals to establish safety policies, rule on requests for allowing high-risk activities, and analyze serious injuries that have occurred in the school district. This committee should develop safety rules that apply districtwide to all teachers. It may determine that certain activities involve too high a risk for the return in student benefit. Acceptable criteria for sport equipment and apparatus may be established by the committee.

The safety committee should include one or more high-level administrators, teachers, health officers (nurse), parents, and students. Remember that school administrators are usually indicted when lawsuits occur, because they are held responsible for program content and curriculum. Their representation on the safety committee is therefore important. Students on the committee may be aware of possible hazards, and parents may often voice concerns overlooked by teachers.

The Emergency Care Plan

Before any emergency arises, prepare yourself by learning about special health and physical conditions of students (Gray, 1993). Most schools have a method for identifying students with special health problems. If a student has a problem that may require treatment, a consent-to-treat form should be on file in case the parent or guardian is unavailable. Necessary first-aid materials and supplies should be available in a kit and be readily accessible.

Establishing procedures for emergency care and notification of parents in case of injury is of utmost importance in providing a high standard of care for students. First aid is the immediate and temporary care given at an emergency before a physician is available. Its purpose is to save life, prevent aggravation of injuries, and alleviate severe suffering. If there is evidence of life-threatening bleeding or if the victim is unconscious or has stopped breathing, you must administer first aid. When already injured persons may be further injured if they are not moved, then moving them is permissible. As a general rule, however, an injured person should not be moved unless absolutely necessary. If there is indication of back or neck injury, the head must be immobilized and should not be moved without the use of a spine board. Remember: The purpose of first aid is to save life. The emergency care plan should consist of the following steps:

1. Administration of first aid to the injured student is the number one priority. Treat only life-threatening injuries. The school nurse should be called to the scene of the accident immediately. Send two students to notify the nurse. Emergency care procedures should indicate whether the student can be moved and in what fashion. It is critical that the individual applying first aid avoid aggravating the injury.

2. Notify parents as soon as possible when emergency care is required. Each student's file should list home and emergency telephone numbers where parents can be reached. If possible, the school should have an arrangement with local emergency facilities so that a paramedic unit can be called immediately to the scene of a serious accident.

3. In most cases, the student should be released to a parent or a designated representative. Policies for transportation of injured students should be established and documented.

4. A student accident report should be completed promptly while the details of the accident are clear. Figure 7.1 is an example of an acci-

FIGURE 7.1   Sample Accident Report Form

STUDENT ACCIDENT REPORT
_____ SCHOOL

In all cases, this form should be filed through the school nurse and signed by the principal of the school. The original will be forwarded to the superintendent's office, where it will be initialed and sent to the head nurse. The second copy will be retained by the principal or the school nurse. The third copy should be given to the physical education teacher if accident is related.

Name of injured _____ Address_____

Phone _____ Grade _____ Homeroom_____ Age_____

Parents of injured _____

Place of accident_____ Date of accident_____

Hour _____ A.M./P.M. Date reported_____ By whom _____

Parent contact attempted at A.M./P.M. _____ Parent contacted at A.M./P.M. _____

DESCRIBE ACCIDENT, GIVING SPECIFIC LOCATION AND CONDITION OF PREMISES _____
_____

NATURE OF INJURY_____
(Describe in detail)

CARE GIVEN OR ACTION TAKEN BY NURSE OR OTHERS_____
_____

REASON INJURED PERSON WAS ON PREMISES _____
(Activity at time-i.e., lunch, physical education, etc.)

STAFF MEMBER RESPONSIBLE FOR STUDENT SUPERVISION AT TIME OF ACCIDENT _____
_____

IS STUDENT COVERED BY SCHOOL-SPONSORED ACCIDENT INSURANCE? _____Yes _____No

MEDICAL CARE RECOMMENDED _____Yes _____No

WHERE TAKEN AFTER ACCIDENT _____
(Specify home, physician, or hospital, giving name and address)

BY WHOM_____ AT WHAT TIME A.M./P.M. _____

FOLLOW-UP BY NURSE TO BE SENT TO CENTRAL HEALTH OFFICE

REMEDIATIVE MEASURES TAKEN_____
(Attach individual remarks if necessary)

School_____ Principal_____

Date _____ Nurse _____

On the back of this sheet, list all persons familiar with the circumstances of the accident, giving name, address, telephone number, age, and location with respect to the accident.

dent form that covers the necessary details. Both the teacher and principal should retain copies and additional copies should be sent to the administrative office.

Personal Protection: Minimizing the Effects of a Lawsuit

In spite of proper care, injuries do occur and lawsuits may be initiated. Two courses of action are necessary to counteract the effects of a suit.

Liability Insurance

Teachers may be protected by school district liability insurance. Usually, however, teachers must purchase their own policies. Most policies provide for legal services to contest a suit and will pay indemnity up to the limits of the policy (liability coverage of $500,000 is most common). Most policies give the insurance company the right to settle out of court. Unfortunately, when this occurs, some may infer that the teacher was guilty even though the circumstances indicate otherwise. Insurance companies usually settle out of court to avoid the excessive legal fees required to try to win the case in court.

Recordkeeping

The second course of action is to keep complete records of accidents. Many lawsuits occur months or even years after the accident, when memory of the situation is fuzzy. Accident reports should be filled out immediately after an injury. Take care to provide no evidence, oral or written, that others could use in a court of law. Do not attempt to make a diagnosis or to specify the supposed cause of the accident in the report.

If newspaper reporters probe for details, avoid describing the accident beyond the basic facts. When discussing the accident with administrators, only the facts recorded on the accident report should be discussed. Remember that school records can be subpoenaed in court proceedings. The point here is not to dissemble, but to be cautious and avoid self-incrimination.

Safety and Liability Checklist

The following checklist can be used to monitor the physical education environment. Any situations that deviate from safe and legally sound practices should be rectified immediately.

Supervision and Instruction

1. Are teachers adequately trained in all of the activities that they are teaching?
2. Do all teachers have evidence of a necessary level of first-aid training?
3. When supervising, do personnel have access to a written plan of areas to be observed and responsibilities to be carried out?

4. Have students been warned of potential dangers and risks, and advised of rules and the reasons for the rules?

5. Are safety rules posted near areas of increased risk?

6. Are lesson plans written? Do they include provisions for proper instruction, sequence of activities, and safety? Are all activities taught listed in the district curriculum guide?

7. When a new activity is introduced, are safety precautions and instructions for correct skill performance always communicated to the class?

8. Are the activities taught in the program based on sound curriculum principles? Could the activities and units of instruction be defended on the basis of their educational contributions?

9. Do the methods of instruction recognize individual differences among students, and are the necessary steps taken to meet the needs of all students, regardless of sex, ability, or disability?

10. Are substitute teachers given clear and comprehensive lesson plans so that they can maintain the scope and sequence of instruction?

11. Is the student evaluation plan based on actual performance and objective data rather than on favoritism or arbitrary and capricious standards?

12. Is appropriate dress required for students? (This does not imply uniforms, only dress [including shoes] that ensures the safety of the student.)

13. When necessary for safety, are students grouped according to ability level, size, or age?

14. Is the class left unsupervised for teacher visits to the office, lounge, or bathroom? Is one teacher ever asked to supervise two or more classes at the same time?

15. If students are used as teacher aides or to spot others, are they given proper instruction and training?

Equipment and Facilities

1. Is all equipment inspected regularly and are the inspection results recorded on a form and sent to the proper administrators?

2. Is a log maintained recording the regular occurrence of an inspection, the equipment in need of repair, and when repairs were made?

3. Are "attractive nuisances" eliminated from the gymnasium and playing field?

4. Are specific safety rules posted on facilities and near equipment?

5. Are the following inspected periodically?
   a. Playing field for presence of glass, rocks, and metal objects
   b. Fasteners holding equipment (such as climbing ropes, horizontal bars, or baskets)

c. Goals for games (such as football, soccer, and field hockey) to be sure that they are fastened securely

d. Padded areas (such as goal supports)

6. Are mats placed under apparatus from which a fall is possible?

7. Are playing fields arranged so participants will not run into each other or be hit by a ball from another game?

8. Are landing pits filled and maintained properly?

Emergency Care

1. Is there a written procedure for emergency care?

2. Is a person properly trained in first aid available immediately following an accident?

3. Are emergency telephone numbers readily accessible?

4. Are telephone numbers of parents available?

5. Is an up-to-date first-aid kit available? Is ice immediately available?

6. Are health folders maintained that list restrictions, allergies, and health problems of students?

7. Are health folders reviewed by instructors on a regular basis?

8. Are students participating in extracurricular activities required to have insurance? Is the policy number recorded?

9. Is there a plan for treating injuries that involves the local paramedics?

10. Are accident reports filed promptly and analyzed regularly?

Transportation of Students

1. Have parents been informed that their students will be transported off campus?

2. Are detailed travel plans approved by the site administrator and kept on file?

3. Are school vehicles used whenever possible?

4. Are drivers properly licensed and vehicles insured?

5. If teachers or parents use their vehicles to transport students, are the students, driver, and car owner covered by an insurance rider purchased by the school district?

References and Suggested Readings

Appenzeller, H. (1970). *From the gym to the jury.* Charlottesville, VA: Michie Company Law Publishing.

Arnold, D. E. (1983). *Legal considerations in the administration of public school physical education and athletic programs.* Springfield, IL: Charles C. Thomas.

Baley, J. A., & Matthews, D. L. (1984). *Law and liability in athletics, physical education, and recreation.* Boston: Allyn and Bacon.

Black, H. C. (1990). *Black's Law Dictionary* (6th ed.). St. Paul, MN: West.

Blucker, J. A., & Pell, S. W. (1986). Legal and ethical issues. *Journal of Physical Education, Recreation, and Dance, 57*, 19–21.

Dougherty, N. J. (Ed.). (1987). *Principles of safety in physical education and sport.* Reston, VA: AAHPERD.

Gray, G. R. (1993). Providing adequate medical care to program participants. *Journal of Physical Education, Recreation, and Dance, 64*(2), 56–57.

Institute for the Study of Educational Policy, Law Division. (1986). *School athletics and the law.* Seattle: University of Washington Press.

Kaiser, R. A. (1984). *Liability and law in recreation, parks, and sports.* Englewood Cliffs, NJ: Prentice-Hall.

Merriman, J. (1993). Supervision in sport and physical activity. *Journal of Physical Education, Recreation, and Dance, 64*(2), 20–23.

Pittman, A. J. (1993). Safe transportation—A driving concern. *Journal of Physical Education, Recreation, and Dance, 64*(2), 53–55.

Stone, W. J. (1977). Running and running tests for Arizona school children. *Arizona JOHPERD, 21*, 15–17.

Strickland, R., Phillip, J. F., & Phillips, W. R. (1976). *Avoiding teacher malpractice.* New York: Hawthorn.

U.S. Consumer Product Safety Commission. (1992). *Handbook for public playground safety.* Washington, DC: U.S. Government Printing Office.

van der Smissen, B. (1990). *Legal liability and risk management of public and private entities.* Cincinnati, OH: Anderson.

Chapter EIGHT

Physical Activity and Fitness

In this chapter, you will learn...

- ◆ *The difference between health-related and skill-related fitness*

- ◆ *Why criterion-reference standards are used to describe minimum standards of health*

- ◆ *Whether today's children are as physically fit as youngsters in earlier decades*

- ◆ *How heredity and trainability affect physical performance differences among children*

- ◆ *Whether instruction should focus on fitness or activity*

- ◆ *Ways to create positive attitudes toward activity*

- ◆ *Procedures for successfully implementing fitness activities and routines*

- ◆ *Fitness activities that are developmentally appropriate for all students*

- ◆ *To teach a wide variety of physical activities that appeal to youngsters*

- ◆ *To develop fitness activities that take advantage of the intermittent activity patterns of youngsters*

Physical education programs can inoculate youngsters with an active lifestyle that promotes health and vitality. Sometimes, administrators and school boards feel that physical education is a subject to be taught after all other subjects have received adequate coverage and support. Schools teach children how to achieve academically in order to live a productive life, and few question the importance of learning to read and write. However, these skills are of little worth when one is near death or suffering from hypokinetic disease. There is no higher priority in life than health. Without it, all other skills lack meaning and utility. Exercise programs for children should be designed to improve their self-confidence rather than undermine it. Fitness activities should be individualized and tailored to the needs of each child to assure the experience is successful. Fitness should be an enjoyable and positive social experience that assures children develop a positive association with activity.

What Is Physical Fitness?

Although it is generally agreed that physical fitness and activity are an important part of the normal growth and development of children, a general definition regarding the precise nature of physical fitness has not been universally accepted. However, most often, physical fitness is divided into two areas: health-related physical fitness and skill-related physical fitness. Although these definitions have curricular implications, classifying fitness into two categories does not lessen the importance of either in the total growth and development of youngsters. Understanding the distinctive features of the various components that make up health-related physical fitness and skill-related physical fitness helps teachers develop proper fitness objectives and goals for elementary physical education.

Health-Related Physical Fitness

Health-related physical fitness includes those aspects of physiological function that offer protection from diseases resulting from a sedentary lifestyle. It can be improved and/or maintained through regular physical activity. Specific components include cardiovascular fitness, body composition (ratio of leanness to fatness), abdominal strength and endurance, and flexibility. These components are currently measured with test batteries, such as the Fitnessgram System (Cooper Institute for Aerobic Research, 1992). The following are the major components of health-related fitness.

Cardiovascular Fitness
Aerobic fitness plays an important role in living a healthy lifestyle and may be the most important element of fitness. Cardiovascular endurance is the ability of the heart, the blood vessels, and the respiratory system to deliver oxygen efficiently over an extended period of time. Activities that stimulate development in this area are walking, jogging, biking, rope jumping, aerobics, swimming, and continuous movement sports such as basketball or soccer.

In contrast to aerobic activity is anaerobic exercise, an activity that is so intense the body cannot supply oxygen at the cellular level. The body is limited to performing this type of activity for a short time. Examples of anaerobic activity are sprinting, running up stairs, or all-out effort in any sport.

Body Composition

Body composition is an integral part of health-related fitness. Body composition is the proportion of body fat to lean body mass. After the thickness of selected skinfolds is measured, the percentage of body fat is calculated. Attaining physical fitness is difficult when an individual's body composition contains a high amount of body fat.

Flexibility

Flexibility is the range of movement through which a joint or sequence of joints can move. Inactive individuals lose flexibility, whereas frequent movement helps retain the range of movement. Through stretching activities, the length of muscles, tendons, and ligaments is increased. The ligaments and tendons retain their elasticity through constant use. Flexibility is important to fitness; a lack of flexibility can be a health problem for individuals. People who are flexible usually maintain good posture and have less low-back pain. Many physical activities demand a range of motion to generate maximum force, such as serving a tennis ball, kicking a soccer ball, and so on.

Muscular Strength and Endurance

Strength is the ability of muscles to exert force—a necessary component for efficient learning of motor skills (Rarick & Dobbins, 1975). Most aerobic activities do not build strength in areas where it is most needed—the arm-shoulder girdle and the abdominal-trunk region. Muscular endurance is the ability to exert force over an extended period. Endurance postpones the onset of fatigue so an activity can be performed for lengthy periods. Most sport activities require muscular endurance, because throwing, kicking, and striking skills have to be performed many times without fatigue.

Skill-Related Physical Fitness

Skill-related fitness includes those physical qualities that enable a person to perform in sport activities. Skill-related fitness is strongly influenced by genetic makeup. All individuals can improve health-related fitness; however, skill-related fitness is more resistant to change because of an individual's genetic endowment. Whereas health-related fitness is important for good health, skill-related fitness is performance oriented and required for athletic prowess. In addition to the health-related aspects that are important to sport performance, specific components making up skill-related fitness are agility, balance, coordination, power, and speed. Table 8.1 shows a number of activities that can be used to improve health- and skill-related physical fitness.

- *Agility* is the ability of the body to change position rapidly and accurately while moving in space. Wrestling and football are examples of sports that require agility.

TABLE 8.1 *Activities for Various Components of Physical Fitness*

Component	Activities
Health Related	
Cardiovascular fitness	Jogging, cross-country skiing, walking, rope jumping, bicycling, swimming, and aerobic dance.
Body composition	Same as cardiovascular fitness.
Abdominal strength and endurance	Sit-ups, selected animal walks, stretching, and twisting.
Flexibility of lower back	Bending and stretching, sitting stretch, partner stretching, and selected animal walks.
Skill Related	
Arm and shoulder girdle strength	Pull-ups, rope climbing, and selected animal walks.
Abdominal strength and endurance	Sit-ups, selected animal walks, bending, stretching, and twisting.
Agility	Selected stunts, agility running, and selected sport skills.
Leg power	Treadmill, vertical jumping, running, and long jump.
Speed	Tortoise and Hare, running in place, and selected leg exercises.
Coordination	Locomotor movements, manipulative skill practice, and specialized sport skills.
Balance	Movements on benches or balance beams, balance stunts, and locomotor movements.

- *Balance* refers to the body's ability to maintain a state of equilibrium while remaining stationary or moving. Maintaining balance is essential to all sports but especially so in the performance of gymnastic activities.

- *Coordination* is the ability of the body to perform smoothly and successfully more than one motor task at the same time. Needed for football, baseball, tennis, soccer, and other sports that require hand-eye and foot-eye skills coordination can be developed by practicing over and over the skill to be learned.

- *Power* is the ability to transfer energy explosively into force. To develop power, a person must practice activities that are required to improve strength, but at a faster rate involving sudden bursts of energy. Skills requiring power include high jumping, long jumping, throwing, and kicking.

- *Speed* is the ability of the body to perform movement in a short period of time. Usually associated with running forward, speed is essential for the successful performance of most sports and general locomotor movement skills.

Which Type of Fitness Should You Teach?

Skill-related fitness components are useful in performing motor tasks related to sport and athletics. The ability to perform well depends on the genetically determined skill of the individual. Asking youngsters to "try harder" only adds to their frustration if they lack natural ability and see skilled friends performing well without excessive effort. When skill-related fitness is taught in elementary school, it should be accompanied with an explanation of why some children can perform well with a minimum of effort whereas others, no matter how hard they try, never excel. There are many examples that can be used to illustrate the situation, such as individual differences in speed, jumping ability, strength, and physical size.

In contrast, health-related physical fitness is less genetically controlled. Health-related fitness helps youngsters understand how much activity is required for good health. Emphasis is placed on the process of activity and participation rather than the product of high-level performance. Regular physical activity necessary for reduction of health risks becomes the locus of instruction. This contrasts with skill-related fitness, which is influenced by genetic traits and abilities, rewards high performance, and rewards students capable of achieving high fitness performance standards.

An important concept emphasized in health-related fitness programs is that of *criterion-referenced health standards.* In the past, fitness tests asked students to compare their performances with the performances of other students regardless of many complicating factors, such as body type, genetic makeup, and age differences. Youngsters have been compared on percentile charts that showed what percentage of the students ranked above and below them. For students who perform poorly, this is a demoralizing process. Newer tests (Cooper Institute for Aerobic Research, 1992) establish minimum levels of performance required for good health. Performance in excess of the minimum is certainly laudable, but not required. This approach educates students to understand that it is critical to maintain health through regular activity rather than compare fitness test performances. In addition, self-improvement is a personal goal rather than a comparison with others.

Are Today's Children Fit?

A popular point of view among teachers and parents is that children today are less fit than children were in the past. This opinion is often used as a justification for more physical education time in the schools. Recent research (Corbin & Pangrazi, 1992) suggests that the fitness of today's youngsters has not degenerated; they do quite well when compared to past students. When data from the last four national surveys of youth fitness conducted by the AAHPERD and/or the President's Council on Physical Fitness and Sports were compared, results showed children and youth today are just as fit as they were in the past. The only items that were used in all four surveys were pull-ups and the flexed arm hang. Youngsters, both boys and girls, showed an increase in performance when these two items were compared over four decades. The only area where children have shown a minor decrease in fitness is body composition (Gortmaker, Dietz, Sobol, & Wehler, 1987); today's youngsters are slightly fatter than they were 20 years ago.

Why Do People Continue to Believe Children Are Unfit?

One reason people believe youngsters are unfit is because definitions of fitness have changed. Fitness testing has evolved from skill-related fitness to health-related fitness and its relationship to good health and feelings of well-being. High performance on fitness test items is not necessary for good health, especially when the performance is based on skill-related items such as the 50-yard dash and the shuttle run. Evidence shows that moderate amounts of health-related physical fitness are enough to contribute to good health (Blair et al., 1989). When health-related fitness test items are compared, today's children perform as well (and better) than those in years past. Modern health standards reveal that the majority of children are fit.

Another contention often made is that today's children are much less active, so they must be much less fit. It is true that children watch much television (American Academy of Pediatrics, 1991). However, whether this equates with inactivity is questionable. Children today are still the most active segment of our society. When daily energy expenditure is examined, it is highest at 6 years of age and gradually reaches a low point at 16 to 18 years of age (Rowland, 1990). It is interesting to note that adults continue to prod youngsters toward better fitness even though adults are the least active age group in our society.

Activity has much less influence on the fitness levels of children than adults. The reason is that children are a somewhat homogenous group. That is, the majority of them are active. Few are totally inactive, unlike many adults, so the effects of adding activity to children's lifestyle usually does not manifest itself in an improved fitness level for the entire group.

Can All Children Meet Similar Standards of Fitness?

Is it a realistic expectation that all children be expected to reach specified standards of fitness? What factors control fitness performance and how much control do youngsters have over their fitness accomplishments? Payne and Morrow (1993) reviewed 28 studies examining training and aerobic performance in children and concluded that improvement is small to moderate in prepubescent children. They stated the following:

> The relatively small-to-moderate increase in pre- to post-aerobic improvement and the weak relationship between type of training program and effect size lead to questions concerning traditional practices when dealing with children and their fitness. Are we expecting too much from traditional physical education or fitness programs? Have award structures, designed to motivate children within these programs or test batteries, been appropriately designed when children appear to elicit only small improvements in aerobic capacity? Clearly, curriculum planners, teachers, fitness directors, exercise physiologists, and physicians need to consider carefully the ramifications of these findings. (p. 312)

Heredity

A significant amount of fitness test performance is explained by heredity (Bouchard, 1990; Bouchard, Dionne, Simoneau, & Boulay, 1992). Various factors such as environment, nutrition, heredity, and maturation affect fitness performance as reflected in physical fitness test scores. Research shows that heredity and maturation strongly impact fitness scores (Bouchard et al., 1992; Pangrazi & Corbin, 1990). In fact, these factors may have more to do with youth fitness scores than activity level. Lifestyle and environmental factors can also make a difference. For example, nutrition is a lifestyle factor that can influence test scores; also, environmental conditions (heat, humidity, and pollution) strongly modify test performances. Fitness performance is only partially determined by activity and training.

Trainability

Some youngsters have a definite advantage on tests because of the types of muscle fibers they inherit. Others inherit a predisposition to perform well on tests. In other words, even in an untrained state, some children score better because of heredity. On the other hand, some youngsters who train will not score as well as others who are untrained because of their genetic predisposition. Beyond heredity lies another factor that predisposes some youngsters to high performance. Recent research has shown that "trainability" is inherited (Bouchard et al., 1992). This implies that some people receive more benefit from training (regular physical activity) than others. As an example, assume that two youngsters perform the same amount of activity throughout a semester. Child A shows dramatic improvement immediately while child B does not. Child A simply responds more favorably to training than child B. Child A inherited a system that is responsive to exercise. Child A not only gets fit and scores well on the test but gets feedback that says "the activity works—it makes me fit." Child B scores poorly, receives no feedback, and concludes that "activity doesn't improve my fitness, so why try?" Because of less sensitivity to training, child B will improve in fitness to a lesser degree than child A and take longer to show improvement. Child B will probably never achieve the fitness level attained by child A.

Physical Maturation

Another factor that impacts fitness performance is physical maturation. Teachers know some youngsters mature faster than others. Sometimes forgotten is how important maturation is in relationship to physical performance. If two youngsters are the same age and sex, but one is physiologically older (advanced skeletal maturation), it is likely the more mature youngster will perform better on tests than the less mature child. Examining fitness norms reveals that children increase their scores as they grow older. In such cases, fitness test scores for an immature active child could be lower than fitness scores of a more mature, less active youngster. Maturation may override the effects of activity among young children. Age also plays a role in fitness performance (Pangrazi & Corbin, 1988). As little as three months difference in age significantly impacts performance in children. Expect older students in the same class with younger children to perform better.

Should teachers assume from this discussion there is little use in helping students become more active? Certainly not. Whereas heredity plays an important role in fitness and in trainability of fitness, all youngsters benefit from regular fitness activity. It simply takes some children longer to benefit from regular physical activity and to show fitness gains. This means less gifted children will need more encouragement and positive feedback, as their improvement will be in smaller increments and of a lesser magnitude.

Should Instruction Focus on Fitness or Regular Activity?

Teachers and parents want to believe that fitness in youngsters is primarily a reflection of the amount of activity children perform on a regular basis. Studies have shown that the relationship of physical fitness to physical activity among children is low (Pate, Dowda, & Ross, 1990; Pate & Ross, 1987; Ross, Pate, Caspersen, Damberg, & Svilar, 1987). If teachers make the mistake of assuming that a child is inactive because of scores on a fitness test, they may be wrong. The concept that activity builds fitness may lead teachers to the conclusion that youngsters who score high on fitness tests are active and those who do not score well are inactive. Physical activity is an important variable in fitness development for adults, but for children and youth, other factors can be of equal or greater importance.

A number of factors impact fitness performance, therefore an important question is: Should instructors emphasize physical fitness performance or participation in regular activity? When examining this question, understand several concepts that can help determine an effective instructional approach. Asking the questions of how many, how fast, or how far places emphasis on the product of fitness. This product orientation places emphasis on the results of fitness testing and performance. To believe that participation in some type of daily activity is important places the focus of instruction on the process of physical activity. A process focus involves activity and participation rather than fitness scores and award systems. Often, exercisers who focus on the product (how fast, how far, how long) of fitness burn out or become discouraged after a short period of time. For example, when running against the clock, improvement continues to the point where it is impossible to go any faster. This lack of improvement can be discouraging to a product-oriented person. In like fashion, emphasizing product outcomes with children can cause them to become discouraged if they fail to reach goals their peers have reached.

All children have the right to a lifetime of physical activity and health. Activity in childhood translates to activity in adulthood (Raitakari, et al., 1994). If schools fail to teach children how to live active lifestyles, the children may not become active and healthy adults. A study conducted by the U.S. Department of Health and Human Services (Ross & Gilbert, 1985) showed that about half of all U.S. children were not developing adequate exercise knowledge and skill needed to develop a healthy cardiovascular system. The same study showed that only about one-third of U.S. youths participate in organized physical education programs. A recent statement issued by the American Academy of Pediatrics (1991) reported that children from the ages of 2 to 12 spend about 25 hours a week watching television. Even in school programs, children may be fortunate to spend 1 hour a week in an organized physical education lesson. Teachers need to place emphasis on developing activity habits that carry over to out-of-school activities. Patterns of activity cannot be developed solely by the school; active lifestyles must be encouraged at home, too.

Some professionals question the value of organized fitness activities in the schools. They express the opinion that since physical education classes meet only once or twice a week, actual fitness changes in children may not occur, making it more important to use the time for skill development. This is a mistake. Youngsters are experiential; that is, they learn from participation and develop perceptions based on those experiences. To avoid taking time to teach exercises and other fitness activities is to circumvent teaching important skills that can be integrated into adult lifestyles. Youngsters must learn during their school experiences that daily activity (independently conducted) is an important habit for a healthy lifestyle. Children are taught how to brush their teeth at a tender age in order that their teeth will last a lifetime. In a similar light, how can teachers justify not teaching children to be active for a few minutes each day to assure that their total health does not decay? Teaching different ways to develop and maintain fitness (even if only one day per week) suggests to students that the school values health and exercise as part of a balanced lifestyle. What better outcome than to teach youngsters to participate in some type of daily activity throughout life?

Continuous high-intensity activity is not prescribed for children. Given what is known about effort to benefit ratios and developmental needs of children, such activity may actually decrease motivation for future activity. From 30 to 60 minutes of moderate-intensity activity accumulated throughout each day is recommended (Corbin, Pangrazi, & Welk, 1994). A similar recommendation is made for adolescents, though continuous moderate to vigorous activity three days a week is encouraged as part of the 30 to 60 minutes of daily activity. Some additional guidelines are offered to assist professionals in making decisions about appropriate activity levels for children and youth.

1. Children should be encouraged to perform high-volume/moderate-intensity activity. Such activity can be accumulated through sporadic activities such as active play performed throughout the day.

2. Lifestyle activity such as walking or riding bikes to and from school or performing active physical tasks at home should be encouraged. Involvement in such activity should be reinforced by teachers so youngsters learn that all moderate activity is beneficial to good health.

3. Students should be allowed to individualize their activity workloads. Encourage children to do the best they can within a time limit. People dislike and fear experiences they perceive to be forced on them from an external source. Voluntary long-term exercise is more probable when individuals are allowed to control the intensity of their activities.

4. Opportunities to learn basic motor skills and develop all parts of health-related physical fitness through appropriate moderate-intensity activity should be included in the activity program.

5. Activity without behavioral change is not enough. Children should begin developing behavioral skills that lead to lifetime activity.

Create Positive Attitudes toward Activity

There are a number of things teachers can do to increase the possibility of students being "turned on" to activity. Fitness activity is neither good nor bad. Rather, how fitness activities are taught determines how youngsters feel about making fitness a part of their lifestyles. The following strategies can make activity a positive learning experience.

Individualize Fitness Activities

Students who are expected to participate in fitness activities and find themselves unable to perform exercises are not likely to develop positive attitudes toward physical activity. Fitness experiences should be designed to allow children to determine their personal workloads. Use time as the workload variable and ask children to do the best they can within a time limit. People dislike and fear experiences they perceive to be forced on them from an external source. Voluntary long-term exercise is more probable when individuals are internally driven to do their best. Fitness experiences that allow children to control the intensity of their workouts offer better opportunity for developing positive attitudes toward activity.

Expose Youngsters to a Variety of Fitness Routines and Exercises

Presenting a variety of fitness opportunities decreases the monotony of doing the same routines week after week and increases the likelihood that students will experience fitness activities that are personally enjoyable. Most youngsters are willing to accept activities they dislike if they know there will be a chance to experience routines they enjoy in the near future. A year-long routine of "calisthenics and running a mile" forces children, regardless of ability and interest, to participate in the same routine whether they like it or not. When youngsters know a new and exciting routine is on the horizon, they are more willing to accept routines they dislike. Avoiding potential boredom by systematically changing fitness activities is a significant way to help students perceive fitness in a positive way.

Give Students Meaningful Feedback about Their Performances

Teacher feedback contributes to the way children view fitness activities. Immediate, accurate, and specific feedback regarding performance encourages continued participation. Provided in a positive manner, this feedback can stimulate children to extend their participation habits outside the confines of the gymnasium. Reinforce all children, not just those who perform at high levels. All youngsters need feedback and reinforcement, even if they are incapable of performing at an elite level.

Teach Physical Skills and Fitness

Physical education programs should concentrate on skill development as well as fitness. Some states mandate fitness testing, which causes some teachers to worry that their students will not pass. Unfortunately, the skill development portion of physical education is often sacrificed to increase the emphasis on teaching for fitness. Physical education programs must develop two major objectives: fitness and skill development. Skills are the tools that most adults use to attain fitness. The majority of individuals maintain fitness through various skill-based activities such as tennis, badminton, swimming, golf, basketball, aerobics, bicycling, and the like. People have a much greater propensity to participate as adults if they feel competent in an activity. School programs must graduate students with requisite entry skills in a variety of activities.

Be a Role Model

Appearance, attitude, and actions speak loudly about teachers and their values regarding fitness. Teachers who display physical vitality, take pride in being active, participate in fitness activities with children, and are physically fit will positively influence youngsters to maintain active lifestyles. It is unreasonable to expect teachers to complete a fitness routine nine times a day, five days a week. However, teachers must exercise with a class periodically to show students they believe in what they ask others to do.

Be Concerned about the Attitudes of Children

Attitudes dictate whether youngsters will participate in activity. Too often, adults want to *force* fitness on children. This can result in insensitivity to the feelings of participants. Training does not equate to lifetime fitness. When youngsters are trained without concern for their feelings, it is possible that the result will be children who hate physical activity. Once a negative attitude is developed, it is difficult to change. This does not mean that youngsters should avoid fitness activity. It means that fitness participation must be a positive experience. Youngsters should not all be funneled into one type of fitness activity. For example, running may be detrimental to the health of obese children, and lean, uncoordinated students may not enjoy contact activities. Additionally, the fitness experience must be a challenge rather than a threat. A challenge is an experience that participants feel they can accomplish. In contrast, a threat appears to be an impossible undertaking—one in which there is no use trying. Fitness goals should be kept within the realm of challenge. A final note: Whether an activity is a challenge or a threat depends on the perceptions of the learner, not the instructor. Listen carefully to students rather than telling them they should "do it for their own good."

Start Easy and Progress Slowly

Fitness development is a journey, not a destination. No teacher wants students to become fit and then quit being active. A rule of thumb to follow is to allow students to start at a level that they can accomplish. This usually means self-directed workloads within a specified time frame. Do not force students into heavy workloads too soon. It is impossible to start a fitness program at a level that is too easy. Start with success and gradually increase the workload. This avoids the discouragement of failure and excessive muscle soreness. When students successfully accomplish activities, they should be taught a system of self-talk that looks at their exercise behavior in a positive light. This helps avoid the common practice of self-criticism when students fail to live up to their own or others' standards.

Use Low-Intensity Activity

Activity should be appropriate to the age of the youngster. The amount of activity needed for good health is somewhat dictated by two variables: the intensity of the activity and the duration of the activity. Most children participate in high-volume/low-intensity activity as they exercise sporadically all day. In contrast, adults usually participate in high-intensity/low-volume activity. The major reason for such activity patterns is available time for exercise. Few adults have time to be active for long periods of time. This contrast of activity styles leads many adults to believe children need to participate in high-intensity activities to receive health benefits. They view children as unfit because they often refuse to participate in high-intensity fitness activities. This focus on high-intensity activity can lead to children becoming discouraged and burned out at an early age. Youngsters are already the most active segment of society (Rowland, 1990), and it is important to maintain and encourage this trait. If the activity is reinforced, the fitness will follow to the extent that it is possible for each child, given heredity and maturation level.

Encourage Lifetime Activity

Teachers want students to exercise throughout their lifetimes. Certain activities may be more likely to stimulate exercise outside of school. There is some evidence (Glasser, 1976) that if the following activity conditions are met, exercise will become positively addicting and a necessary part of one's life. These steps imply that many individual activities such as walking, jogging, hiking, biking, and the like are activities that students might regularly use for fitness during adulthood.

1. The activity must be noncompetitive; the student chooses and wants to do it.
2. The activity must not require a great deal of mental effort.
3. The activity can be done alone, without a partner or teammates.
4. Students must believe in the value of the exercise for improving health and general welfare.

5. Participants must believe that the activity will become easier and more meaningful if they persist. To become addicting, the activity must be done for at least six months.

6. The activity should be accomplished in such a manner that the participant is not self-critical.

Develop a Varied Approach to Fitness

Effective fitness routines should include a variety of different experiences. For generations, youngsters have grown up thinking physical fitness can be achieved only through running laps and performing calisthenics. When organizing fitness instruction, consider some of the following. Units of fitness instruction should vary in length depending on the age of the youngster. Kindergarten through second-grade youngsters need to experience a variety of routines in order to maintain a high level of motivation and understand the different faces of fitness. During these years, exposure to many different types of activities is more important than a progressive, demanding fitness routine. The first experiences of fitness instruction must be positive and enjoyable. As children mature, units can be extended to two weeks. In spite of the varying length of units, one principle is followed: *There are many methods for developing fitness, none of which is best for all children.* Offer a variety of routines and activities so that youngsters learn that fitness is not lockstep and unbending. The fitness approach should offer activities that allow all types of youngsters to find success during the school year.

Fitness routines become more structured as youngsters grow older. Most of the activities listed for kindergarten through second-grade children are unstructured and allow for wide variation of performance. For older children, emphasis on proper technique and performance increases. However, this is not to imply that every student must do every activity exactly the same. It is unrealistic to believe an obese youngster will be able to perform at a level similar to a lean child. Allow for variation of performance while emphasizing the importance of "doing your best."

Implementing Fitness Routines

Fitness activity occurs during a 7- to 10-minute portion of the daily lesson. The following are suggestions to aid in the successful implementation of fitness routines.

1. Fitness instruction should be preceded by a 2- to 3-minute warm-up period. The introductory activity is useful for this purpose because it allows youngsters an opportunity to "loosen up" and prepare for strenuous activity.

2. The fitness portion of the daily lesson, including warm-up, should not extend beyond 10 to 13 minutes. Some argue that more time is needed to develop adequate fitness. A higher level of fitness might

be developed if more time were devoted to the area. However, the reality of the situation is that most teachers are only allowed a 20- to 30-minute period of instruction. Since skill instruction is part of a balanced physical education program, compromise is necessary to assure that all phases of the program are covered.

3. Activities should be vigorous in nature, exercise all body parts, and cover the major components of fitness. Children are capable performers when workloads are geared to their ages, fitness levels, and abilities.

4. A variety of fitness routines comprising sequential exercises for total body development is the recommended alternative to a year-long program of regimented calisthenics. A diverse array of routines that appeal to the interest and fitness levels of children should replace the traditional approach of doing the same routine day in and day out. (The remainder of this chapter describes various fitness activities that can be implemented with children.)

5. The fitness routine should be conducted during the first part of the lesson. Relegating fitness to the end of the lesson does little to enhance the image of exercise. Further, by having the exercise phase of the lesson precede skill instruction, the concept "You get fit to play sport, you do not play sport to get fit" is reinforced.

6. Assume an active role in fitness instruction. Children respond positively to role modeling. A teacher who actively exercises with children, hustles to assist those youngsters having difficulty performing selected exercises, and is able to make exercise fun begins to instill in children the value of an active lifestyle.

7. Various forms of audio or visual assistance should be used to increase children's motivation. Background music, colorful posters depicting exercises, tambourine or drum assistance to provide rhythmical accompaniment for activity, and other instructional media aids can assist in making vigorous activity more enjoyable.

8. When determining workloads for children, alternatives are time or repetitions. It is best to base the workload on *time* instead of a specified number of repetitions because youngsters can adjust their workloads within the time allotment. Having a class perform as many push-ups (or push-up challenges) as possible in a given amount of time (in contrast to requiring that the entire class complete 15 push-ups) results in more children feeling successful.

9. Teachers can use audiotapes to time fitness activity segments so they are free to move throughout the area and offer individualized instruction. (Specifications for the length of segments are listed with the fitness routines described in the lesson plans.)

10. Fitness activities should never be assigned as punishment. Such a practice teaches students that push-ups and running are things that they do when they misbehave. The opportunity to exercise should be a privilege as well as an enjoyable experience. Take a positive

approach and offer students a chance to jog with a friend when they do something well. This not only allows them the opportunity to visit with the friend, but to exercise on a positive note. Be an effective salesperson; sell the joy of activity and benefits of physical fitness to youngsters.

Fitness Activities for Children in Kindergarten through Grade 2

Fitness activities for young children should have the potential to develop components of physical fitness and exercise the various body areas. All the fitness routines that follow are designed to combine strength and flexibility activities with cardiovascular activity. For most routines, strength and flexibility activities are listed. Strength and flexibility activities should be alternated with cardiovascular activities. The introductory activity and fitness development activity should combine to provide broad coverage by including activities for each of these five areas: trunk, abdomen, arm-shoulder girdle, legs and cardiorespiratory system, and flexibility.

Fitness Challenges

Many selected movement challenges can be used to develop fitness routines for children at this level. Nonlocomotor activities should be alternated with locomotor activities to avoid excessively fatiguing youngsters. When youngsters are pushed too hard aerobically, they express their fatigue in many different manners (i.e., complaining, quitting, misbehaving, or sitting out). Effective fitness instructors are keenly aware of how far to push and when to ease up. Instruction and activities should be sensitive to the capacities of youngsters.

Arm-Shoulder Girdle Development
The following are examples of movement challenges that can be issued to help youngsters develop arm-shoulder girdle strength. All the challenges encourage youngsters to support their body weight with the arms and shoulders.

1. Practice taking the weight completely on your hands.
2. In crab position, keep your feet in place and make your body go in a big circle. Do the same from the push-up position.
3. In crab position, go forward, backward, and to the side. Turn around, move very slowly, and so on.
4. Successively from standing, supine, and hands-knees positions: Swing one limb (arm or leg) at a time, in different directions and at different levels.
5. Combine two limb movements (arm-arm, leg-leg, or arm-leg combinations) in the same direction and in opposite directions. (Vary the levels.)

6. Swing the arms or legs back and forth and go into giant circles. In supine position, make giant circles with your feet.

7. In a bent-over position, swing the arms as if swimming. Try a backstroke or a breaststroke. What does a sidestroke look like?

8. Make the arms go like a windmill. Turn the arms in different directions. Accelerate and decelerate.

9. How else can you circle your arms?

10. Pretend that a swarm of bees is around your head. Brush them off and keep them away.

The push-up and crab positions are excellent for developing upper-body strength. Allow students to rest with one knee on the floor in the up position rather than lying on the floor. Students should be allowed to select a challenge they feel able to accomplish rather than being forced to fail trying to do push-ups. Many of the directives listed for the push-up position can be used for the crab position. A way to develop a sequence of push-up challenges is to begin with one knee on the floor while practicing a number of challenges. As youngsters develop strength, they can make a controlled descent to the floor from the up position. The following are examples of movement challenges that can be done with one knee down (beginning) or in the regular push-up (more challenging) position.

Push-Up Position Challenges

1. Hold your body off the floor (i.e., push-up position).

2. Wave at a friend. Wave with the other arm. Shake a leg at someone. Do these challenges in the crab position.

3. Lift one foot high. Now the other foot.

4. Bounce both feet up and down. Move the feet out from each other while bouncing.

5. Inch the feet up to the hands and go back again. Inch the feet up to the hands and then inch the hands out to return to the push-up position.

6. Reach up with one hand and touch the other shoulder behind the back.

7. Lift both hands from the floor. Try clapping the hands.

8. Turn over so that the back is to the floor. Now complete the turn to push-up position.

9. Walk on your hands and feet. Try two hands and one foot. Walk in the crab position (tummy toward the ceiling).

10. With one knee on the ground, touch your nose to the floor between your hands. As you get stronger, move your head forward a little and touch your nose to the floor. (The farther the nose touches the floor in front of the hands, the greater the strength demands.)

11. Lower the body an inch at a time until the chest touches the floor. Return to the up position any way possible.

12. Pretend you are a tire going flat. Gradually lower yourself to the floor as if you were a tire going flat.

Trunk Development

Movements that include bending, stretching, swaying, twisting, reaching, and forming shapes are important inclusions. No particular continuity exists, except that a specified approach should move from simple to more complex. A logical approach is to select one or more movements and to use them as the theme for the day. Vary the position the child is to take: standing, lying, kneeling, or sitting. From the selected position, stimulate the child to varied movements based on the theme for the day. Examples of different trunk movements follow.

Bending

1. Bend in different ways.
2. Bend as many parts of the body as you can.
3. Make different shapes by bending two, three, and four parts of the body.
4. Bend the arms and knees in different ways and on different levels.
5. Try different ways of bending the fingers and wrist of one hand with the other. Use some resistance. (Explain resistance.) Add body bends.

Stretching

1. Keep one foot in place and stretch your arms in different directions; move with the free foot. Stretch at different levels.
2. Lie on the floor, stretch one leg different ways in space. Stretch one leg in one direction and the other in another direction.
3. Stretch as slowly as you can and then snap back to original position.
4. Stretch with different arm-leg combinations in several directions.
5. See how much space on the floor you can cover by stretching.
6. Combine bending and stretching movements.

Swaying and Twisting

1. Sway your body back and forth in different directions. Change the position of your arms.
2. Sway your body, bending over.
3. Sway your head from side to side.
4. Select a part of the body and twist it as far as you can in one direction and then in the opposite direction.
5. Twist your body at different levels.
6. Twist two or more parts of your body at the same time.

7. Twist one part of your body while untwisting another.

8. Twist your head to see as far back as you can.

9. Twist like a spring. Like a screwdriver.

10. Stand on one foot and twist your body. Untwist.

11. From a seated position, make different shapes by twisting.

Abdominal Development

The basic position for exercising the abdominal muscles is supine on the floor or on a mat. Challenges should lift the upper and lower portions of the body from the floor, either singly or together. Since kindergarten through second-grade children are top heavy, (large head, small body), they will find it difficult to perform most abdominal exercises. Therefore, early abdominal development should begin with youngsters lying on the floor and lifting the head. This is followed by starting in a sitting position and gradually lowering (with head tucked) the upper body to the floor. The following are challenges teachers can use to stimulate children to develop abdominal and shoulder girdle strength. In addition, selected abdominal exercises (pages 180–183) can be modified to provide suitable challenges. The approach should be informal, using directives such as, "Can you …?" or "Show me how you can …."

1. Lift your head from the floor and look at your toes. Wink your right eye and wiggle your left foot. Reverse.

2. In a supine position, "wave" a leg at a friend. Use the other leg. Use both legs.

3. Lift your knees up slowly, an inch at a time.

4. Pick your heels up about 6 inches off the floor and swing them back and forth. Cross them and twist them.

5. Sit up any way you can and touch both sets of toes with your hands.

6. Sit up any possible way and touch your right toes with your left hand. Do it the other way.

7. In a sitting position, lean the upper body backward without falling. How long can you hold this position?

8. From a sitting position, lower the body slowly to the floor. Vary the positions of the arms (across the tummy, the chest, and above the head).

9. From a supine position, curl up by pulling up on your legs.

10. From a supine position, hold your shoulders off the floor.

11. From a supine position, lift your legs and head off the floor.

Leg and Cardiorespiratory Development

Leg and cardiorespiratory development activities can include a range of movement challenges, either in general space or in place. Youngsters fatigue and recover quickly. Take advantage of this trait by alternating cardiorespiratory activities with arm, trunk, and abdominal exercises.

Running Patterns

Running in different directions

Running in place

Running and stopping

Running and changing direction on signal

Jumping and Hopping Patterns

Jumping in different directions back and forth over a spot

Jumping or hopping in, out, over, and around hoops, individual mats, or jump ropes laid on the floor

Jumping or hopping back and forth over lines, or hopping down the lines

Rope Jumping

Individual rope jumping—allow choice

Combinations

Many combinations of locomotor movements can be suggested, such as run, leap, and roll, or run, jump-turn, and shake. Other combinations can be devised. Following are possible challenges that might be used.

1. Do some running steps in place without stopping.
2. Skip or gallop for 30 seconds.
3. Slide all the way around the gymnasium.
4. Alternate hopping or jumping for 30 seconds with 30 seconds of rest.
5. Jump in place while twisting the arms and upper body.
6. Do 10 skips, 10 gallops, and finish with 30 running steps.
7. Hold hands with a friend and do 100 jumps.
8. Jump rope as many times as possible without missing.
9. Hop back and forth over this line from one end of the gym to the other.
10. Try to run as fast as you can. How long can you keep going?

Animal Movements

Animal movements are excellent activities for developing fitness because they develop cardiovascular endurance and strength. They are particularly enjoyable for primary-grade children because the students can mimic the sounds and movements of the animals. Most of the animal movements are done with the body weight on all four limbs, which assures development of the arms and shoulders. Children can be challenged to move randomly throughout the area, across the gymnasium, or between cones delineating a specific distance. The distance moved can be lengthened or the amount of time each walk is performed can be increased to assure that overload occurs. To avoid excessive fatigue, alternate the animal movements with stretching activities. The following are examples of animal walks that can be used. Many more can be created simply by asking students to see if they can move like a ... (specific animal).

- *Puppy Walk.* Move on all fours (not the knees). Keep the head up and move lightly.
- *Lion Walk.* Move on all fours while keeping the back arched. Move deliberately and lift the "paws" to simulate moving without sound.
- *Elephant Walk.* Move heavily throughout the area, swinging the head back and forth like an elephant's trunk.
- *Seal Walk.* Sit on the floor and use the arms to propel the body. Allow the legs to drag along the floor much as a seal would move.
- *Injured Coyote.* Move using only three limbs. Hold the injured limb off the floor. Vary the walk by specifying which limb is injured.
- *Crab Walk.* Move on all fours with the tummy facing the ceiling. Try to keep the back as straight as possible.
- *Rabbit Jump.* Start in a squatting position with the hands on the floor. Reach forward with the hands and support the body weight. Jump both feet toward the hands. Repeat the sequence.

Fitness Games

Fitness games are excellent for cardiovascular endurance and create a high degree of motivation. Emphasis should be placed on all students moving. One of the best ways to assure this occurs is to play games that do not eliminate players. This usually means players who tag someone are no longer "it" and the person tagged becomes "it." This makes it less easy to tell who is "it," which is desirable since players cannot stop and stand when the "it" player is a significant distance from them. If various games stipulate a "safe" position, allow the player to remain in this position for a maximum of 5 seconds. This assures activity continues. Because fitness games focus on cardiovascular fitness, alternate the games with strength and flexibility activities. The following are examples of games that can be played.

- *Stoop Tag.* Players cannot be tagged when they stoop.
- *Back-to-Back Tag.* Players are safe when they stand back to back with another. Other positions can be designated such as toe to toe, knee to knee, and so on.
- *Train Tag.* Form groups of three or four and make a train by holding the hips of the other players. Three or four players are designated as "it" and try to hook onto the rear of the train. If "it" is successful, the player at the front of the train becomes the new "it."
- *Color Tag.* Players are safe when they stand on a specified color. The "safe" color may be changed by the leader at any time.

- *Elbow Swing Tag.* Players cannot be tagged as long as they are performing an elbow swing with another player.
- *Balance Tag.* Players are safe when they are balanced on one body part.
- *Push-Up Tag.* Players are safe when they are in a push-up position. Other exercise positions, such as bent knee curl-up, V-up, and crab position, can be used.
- *Group Tag.* The only time a player is safe is when all are in a group (stipulated by the leader) holding hands. For example, the designated number might be 4, which means that students must be holding hands in groups of four to be safe.

Miniature Challenge Courses

A miniature challenge course (see Figure 8.1) can be set up indoors or outdoors. The distance between the start and finish lines depends on the type of activity. To begin, a distance of about 30 feet is suggested, but this can be adjusted. Cones can mark the course boundaries. The course should be wide enough for two children at a time to move down it.

Each child performs the stipulated locomotor movement from the start to the finish line, then turns and jogs back to the start. The movement is continuous. Directions should be given in advance so that no delay occurs. The number of children on each course should be limited to normal squad size or fewer. The following movements can be stipulated:

- All types of locomotor movements: running, jumping, hopping, sliding, and so on
- Movements on the floor: crawling, bear walk, seal crawl, and the like
- Movements over and under obstacles or through tires or hoops

Parachute Fitness Routines

The parachute has been a popular item in elementary physical education for many years. Usually used to promote teamwork, provide maximum partici-

FIGURE 8.1   *Miniature Challenge Course*

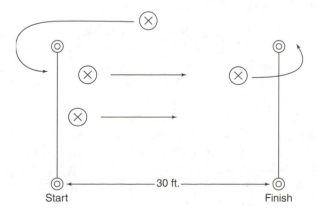

pation, stimulate interest, or play games, the parachute has been overlooked as a tool to develop physical fitness. By combining vigorous shaking movements, locomotor circular movement, and selected exercises while holding onto the chute, exciting fitness routines can be developed.

Walk, Trot, and Sprint

Four cones can outline a square or rectangular area 30 to 40 yards on a side. (Indoors, the circumference of the gymnasium is used.) Children are scattered around the perimeter, all facing in the same direction. The signals are given with a whistle. On the first whistle, children begin to walk. On the next whistle, they change to a trot. On the third whistle, they run as rapidly as they can. Finally, on the fourth whistle, they walk again. The cycle is repeated as many times as the capacity of the children indicates. Faster-moving youngsters should pass on the outside of the area.

Another way to signal change is by drumbeat. One drumbeat signals walk, two beats signals trot, and three means run. This allows the teacher to present the three movements in different order. Different locomotor movements such as running, skipping, galloping, and sliding can be used for variation. At regular intervals, students should be stopped so that they can perform various stretching activities and strength development exercises. This will allow short rest periods between bouts of activity. Examples of activities might be one-leg balance, push-ups, curl-ups, touching the toes, and any other challenges.

Jump Rope Exercises

Jump ropes form the basis of a number of exercises and aerobic activities. Each youngster should have a jump rope and space for jumping. Recorded music with taped intervals of silence is an excellent method for alternating periods of rope jumping and exercises. During the periods of silence, youngsters perform an exercise; during the music, children pick up their ropes and begin jumping. The lesson plan book contains a suggested rope jumping routine.

Four-Corners Movement

A rectangle is formed by four cones. The student moves around the rectangle. Each time children go around a corner, they change their movement pattern. On long sides, rapid movement such as running, skipping, or sliding should be designated. Moving along short sides, students can hop, jump, or do animal walks. Vary clockwise and counterclockwise directions. On signal, youngsters stop and perform flexibility and strength development challenges.

Using the four-corners ideas as a basis, other combinations can be devised. For example, the pattern in Figure 8.2 requires running along one of the long sides of the area and sliding along the other. One of the short sides has mats and requires three forward rolls, while the other short side requires an animal walk on all fours.

FIGURE 8.2   Four-Corners Movement Formation

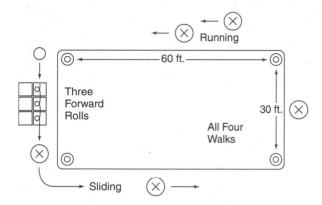

Another variation that stimulates interest in children is to place different equipment around the perimeter of the area. This could be on the inside or outside of the area where youngsters are moving. On signal, youngsters stop and pick up a piece of equipment and manipulate it for a specified time. By interspersing four-corners movement (aerobic movement) with equipment handling (resting), teachers implement interval training. Equipment that can be used might be beanbags, scooters, balance beams, benches, balls, and hoops.

Measurements can vary according to the ages of the children and the movement tasks involved. Outdoors, four rectangles can be laid out. Indoors, at least two should be established. Too much crowding and interference occur when only one rectangle is used for the average-sized class.

Other Fitness Challenges and Routines

Astronaut drills (pages 194–195) can be modified for primary-grade children. Circuit training (pages 191–194) can also be adapted to fit the needs of youngsters at this level. Stations can include challenging or manipulative activities on an informal basis in addition to exercise routines. Exercises to music (pages 190–191) can be adapted by combining music and movement challenges.

Fitness Activities for Children in Grades 3 through 6

In contrast to the program of activities kindergarten through second-grade children, emphasis on fitness for children in grades 3 through 6 shifts to exercises and routines, with less focus on exploratory movement. Starting off the year with teacher-leader exercises is suggested, as these are the basic exercises used in other routines.

Instructional Procedures for Fitness Activities

1. Students should move into an appropriate formation quickly. Methods for accomplishing this include scattering so each student has suf-

ficient personal space, going to prearranged places (numbers painted on the floor help), and using extended squad formation. (Squads stay in line but spacing is increased between members.)

2. When introducing a new exercise, demonstrate briefly how it is to be done. Explain the purpose of the exercise and its value, including the muscle groups involved. Take children through the exercise by parts (count by count) until it is mastered, and then speed up to normal tempo.

3. Beginning dosages for exercises should start at a level where all children will succeed. The best way to assure success is to allow students to adjust the workload to suit their capabilities. Using a specified amount of time per exercise will allow a less gifted child to perform successfully. All children should not be expected to perform exactly the same workload. Allow for individual differences by offering dosages in time and asking children to do the best they can within the time constraint.

4. For some exercises, allow students to select a modified activity in order to meet success. For example, some students may not be able to perform a push-up. Rather than asking them to continue to fail with this task, ask them to select a different push-up challenge (pages 164–165). This also is effective with abdominal activities (page 166).

5. Postural alignment should be maintained. In exercises in which the arms are held in front, to the sides of the body, or overhead, the abdominal wall needs to be tensed and flattened for proper positioning of the pelvis. In most activities, the feet should be pointed forward, the chest up, and the head and shoulders in good postural position.

6. Exercises, in themselves, are not sufficient to develop cardiovascular endurance. Additional aerobic activity in the form of jogging, rope jumping, walking, or some other activity is needed to round out fitness development.

Harmful Practices and Exercises

The following points contraindicate certain exercise practices and should be considered when offering fitness instruction. For in-depth coverage of contraindicated exercises, see Lindsey and Corbin (1989) and Corbin and Lindsey (1994).

1. The following techniques (Macfarlane, 1993) should be avoided when performing abdominal exercises that lift the head and trunk off the floor:
   a. Avoid placing the hands behind the head or high on the neck. This may cause hyperflexion and injury to the discs when the elbows swing forward to help pull the body up.
   b. Keep the knees bent. Straight legs cause the hip flexor muscles to be used earlier and more forcefully, making it difficult to maintain proper pelvic tilt.

c. Don't hold the feet on the floor. Having another student secure the feet places more force on the lumbar vertabrae and may lead to lumbar hyperextension.

d. Don't lift the buttocks and lumbar region off the floor. This also causes the hip flexor muscles to contract vigorously.

2. Two types of stretching activity have been used to develop flexibility. *Ballistic stretching* (strong bouncing movements) formerly was the most common stretching used, but it has been discouraged for many years because it was thought to increase delayed onset muscle soreness. The other flexibility activity, *static stretching*, involves increasing the stretch to the point of discomfort, backing off slightly to where the position can be held comfortably, and maintaining the stretch for an extended time. Static stretching has been advocated because it was thought to reduce muscle soreness and prevent injury. However, a recent study (Smith et al., 1993) has disputed the muscle soreness and tissue damage theory with findings that showed ballistic and static stretching both produced increases in muscle soreness. In fact, the static stretching actually induced significantly more soreness than did ballistic stretching. Until findings show otherwise, it is probably acceptable to use either type of stretching to improve flexibility.

3. If forward flexion is done from a sitting position in an effort to touch the toes, the bend should be from the hips, not from the waist, and should be done with one leg flexed.

4. Straight-leg raises from a supine position should be avoided because they may strain the lower back. The problem can be somewhat alleviated by placing the hands under the small of the back, but it is probably best to avoid such exercises.

5. Deep knee bends (full squats) and the duck walk should be avoided. They may cause damage to the knee joints and have little developmental value. Much more beneficial is flexing the knee joint to 90 degrees and returning to a standing position.

6. When doing stretching exercises from a standing position, the knees should not be hyperextended. The knee joint should be relaxed rather than locked. Have students do their stretching with bent knees; this will remind them not to hyperextend the joint. In all stretching activities, participants should be allowed to judge their range of motion. Expecting all students to be able to touch their toes is an unrealistic goal. If concerned about touching the toes from this position, do so from a sitting position with one leg flexed.

7. Activities that place stress on the neck should be avoided. Examples of activities in which caution should be used are the Inverted Bicycle, the Wrestler's Bridge, and abdominal exercises with the hands behind the head.

8. Avoid the so-called hurdler's stretch. This activity is done in the sitting position with one leg forward and the other leg bent and to the rear. Using this stretch places undue pressure on the knee joint of the bent leg. Substitute a stretch using a similar position with one leg

straight forward and the other leg bent with the foot placed in the crotch area.

9. Avoid stretches that demand excessive back arching (such as while lying in prone position, the student reaches back and grabs the ankles). By pulling and arching, the exerciser can hyperextend the lower back. This places stress on the discs and stretches the abdominal muscles (not needed by most people).

Exercises for Developing Fitness Routines

Exercises selected fall into the following five categories: flexibility, arm-shoulder girdle, abdominal, leg and agility, and trunk-twisting and bending. In any one class session, the exercises should number from 6 to 10. Included in each lesson should be two exercises from the arm-shoulder girdle group and at least one from each of the other categories. Specific exercises should be changed at times, with a minimum of 12 exercises being included in the year's experiences.

Several approaches ensure variety in exercise selection. One system is to select a basic group of exercises. Assume that 12 exercises are selected. These could be divided into two sets of 6 each, with the selection meeting the standards of category coverage previously discussed. Some teachers like to alternate sets day by day. Others prefer to have one set in effect for a week or two before changing. Another method is to make sets of exercises on cards, using a different-colored card for each of the categories. In this manner, teachers can be assured of full developmental coverage by having students select a card from each color group, with the stipulation of two from the arm-shoulder girdle group.

Recommended exercises are presented under each of the five categories. Stress points, modifications, variations, and teaching suggestions are presented when appropriate. Teachers can supplement the listed exercises with some of their choice, provided that the exercises are fundamentally sound. A beginning dosage is offered as a starting point for teachers who are meeting a group of youngsters for the first time.

Flexibility Exercises

Many exercises contribute to the development of flexibility. Those included in this section, however, have flexibility as their main goal.

Bend and Twist
Starting Position: Stand with the arms crossed, hands on opposite shoulders, knees slightly flexed, and feet shoulder width apart.

Movement: Bend forward at the waist (count 1). Twist the trunk and touch the right elbow to the left knee (count 2). Twist in the opposite direction and touch the left elbow to the right knee (count 3). Return to the starting position (count 4). Knees can be flexed.

FIGURE 8.3   Sitting Stretch Position

Sitting Stretch

Starting Position: Sit on the floor with one leg extended forward and the other bent at the knee. The foot is placed in the area of the crotch. The toes of the extended foot are touched with the fingertips of both hands as the chest gradually moves forward (see Figure 8.3).

Movement: Gradually bend forward, taking three counts to bend fully. Recover to sitting position on the fourth count.

Stress Point: Bend from the hips.

Partner Rowing

Starting Position: Partners sit facing each other, holding hands with palms touching and fingers locked. The legs are spread and extended to touch soles of partner's feet.

Movement: One partner bends forward, with the help of the other pulling backward, to try to bring the chest as close to the floor as possible (see Figure 8.4). Reverse direction. Pairs should work individually.

FIGURE 8.4   Partner Rowing

Variation: Steam Engine. With both partners in the sitting position, alternate pulling hands back and forth like a pair of steam engine pistons. Do eight sets, right and left combined twists.

Lower Leg Stretch
Starting Position: Stand facing a wall with the feet about shoulder width apart. Place the palms of the hands on the wall at eye level (see Figure 8.5).

Movement: Slowly walk away from the wall, keeping the body straight, until the stretch is felt in the lower portion of the calf. The feet should remain flat on the floor during the stretch.

Achilles Tendon Stretch
Starting Position: Stand facing a wall with the forearms on it. Place the forehead on the back of the hands. Back 2 to 3 feet away from the wall, bend, and move one leg closer to the wall.

FIGURE 8.5   *Lower Leg Stretch*

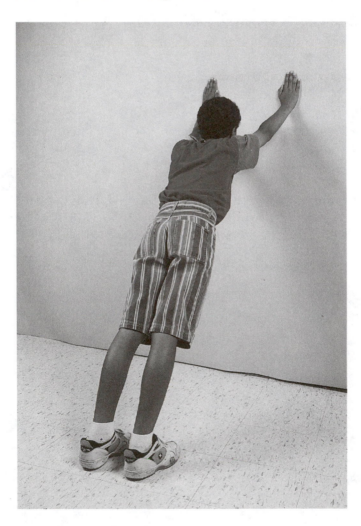

Movement: Flex the bent leg with the foot on the floor until the stretch is felt in the Achilles tendon area. The feet should remain flat on the floor as the leg closer to the wall is flexed. Repeat, flexing the other leg.

Body Twist

Starting Position: Sit on the floor with the left leg straight. Lift the right leg over the left leg and place it on the floor outside the left knee (see Figure 8.6). Move the left elbow outside the upper right thigh and use it to maintain pressure on the leg. Lean back and support the upper body with the right hand.

Movement: Rotate the upper body toward the right hand and arm. Reverse the position and stretch the other side of the body.

Standing Hip Bend

Starting Position: Stand with the knees slightly flexed, one hand on the hip and the other arm overhead.

Movement: Bend to the side with the hand resting on the hip. The arm overhead should point and move in the direction of the stretch with a slight bend at the elbow. Reverse and stretch the opposite side.

Arm-Shoulder Girdle Exercises

Arm-shoulder girdle exercises for this age group include both arm-support and free-arm types.

Push-Ups

Starting Position: Assume the push-up position, with the body straight from head to heels.

FIGURE 8.6   *Body Twist*

Movement: Keeping the body straight, bend the elbows and touch the chest to the ground; then straighten the elbows, raising the body in a straight line.

Stress Points: The movement should be in the arms. The head is up, with the eyes looking ahead. The chest should touch the floor lightly, without receiving the weight of the body. The body remains in a straight line throughout, without sagging or humping.

Modification: Many youngsters develop a dislike for push-ups because they are asked to perform them without any modification. Allow youngsters to judge their strength and choose a push-up challenge (pages 164–165) they feel able to accomplish. Instead of asking an entire class to perform a specified number of push-ups, personalize the workload by allowing each youngster to accomplish as many repetitions as possible of a self-selected push-up challenge in a specified amount of time. This creates a positive experience and feeling about this important exercise.

Reclining Pull-Ups
Starting Position: One pupil lies in supine position. Partner is astride, with feet alongside the reclining partner's chest. Partners grasp hands with interlocking fingers, with some other suitable grip, or with an interlocked wrist grip.

Movement: The pupil on the floor pulls up with arms until the chest touches the partner's thighs. The body remains straight, with weight resting on the heels (see Figure 8.7). Return to position.

Stress Points: The supporting student should keep the center of gravity well over the feet by maintaining a lifted chest and proper head position. The

FIGURE 8.7   Reclining Pull-Ups

lower student should maintain a straight body during the pull-up and move only the arms.

Variation: Raise as directed (count 1), hold the high position isometrically (counts 2 and 3), return to position (count 4).

Triceps Push-Ups
Starting Position: Assume the inverted push-up position with the arms and body held straight.

Movement: Keeping the body straight, bend the elbows and touch the seat to the ground, then straighten the elbows and raise the body.

Stress Points: The fingers should point toward the toes or be turned in slightly. The body should be held firm with movement restricted to the arms.

Arm Circles
Starting Position: Stand erect, with feet apart and arms straight out to the side.

Movement: Do forward and backward circles with palms facing forward, moving arms simultaneously. The number of circles executed before changing can be varied.

Stress Points: Avoid doing arm circles with palms down (particularly backward circles) as it stresses the shoulder joint. Correct posture should be maintained, with the abdominal wall flat and the head and shoulders held back.

Crab Kick
Starting Position: Crab position, with the body supported on the hands and feet and the back parallel to the floor. The knees are bent at right angles. On all crab positions, keep the seat up and avoid body sag.

Movement: Kick the foot forward and extend the right leg (counts 1 and 2). Repeat with the left leg (counts 3 and 4). Continue alternating legs.

Crab Alternate-Leg Extension
Starting Position: Assume crab position.

Movement: On count 1, extend the right leg forward so that it rests on the heel. On count 2, extend the left leg forward and bring the right leg back. Continue alternating.

Crab Full-Leg Extension
Starting Position: Assume crab position.

Movement: On count 1, extend both legs forward so that the weight rests on the heels. On count 2, bring both feet back to crab position.

Crab Walk
Starting Position: Assume crab position.

Movement: Move forward, backward, sideward, and turn in a small circle right and left.

Flying Angel
Starting Position: Stand erect, with feet together and arms at sides.

Movement: In a smooth, slow, continuous motion, raise the arms forward with elbows extended and then upward, at the same time rising up on the toes and lifting the chest, with eyes following the hands. Lower the arms sideward in a flying motion and return to starting position.

Stress Points: The abdominal wall must be kept flat throughout to minimize lower back curvature. The head should be back and well up. The exercise should be done slowly and smoothly, under control.

Variation: Move the arms forward as if doing a breaststroke. The arms are then raised slowly, with hands in front of the chest and elbows out, to full overhead extension. Otherwise, the movement is the same as the Flying Angel.

Abdominal Exercises

For most exercises stressing abdominal development, start from a supine position on the floor or on a mat. For children who have weak abdominal muscles, begin by first lifting and holding the head off the floor. This action tightens the abdominal muscles. Increased challenge can gradually occur by lifting the legs, the upper body, or both at the same time. If the upper body is lifted, the movement should begin with a roll-up (curling) action, moving the head first so the chin makes contact or near contact with the chest, thus flattening and stabilizing the lower back curve. The bent-knee position isolates the abdominal muscles and avoids stressing the lower back region. When doing abdominal exercises, avoid lifting the trunk up to the sitting position (past 45 degrees) since it may cause pain and exacerbate back injury in susceptible individuals (Macfarlane, 1993). The benefits of abdominal exercise are gained when the trunk is moved from the floor to approximately a 45-degree angle (see Figure 8.8). Beyond 45 degrees, excessive stress may be placed on the back and there is little benefit to the abdominal muscle group.

Many youngsters develop a dislike for abdominal work in the early school years because they are top heavy (large head, small body) and unable to successfully lift their upper bodies off the floor. To assure success, allow students to choose an abdominal challenge (page 166) they feel able to accomplish. Instead of asking an entire class to perform a specified number of curl-ups, personalize the workloads by allowing youngsters to accomplish as many repetitions as possible in a specified amount of time using a self-selected abdominal challenge.

FIGURE 8.8   Curl-Up to a 45-Degree Angle

Reverse Curl

Starting Position: Lie on the back with the hands on the floor to the sides of the body.

Movement: Curl the knees to the chest. The upper body remains on the floor. As abdominal strength increases, the child should lift the buttocks and lower back off the floor.

Stress Points: Roll the knees to the chest and return the feet to the floor after each repetition. The movement should be controlled, with emphasis on the abdominal contraction.

Variations: (1) Hold the head off the floor and bring the knees to the chin. (2) Instead of returning the feet to the floor after each repetition, move them 1 or 2 inches off the floor. This activity requires greater abdominal strength as there is no resting period (feet on floor).

Pelvis Tilter

Starting Position: Lie on the back with the feet flat on the floor, knees bent, arms out in wing position, and palms up.

Movement: Flatten the lower back, bringing it closer to the floor by tensing the lower abdominals and lifting up on the pelvis. Hold for 8 to 12 counts. Tense slowly and release slowly.

Knee Touch Curl-Up

Starting Position: Lie on the back, with the feet flat and the knees bent, and with the hands flat on top of the thighs.

Movement: Leading with the chin, slide the hands forward until the fingers touch the kneecaps and gradually curl the head and shoulders until the shoulder blades are lifted off the floor (see Figure 8.9). Hold for eight counts

FIGURE 8.9   Knee Touch Curl-Up

and return to position. To avoid stress on the lower back, the performer should not curl up to the sitting position.

Curl-Up
Starting Position: Lie on the back with the feet flat, knees bent and arms on the floor at the side of the body with palms down.

Movement: Lift the head and shoulders to a 45-degree angle and then back in a two-count pattern. The hands should slide forward on the floor 3 to 4 inches. The curl-up can also be done as an eight-count exercise, moving up on one count, holding for six counts, and moving down on the last count.

Stress Points: Roll up, with the chin first. Do not lift the hands off the floor.

Curl-Up with Twist
Starting Position: Lie on the back with the feet flat and the knees bent. The arms are folded and placed across the chest with hands on shoulders.

Movement: Do a partial curl-up and twist the chest to the left. Repeat, turning the chest to the right (see Figure 8.10).

Variations: (1) Touch the outside of the knee with the elbow. (2) Touch both knees in succession. The sequence is up, touch left, touch right, and down.

Leg Extension
Starting Position: Sit on the floor with legs extended and hands on hips.

Movement: With a quick, vigorous action, raise the knees and bring both heels as close to the seat as possible. The movement is a drag with the toes touching lightly. Return to position.

FIGURE 8.10   *Curl-Up with Twist*

Variation: Alternate bringing the knees to the right and left of the head.

Abdominal Cruncher
Starting Position: Lie in supine position with feet flat, knees bent, and palms of hands cupped over the ears (not behind the head). An alternate position is to fold the arms across the chest and place the hands on the shoulders.

Movement: Tuck the chin and curl upward until the shoulder blades leave the floor. Return to the floor with a slow uncurling.

Variation: Lift the feet off the floor and bring the knees to waist level. Try to touch the right elbow to the left knee and vice versa while in the crunch position.

Leg and Agility Exercises

Leg and agility exercises should feature rhythmic, graceful motion with emphasis on control.

Running in Place
Starting Position: Stand with arms bent at the elbows.

Movement: Run in place. Begin slowly, counting only the left foot. Speed up somewhat, raising the knees to hip height. Then run at full speed, raising the knees hard. Finally, slow down. The run should be on the toes.

Variations: (1) Tortoise and Hare. Jog slowly in place. On the command "Hare," double the speed. On the command "Tortoise," slow the tempo to original slow jogging pace. (2) March in place. Lift the knees high and swing the arms up. Turn right and left on command while marching. Turn completely around to the right and then to the left while marching. (3) Fast Stepping. Step in place for 10 seconds as rapidly as possible. Rest for 10 seconds and repeat five or more times.

Jumping Jack
Starting Position: Stand at attention.

Movement: On count 1, jump to a straddle position with arms overhead. On count 2, recover to starting position.

Variations: (1) Begin with the feet in a stride position (forward and back). Change feet with the overhead movement. (2) Instead of bringing the feet together when the arms come down, cross the feet each time, alternating the cross. (3) On the completion of each set of eight counts, do a quarter-turn right. (After four sets, the child is facing in the original direction.) Do the same to the left. (4) Modified Jumping Jack. On count 1, jump to a straddle position with arms out to the sides, parallel to the floor, and palms down. On count 2, return to position.

Treadmill
Starting Position: Assume push-up position, except that one leg is brought forward so that the knee is under the chest.

Movement: Reverse the position of the feet, bringing the extended leg forward. Change back again so that the original foot is forward. Continue rhythmically alternating feet.

Stress Points: The head should be kept up. A full exchange of the legs should be made, with the forward knee coming well under the chest each time.

Power Jumper
Starting Position: Begin in a semicrouched position, with knees flexed and arms extended backward.

Movement: Jump as high as possible and extend the arms upward and overhead.

Variations: (1) Jump and perform different turns (i.e., quarter, half, full). (2) Jump and perform different tasks (i.e., heel click, heel slap, clap hands, catch an imaginary pass, snare a rebound).

Trunk-Twisting and Bending Exercises

Many exercises involve twisting or bending; a few involve both. The twisting or bending should be done throughout the full range of movement. Movements should be large and vigorous.

Trunk Twister

Starting Position: Stand with feet shoulder width apart and pointed forward. The hands are cupped and placed loosely over the shoulders, with the elbows out and the chin tucked.

Movement: Bend downward, keeping the knees relaxed. Recover slightly. Bend downward again and simultaneously rotate the trunk to the left and then to the right (see Figure 8.11). Return to original position, pulling the head back, with chin in.

Bear Hug

Starting Position: Stand with feet comfortably spread and hands on hips.

Movement: Take a long step diagonally right, keeping the left foot anchored in place. Tackle the right leg around the thigh by encircling the thigh with both arms. Squeeze and stretch. Return to position. Tackle the left leg. Return to position.

Stress Point: The value in flexibility comes from slow, controlled stretching.

Side Flex

Starting Position: Lie on one side with lower arm extended overhead. The head rests on the lower arm. The legs are extended fully, one on top of the other.

FIGURE 8.11 Trunk Twister

FIGURE 8.12   Side Flex

Movement: Raise the upper arm and leg diagonally (see Figure 8.12). Repeat for several counts and change to the other side.

Body Circles
Starting Position: Stand with feet shoulder width apart, hands on hips, and body bent forward.

Movement: Make a complete circle with the upper body. A specified number of circles should be made to the right and the same number to the left.

Variations: (1) Circle in one direction until told to stop, then reverse direction. (2) Change to a position in which the hands are on the shoulders and the elbows are kept wide. Otherwise, the exercise is the same. (This is more demanding than the regular Body Circles.)

Windmill
Starting Position: Stand with feet shoulder width apart and arms extended sideward with palms down.

Movement: Bend and twist at the trunk, bringing the right hand down to the left toes. Recover to starting position. Bend and twist again, but bring the left hand to the right toes. Recover to starting position.

Stress Point: The arms and legs should be kept straight throughout.

Partner-Resistance Exercises

Partner-resistance exercises are useful for building strength, but produce little increase in cardiorespiratory endurance. Consequently, they should be used in conjunction with activities that demand considerable endurance, such as Aerobic Fitness Routines, jogging, or Astronaut Drills. Partner resistance exercises can strengthen specific muscle groups and are useful for helping the physically underdeveloped child. The exercises are simple and enjoyable; children can do them as homework with their parents or friends. Children should be made aware of the muscle group developed by each exercise.

Partners should be somewhat matched in size and strength so that they can challenge each other. The exercises are performed throughout the full range of motion at each joint and should take 8 to 12 seconds to complete. The partner providing the resistance counts the duration of the exercise; positions are then reversed.

Arm Curl-Up

The exerciser keeps the upper arms against the sides with the forearms and palms forward. The partner's fists are put in the exerciser's palms (see Figure 8.13). The exerciser attempts to curl the forearms upward to the shoulders. To develop the opposite set of muscles, partners reverse hand positions. Push down in the opposite direction, starting at shoulder level.

FIGURE 8.13   Arm Curl-Up

Forearm Flex

The exerciser extends the arms and places the hands, palms down, on the partner's shoulders. The exerciser attempts to push the partner into the floor. The partner may slowly stoop lower to allow the exerciser movement through the range of motion. Try with the palms upward.

Fist Pull-Apart

The exerciser places the fists together in front of the body at shoulder level. The exerciser attempts to pull the hands apart while the partner forces them together with pressure on the elbows. As a variation, with fists apart, the exerciser tries to push them together. The partner applies pressure by grasping the wrists and holding the exerciser's fists apart.

Butterfly

The exerciser starts with arms straight and at the sides. The partner, from the back, attempts to hold the arms down while the exerciser lifts with straight arms to the sides. Try with arms above the head (partner holding) to move them down to the sides.

Camelback

The exerciser is on all fours with head up. The partner pushes on the exerciser's back, while the exerciser attempts to hump the back like a camel.

Back Builder

The exerciser spreads the legs and bends forward at the waist with head up. The partner faces the exerciser and places clasped hands behind the exerciser's neck. The exerciser attempts to stand upright while the partner pulls downward (see Figure 8.14).

Scissors

The exerciser lies on one side, while the partner straddles the exerciser and holds the upper leg down. The exerciser attempts to raise the top leg. Reverse sides and lift the other leg.

Bear Trap

Starting from a supine position on the floor, spread the legs and then attempt to move them together. Resistance is provided by the partner, who tries to keep the legs apart.

Knee Bender

The exerciser lies in prone position with legs straight and arms pointing ahead on the floor. The partner places the hands on the back of the exerciser's ankles. The exerciser attempts to flex the knees while the partner applies pressure (see Figure 8.15). Try in the opposite direction, starting with the knee joint at a 90-degree angle.

FIGURE 8.14   Back Builder

FIGURE 8.15   Knee Bender

Push-Up with Resistance

The exerciser is in push-up position with arms bent, so that the body is about halfway up from the floor. The partner straddles or stands alongside the exerciser's head and puts pressure on the top of the shoulders by pushing down lightly. The amount of pressure takes judgment by the partner. Too much causes the exerciser to collapse.

Developing Physical Fitness Routines

When planning fitness routines, establish variety in activities and include different approaches. This tends to minimize the inherent weaknesses of any single routine. Design routines that exercise all major parts of the body. Additionally, when sequencing fitness activities into a routine, try not to overload the same body part with two sequential exercises. For example, if push-ups are being performed, the next exercise should not be crab walking, as it also stresses the arm-shoulder girdle.

Exercise dosage for youngsters should be administered in time rather than repetitions. It is unreasonable to expect all youngsters to perform the same number of exercise repetitions. Fitness performance is controlled by a number of factors, including genetics and trainability, making it impossible for all children to do the same workload. When time is used to determine the workload, each child can personalize the amount of activity performed within the time constraints. It is reasonable to expect a gifted youngster to be able to perform more repetitions in a certain amount of time than a less genetically endowed child. An obese youngster may not be able to perform as many push-ups as a leaner peer. Develop positive attitudes toward activity by asking youngsters to do the best they can within the time allotted.

Student Leader Exercises

At times, select students to lead either single exercises or an entire routine. Students need prior practice if they are to lead their peers effectively in a stimulating exercise session. Teachers should ask for volunteers and allow students to practice ahead of time. Children should not be forced to lead, because this can result in failure for both the child and the class. See the lesson plan book for a suggested routine.

Squad Leader Exercises

Squad leader exercises provide students with an opportunity to lead exercises in a small group. This approach is an effective method for teaching students how to lead others and to help them learn how a well-balanced fitness routine takes place. A student within each squad is given a task card specifying a sequence of exercises (see following sample routine). After the first student has led the exercise for the desired amount of time, the card is passed to another member of the squad, who becomes the leader. Exercises can be placed in groups on the task card (arm-shoulder girdle, abdominal strength, leg strength, etc.). Each new leader then selects an exercise from a different group of exercises. This will help assure that a balanced fitness routine results. See the lesson plan book for a suggested routine.

Exercises to Music

Exercises to music add another dimension to developmental experiences. Many commercial record sets with exercise programs are available, but an effective approach is to rely on the tape recorder. Most media departments in schools have equipment that will allow music to be mixed with vocal instructions onto audiotape cassettes. (Ask the school media department if the school has a mixer.) This approach gives teachers control over the selection, sequence, and amount of time, and allows the routine to be adapted to the particular needs and characteristics of the group. Starting and stopping exercises can easily be incorporated into the taped sequences.

Taped music is an excellent way to time the length of exercise bouts. For example, if doing random moving, students could run/walk as long as the music is playing and stretch when it pauses. If the music is pretaped, it will free teachers from having to time the intervals. Other exercise modules that work well with music are Circuit Training, Aerobic Fitness Routines, Continuity Exercises, Astronaut Drills, Squad Leader Exercises, and Rope Jumping Exercises.

A way to identify music that will motivate students is to ask them to bring a compact disk or tape they own. Review the music to see if it is offensive to any parents or other students. After screening, the music can be recorded. When a teacher feels comfortable with narrating the tape, speaking can be mixed with the music.

Circuit Training

Circuit training incorporates several stations, each with a designated fitness task. Students move from station to station, generally in a prescribed order, completing the designated fitness task at each station. Exercise tasks constituting the circuit should contribute to the development of all parts of the body. In addition, activities should contribute to the various components of physical fitness (strength, power, endurance, agility, and flexibility).

Instructional Procedures

1. Each station provides an exercise task that the child can learn and perform without the aid of another child. Exercises that directly follow each other should make demands on different parts of the body. In this way, demands at any one station do not cause local fatigue that could affect the ability to perform the next task.

2. Before beginning the course, giving students sufficient instruction in the activities is important so that they can perform correctly at each station.

3. Distribute the class so similar numbers of children are starting the circuit at each station. This method keeps the demands on equipment low and the activity high. For example, if there are 30 children for a circuit of six stations, then 5 children start at each spot.

4. A tape recorder can be used effectively to give directions for the circuit. Music, whistle signals, and even verbal directions can be prerecorded. The tape provides a rigid time control and gives a measure of consistency to the circuit. Using tapes also frees a teacher for supervisory duties.

5. The number of stations can vary but probably should be no fewer than six and no more than nine. Signs at the different stations can

include the name of the activity and any necessary cautions or stress points for execution. When children move between lines as limits (as in the Agility Run), traffic cones or beanbags can be used to mark the designated boundaries.

Timing and Dosage

In general, a fixed time limit at each station is easiest for Circuit training. Children do their personal best during the time allotted at a station. Progression can be assured by increasing the amount of time at each station. About 30 to 40 seconds to exercise at station with a 10-second interval allotted to allow children to move from one station to the next. Students may start at any station, as designated, but they must follow the established station order.

A second method of timing is to sound only one signal for the change to the next station. With this plan, the child ceases activity at one station, moves to the next, and immediately begins the task at that station without waiting for another signal.

The activity demands of the circuit can be increased by changing the exercises to more strenuous ones. For example, a station could specify knee or bench push-ups and later change to regular push-ups, a more demanding exercise. Another method of increasing intensity is to have each child run a lap around the circuit area between station changes. Cardiovascular endurance can be enhanced by dividing the class into halves. One half exercises on the circuit while the other is running lightly around the area. On signal to change, the runners go to the circuit and the others run.

Suggested Activities

A circuit should always include activities for exercising the arm-shoulder girdle and for strengthening the abdominal wall. A variety of activities are suggested and classified in the following section. One activity can be selected from each classification.

General Body Activities

- Rope Jumping: Use single-time speed only.
- Jumping Jacks
- Running in Place: Lift the knees.
- Arm-Shoulder Girdle Exercises
- Crab Walk: Two parallel lines are drawn 6 to 8 feet apart. Start with hands on one line and feet pointing toward the other. Move back and forth between the lines in crab position, touching one line with the heels and the other with the hands.
- Crab Kick: Start in crab position and alternate with the right and the left foot kicking toward the ceiling.

Leg Exercises

- Step-Ups: One bench is needed for every three children at this station. Begin in front of the bench, stepping up on the bench with the left foot and then up with the right foot. Now step down in rhythm, left and then right. The next class period, begin with the right foot to secure comparable development. Be sure that the legs are fully extended and that the body is erect when on top of the bench.

- Treadmill
- Straddle Bench Jumps: Straddle a bench and alternate jumping to the top of the bench and back to the floor. Since the degree of effort depends on the height of the bench, benches of various heights should be considered. These can be constructed in the form of small, elongated boxes 4 feet long and 10 inches wide, with height ranging from 8 to 10 inches. A 4-foot-long box accommodates two children at a time.
- Agility Run—Touch with the Toes: Two lines are established 15 feet apart. Move between the two lines as rapidly as possible, touching one line with the right foot and the other with the left.
- Agility Run—Touch with the Hand: Same as above, except touch the lines with alternate hands instead of with the feet.

Arms and Shoulders

- Standing Arm Circles
- Lying Arm Circles: Lie prone, with arms out to the sides. Alternate forward and backward arm circling, changing after five circles in each direction. The head and shoulders are lifted from the ground during the exercise.
- Reverse Curls
- Alternate Toe Touching: Begin on the back with arms extended overhead. Alternate by touching the right toes with the left hand and vice versa. Bring the foot and the arm up at the same time and return to the flat position each time.

Flexibility and Back Exercises

- Bend and Twist
- Windmill
- Trunk Twister

Other exercises, stunts, and movements can be used, some in combination. In leg exercises, for example, the task can be designated as 25 running steps in place and then 5 rabbit jumps in place, with the whole task repeated. If the gymnasium is equipped with chinning bars, horizontal ladders, and climbing ropes, circuits can make use of these. Some activities—basketball dribbling, traveling over and under obstacles, tumbling stunts, and manipulative activities—can be included as station tasks to liven things up. Hula-hoop activities are attractive, and gym scooters add a different dimension to many routine movements.

Outdoor Circuits

An outdoor circuit can combine running and station tasks. When a time change is signaled, each participant runs one lap around the area counter-clockwise past the station just performed and on to the next station. This is repeated until each station has been completed. Stations should be located inside the track so that there is no interference with the runners. This type of circuit can also be used with a jogging trail, and is sometimes called a *par-course.* At specified points, different tasks can be performed along the course.

Continuity Drills

Continuity drills originated in Europe. These exercises, done snappily and with vigor, are enjoyable experiences for youngsters. Children are scattered, each with a jump rope. They alternate between rope jumping and exercises. A specified time period governs the length of the rope-jumping episode, which should be done in fast time (single jumps). At the signal to stop rope jumping, children drop the ropes and immediately take position for the exercise selected. Many of the exercises can use a two-count rhythm. When children are positioned for the exercise, the leader says, "Ready!" The class completes one repetition of the exercise and responds, "One, two!" This repeats for each repetition. To increase the enjoyment, the leader can say, "P.E.!" and the class will perform the exercise and respond with, "is fun!" A number of brief phrases can be used such as, "Work hard; keep fit." To enable a successful experience for children, modify the push-up and abdominal challenges (pages 164-166). See the lesson plan book for a suggested routine.

Hexagon Hustle

A large hexagon is formed using six cones. Students perform the "hustle" by moving around the hexagon, changing their movement patterns every time they reach one of the six points in the hexagon. On signal, the "hustle" stops and selected exercises are performed. See the lesson plan book for a suggested routine.

Instructional Procedures

1. To create a safer environment, children should move in the same direction around the hexagon.
2. Laminated posters, with colorful illustrations, should be placed by the cones to inform children of the new movement to be performed.
3. Faster children should be encouraged to pass on the outside of slower children.
4. The direction of the "hustle" should be changed after every exercise segment.

Astronaut Drills

Astronaut Drills are performed in circular or scatter formation. Routines are developed by moving using various locomotor movements, alternated with stopping and performing exercises in place. The following movements and tasks can be incorporated in the routine.

1. Various locomotor movements, such as hopping, jumping, running, sliding, skipping, giant steps, and walking high on the toes.
2. Movement on all fours—forward, backward, or sideward—with respect to the direction of walking. Repeat backward and forward using the Crab Walk.
3. Stunt movements, such as the Seal Walk, Gorilla Walk, and Rabbit Jump.
4. Upper torso movements and exercises that can be done while walking, such as arm circles, bending right and left, and body twists.
5. Various exercises are performed when stopped. A balance of arm-shoulder girdle and abdominal exercises should be included.

Astronaut Drills can be adapted successfully to any level. The type of movements selected will determine the strenuousness of the routine. Children who lag can move toward the inner part of the circle, while more active children pass on the outside. Enjoyment comes from being challenged by a variety of movements. See the lesson plan book for a suggested routine.

Challenge Courses

Challenge courses are popular with students as they move through the course with proper form rather than run against a time standard. The course is designed to exercise all parts of the body through a variety of activities. By including running, vaulting, agility tasks, climbing, hanging, crawling, and other activities, teachers can ensure good fitness demands. A variety of courses can be designed, depending on the length of the course and the tasks included. Some schools have established permanent courses similar to commercial parcourses. A sample indoor course, including a climbing rope, is diagrammed in Figure 8.16.

Aerobic Fitness Routines

Aerobic fitness is a popular activity for people of all ages. Music increases effort, duration, and intensity, while reducing the repetitiveness associated with fitness tasks. These routines are a mixture of various locomotor movements, dance steps, swinging movements, and stretching challenges.

Aerobic fitness routines generally follow one of two patterns. The first is the leader type, in which students follow the actions of a leader. The second involves choreography based on a piece of music. In the leader type, when the music begins, the leader performs a series of movements and the other students follow. This is the best choice for elementary school students. Teachers may lead, although skilled students are able to do an excellent job. There are few limits to the range of activities a leader can present. Manipulative equipment (e.g., balls, jump ropes, hoops, wands) can be integrated into the movement activities.

FIGURE 8.16   *Indoor Challenge Course*

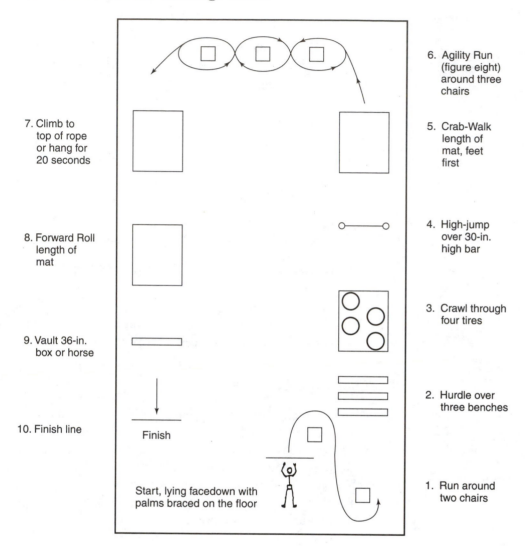

The second method is a formal routine. For elementary school children, routines should be kept uncomplicated. When the music has run through a repetition or phrase, the movement patterns can change. Children can design routines to the music of their choice. For most routines, music should have a tempo of 120 to 140 beats per minute.

Instructional Procedures

1. Use movement increments that are organized by units of 4, 8, or 16 counts. When phrases in the music are repeated, it is often desirable to repeat the previous step.

2. Vary the movements so that stretching and flowing movements are alternated with the more strenuous aerobic activities.

3. Steps should be relatively simple. Students should focus on increasing their fitness levels rather than becoming competent rhythmic per-

formers. Stress continuous movement (moving with the flow) rather than perfection of routines. Running and bouncing steps that children can follow easily are effective and motivating.

4. Routines motivate more children when they are not rigid. Youngsters should not have to worry about being out of step. Both boys and girls should feel comfortable with the activity.

5. Establish cue words to aid youngsters in following routines (e.g., "Bounce," "Step," "Reach," "Jump").

Basic Steps

The following are examples of basic steps and movements that can be used to develop a variety of routines. The majority are performed to a count of 4, although this can be varied depending on the skill of the participants and the goals of the teacher.

Running and Walking Steps

1. Do directional runs—forward, backward, diagonal, sideways, and turning.

2. Do rhythmic runs, with a specific movement on the fourth beat. Examples are knee lift, clap, jump, jump-turn, and hop.

3. Run with flair. Run while lifting the knees, kicking up the heels, or slapping the thighs or heels; or run with legs extended as in the goose step.

4. Run with arms in various positions—on the hips, in the air above the head, and straight down.

Movements on the Floor

1. *Side Leg Raises.* Do these with a straight leg while lying on the side of the body.

2. *Alternate Leg Raises.* While on the back, raise one leg to meet the opposite hand. Repeat, using the opposite leg or both legs.

3. *Rhythmic Push-Ups.* Do these in 2- or 4-count movements. A 4 count would be as follows: halfway down (count 1), nose touched to the floor (count 2), halfway up (count 3), and arms fully extended (count 4).

4. *Crab Kicks and Treadmills.* Do these to 4 counts.

Upright Rhythmic Movements

1. Do lunge variations. Perform a lunge, stepping forward on the right foot while bending at the knee, and extending the arms forward and diagonally upward (counts 1 and 2). Return to starting position by bringing the right foot back and pulling the arms into a jogging position (counts 3 and 4). The lunge is varied by changing the direction of the move and the depth and speed of the lunge.

2. *Side Bends.* Begin with the feet apart. Reach overhead while bending to the side. This movement is done to four beats: bend (count 1), hold (counts 2 and 3), and return (count 4).

3. *Reaches.* Reach upward alternately with the right and left arms. Reaches can be done sideways also and are usually 2-count movements. Fast alternating 1-count movements can be done, too.

4. *Arm and Shoulder Circles.* Make Arm Circles with either one or both arms. Vary the size and speed of the circles. Shoulder shrugs can be done in a similar fashion.

Jumping Jack Variations

1. Jump with arms alternately extended upward and then pulled in toward the chest.

2. Do Side Jumping Jacks with regular arm action while the feet jump from side to side or forward and backward together.

3. Do variations with the feet—forward stride alternating, forward and side stride alternating, kicks or knee lifts added, feet crossed, or heel-toe movements (turning on every fourth or eighth count).

Bounce Steps

1. Bounce and clap. This is similar to a slow-time jump rope step. Clap on every other bounce.

2. Bounce, turn, and clap. Turn a quarter or half turn with each jump.

3. Three bounces and clap. Bounce three times and bounce and clap on the fourth beat. Turns can be performed.

4. Bounce and rock side to side. Transfer the weight from side to side, or forward and backward. Add clapping or arm swinging.

5. Bounce with body twist. Hold the arms at shoulder level and twist the lower body back and forth on each bounce.

6. Bounce with floor patterns. Bounce and make different floor patterns such as a box, diagonal, or triangle.

7. Bounce with kick variations. Perform different kicks such as knee lift and kick; double kicks; knee lift and slap knees; and kick and clap under knees. Combine the kicks with 2- or 4-count turns.

Activities with Manipulative Equipment

1. Use a jump rope. Perform basic steps such as forward and backward, and slow and fast time. Jump on one foot, cross the arms, and, while jogging, swing the rope from side to side with the handles in one hand.

2. Use beanbags. Toss and catch while performing various locomotor movements. Use different tosses for a challenge.

3. Use a hula hoop. Rhythmically swing the hoop around different body parts. Perform different locomotor movements around and over hoops.

4. Try movements with balls. Bounce, toss, and dribble, and add locomotor movements while performing tasks.

Aerobic Fitness and Partner-Resistance Exercises

Partner-resistance exercises develop strength but offer little aerobic benefit.
Combining them with Aerobic Fitness Routines offers a well-balanced routine. Descriptions of partner-resistance exercises are found on pages 187–
189. Allow enough time so each partner has the opportunity to resist and
exercise. See the lesson plan book for a suggested routine.

Sport-Related Fitness Activities

Many sport activities can be modified to place fitness demands on students.
An advantage of sport-related fitness activities occurs because many children
are highly motivated by sport activities. This motivates students to put forth
a better fitness effort since they enjoy the activity. Thoughtful preplanning
and creative thinking can result in drills that teach sport skills as well as provide fitness benefits. The following are some examples of fitness adaptations
of sports skills.

Baseball/Softball

1. *Base Running.* Set up several diamonds on a grass field. Space the
class evenly around throughout the base paths. On signal, the children run to the next base, round the base, take a lead, then run to
the next base. Faster runners may pass on the outside.

2. *Lead-Up Games.* Children waiting on deck to bat and those in the
field perform selected activities (skill or fitness related) while waiting
for the batter to hit.

3. *Position Responsibility.* Start children at various positions on the
field. On command, children are free to move quickly to any other
position. Upon reaching that position, each child is to display the
movement most frequently practiced at that position (e.g., shortstop
fields ball and throws to first base). Continue until all players have
moved to each position.

Basketball

1. *Dribbling.* Each child has a basketball or playground ball. Assign one
or more people to be "it." On command, everyone begins dribbling
the ball and avoids being tagged by those who are "it." If tagged, that
child becomes the new "it." A variation is to begin the game by "its"
not having a ball. Their objective is to steal a ball from classmates.

2. *Dribbling, Passing, Rebounding, Shooting, and Defense.* Using the
concept of a circuit, assign selected basketball skills to be performed
at each station. Be sure that there is ample equipment at each station
to keep all youngsters active. Movement from one station to another
should be vigorous and include a stop for exercise.

3. *Game Play.* Divide the class into four teams. Two teams take the court and play a game of basketball. The other teams assume a position along respective sidelines, and practice a series of exercises. The playing and exercising teams change positions at the conclusion of the exercise sequence.

Football

1. *Ball Carrying.* Divide the class into four to six squads. The first person in line carries the ball while zigzagging through prearranged boundary cones. The remainder of the squad performs a specific exercise. Upon completing the zigzag course, the first person hands off to the next person in line. This hand-off signifies a change in exercise for the remainder of the squad.

2. *Punting.* With partners, one child punts the ball to the other. After the receiver has the ball, the object is to see which child can get to the partner's starting position first. Repeat, with the receiver becoming the punter.

3. *Forward Passing.* Divide the children into groups of no more than four. Children practice running pass patterns. Rotate the passing responsibility after every six throws.

Volleyball

1. *Rotating.* Place youngsters in the various court positions. Teach them the rotational sequence. As they reach a new court position, have them complete several repetitions of a specific exercise. On command, rotate to the next position. Select activities that exercise components of fitness to enhance volleyball skill development.

2. *Serving.* Divide the class evenly among available volleyball courts. Starting with an equal number of children and a number of balls on each side of the net, begin practicing the serve. At the conclusion of each successful serve, the children run around the net standard to the other side of the net and retrieve a ball and serve.

3. *Bumping and Setting.* Using the concept of the circuit, establish several stations to practice the bump and set. Movement from station to station is vigorous and should contain a special stop for exercise.

Soccer

1. *Dribbling.* Working with a partner, have one child dribble the ball around the playground with the partner following close behind. On signal, reverse roles.

2. *Passing and Trapping.* Working with partners or small groups, devise routines that cause the players to move continuously (e.g., jogging, running in place, performing selected exercises while waiting to trap and pass the soccer ball).

3. *Game Play.* Divide the class into teams of three or four players per team. Organize the playground area to accommodate as many soccer

fields as necessary to allow all teams to play. Make the fields as large as possible.

Sample Routine

By combining sport skills that are active, a variety of fitness routines can be developed. The following routine is an example of sport skills incorporated into an eight-station outdoor circuit.

- *Station 1: Soccer Dribble.* Using only the feet, dribble the soccer ball to a predetermined point and back as many times as possible in the time provided.
- *Station 2: Basketball Chest Pass.* With a partner, practice the chest pass. To place additional demands on the arm muscles, increase the distance of the pass.
- *Station 3: Football Lateral.* Moving up and down the field, children practice lateralling the ball to one another.
- *Station 4: Softball Batting.* Each child has a bat and practices proper swing technique. Be sure to allow ample space between hitters.
- *Station 5: Continuous Running Long Jump.* Children take turns practicing the running long jump. After one child completes a jump successfully, the next one begins running down the runway. The activity should be continuous, with station members always moving.
- *Station 6: Soccer Inbounds Pass.* With partners, practice the overhead inbounds pass. Keep the ball overhead and propel the ball forward with a flick of the wrist and proper arm motion.
- *Station 7: Field Hockey Passing.* With partners, pass the field hockey ball back and forth between partners while moving up and down the field.
- *Station 8: Fielding a Softball.* With partners, practice fielding a thrown ground ball. Make the activity more challenging by throwing the ball so that the partner has to move to field the ball.

Walking and Jogging

Jogging and walking, fitness activity appropriate for all ages, can lead to regular activity habits and a lifelong exercise program. *Jogging* is defined as easy, relaxed running at a pace that can be maintained for long distances without undue fatigue or strain. Jogging and walking are unique because they require no special equipment, can be done almost anywhere, are individual activities, consume relatively little time, and are not geared to a particular time of day. For most people, this type of regular activity is an exercise in personal discipline that can enhance self-image and raise the confidence level.

Instructional Procedures

1. Allow youngsters to find a friend with whom they want to jog or walk. This usually results in a friend of similar ability level. A way to

judge correct pace is to talk with a friend without undue stress. If students are too winded to talk, they are probably running too fast. Finding a friend helps assure the experience is positive and within the student's aerobic capacity.

2. Jogging and walking should be done in any direction so children are unable to keep track of the distance covered. Doing laps on a track is a sure way to discourage less able youngsters. They finish last and are open to chiding by the rest of the class.

3. Jogging and walking should be done for a specified time rather than a specified distance. Why should all youngsters have to run the same distance? This goes against the philosophy of accompanying individual differences and varying aerobic capacities. Running or walking for a set amount of time allows less able children to move without fear of ridicule.

4. Do not be concerned about foot action, since children naturally select a style that is most comfortable. Arm movement should be easy and natural, with elbows bent. The head and upper body is held up and back. The eyes look ahead. The general body position in walking and jogging is erect but relaxed. Jogging on the toes should be avoided.

5. Jogging and walking should not be a competitive, timed activity. Each youngster should move at a self-determined pace. Racing belongs in the track program. Another reason to avoid speed is that racing keeps youngsters from learning to pace themselves. To develop endurance and gain health benefits, it is best to move for a longer time at a slower speed than to run at top speed for a shorter distance.

Continuous Movement Program

The continuous movement program (CMP) can be used to augment physical education classes and help children develop an effective conditioning program. This program is an effective method for classroom teachers to use to increase daily activity in a minimal amount of time (Erickson, 1980; Wilcox, 1980). To administer the program, take your class outside to move in any direction at a self-selected speed. Some youngsters may choose to jog, while others will want to maintain a brisk walking pace. Minimum responsibility for the teacher is to clock the specified time period and encourage youngsters to keep moving.

Continuous movement is a safe physical education activity. The chance of injury or physiological damage occurring is minimal, because youngsters are allowed to monitor and control their workloads. Progression should be slow (gradually increase the amount of time) and emphasis is on moving rather than how much or how fast students are performing.

Motivational Techniques
The following are suggestions that help increase a youngster's level of motivation to walk and jog. All of the suggestions are designed to improve phys-

ical conditioning and increase the amount of knowledge allied to the experience.

1. Set up a number of exercise trails on the playground. Trails should be different lengths so students can increase their workloads as their fitness levels improve. Students can keep track of their "mileage" by recording it on a class chart.

2. Walk and jog across the United States by posting a map of the country in the classroom. Each day, the mileage of all the students is added together and the distance plotted on the map. This helps the class work together for a common cause and all can feel as though they are making a meaningful contribution.

3. Develop a walking and jogging course that utilizes playground equipment for strength development. Most playgrounds have chin-up bars, monkey bars, climbing equipment, and parallel bars. Develop a circuit where youngsters have to jog between each strength development station.

4. Develop an after-school activity club. A great deal of time and energy is spent on developing competitive sport programs emphasizing skill-related fitness even though a majority of students do not possess the genetic traits to become outstanding athletes. The attractiveness of an activity club is that all students, regardless of genetic talent, can participate in health-related activities. The club should teach a large number of activities such as bicycling, hiking, power walking, cross-country running, and rope jumping.

5. Using manipulative equipment while walking or jogging is an effective technique for encouraging movement. Examples include playing catch with a football or Frisbee while walking, kicking a soccer ball while running, or running while jumping rope.

Interval Training Activities

Basically all the fitness routines in this chapter take advantage of interval training principles. Interval training can be used effectively with elementary school children, as they fatigue and recover quickly. This training involves alternating work and recovery intervals. Intervals of work (large muscle movement dominated by locomotor movements) and recovery (dominated by nonlocomotor activity or walking) are alternated at regular timed intervals.

Interval training can also be done by monitoring the heart rate. The work interval is continued until the heart rate reaches the target zone and is followed by a recovery interval. A common example of interval training is alternating 30 seconds of jogging with 30 seconds of walking. However, with elementary school children, this can be boring. The following are examples of motivating activities that can be alternated with recovery activities.

- *High Fives.* Youngsters run around the area and, on signal, run to a partner, jump, and give a "high five." Various locomotor movements are used as well as different styles of the "high five."

- *Over and Under.* Students find a partner. One partner makes a bridge on the floor while the other moves over, under, and around the bridge. This continues until a signal is given to "switch," which notifies them to change positions. This assures one child will be moving (working) while the other is resting. Try different types of bridges and movements to offer variety to the activity.

- *Rope Jump and Stretch.* Each student has a jump rope and is jumping it during the work interval. On signal, the student performs a stretch using the jump rope. An example is to fold the rope in half and hold it overhead while stretching from side to side and to the toes.

- *Stick and Stretch.* Working with a partner, one partner is "it" and tries to stick like glue to the partner, who attempts to escape. Students should move under control. Upon signal, "it" leads the other person in a stretching (resting) activity. On the next signal, the roles are reversed.

- *Rubber Band.* Students move throughout the area. On signal, they time a move to the center of the area. Upon reaching the center simultaneously, they jump upward and let out a loud "Yea!" or similar exhortation and resume running throughout the area. A key to the activity is to synchronize the move to the center. After a number of runs, take a rest and stretch, or walk.

Each of these activities just described is used for work intervals. Recovery intervals are characterized by strength development or stretching activities. Using timed intervals of music is an effective approach for motivating youngsters. For a start, tape 30 seconds of music followed by 30 seconds of silence, taping a series of these alternating music and silent intervals. The music sequence signals youngsters to perform the work interval while the silent interval is time for performing stretching or strength development activities. This frees the teacher to help youngsters and assures that intervals are timed accurately. As youngsters become more fit, the length of the music bouts can be increased by making a new recording. Changing the music on a regular basis keeps children motivated.

Partner Fitness Challenges

Partner challenges are fitness activities that are used with intermediate-grade youngsters. They can be used to develop aerobic endurance, strength, and flexibility. Another advantage of partner challenges is that they can be performed indoors as a rainy-day activity. It is best if youngsters are paired with someone of similar ability and size. Telling youngsters to pair up with a friend usually helps assure they will select a partner who is caring and understanding. Emphasis should be placed on continuous movement and activity. The following are examples of partner activities that are challenging and enjoyable.

- *Circle Five.* Partner 1 stands stationary in the center of the circle with one palm up. Partner 2 runs in a circle around 1 and "gives a high five" when passing the upturned palm. The size of the circle should be gradually increased. Reverse roles on signal.

- *Foot Tag.* Partners stand facing each other. On signal, they try to touch each other's toes with their feet. Emphasize the importance of a touch, as contrasted to a stamp or kick.

- *Knee Tag.* Partners stand facing each other. On signal, they try to tag the other person's knees. Each time a tag is made, a point is scored. Play for a designated amount of time.

- *Mini-Merry-Go-Round.* Partners face each other with the feet nearly touching and the hands grasped in a double wrist grip. Partners slowly lean backward while keeping the feet in place until the arms are straight. Spin around as quickly as possible. It is important that partners be of similar size.

- *Around and Under.* One partner stands with the feet spread shoulder-width apart and hands held overhead. The other partner goes between the standing partner's legs, stands up, and slaps the partner's hands. Continue the pattern for a designated time.

- *Ball Wrestle.* Both partners grasp an 8-inch playground ball and try to wrestle it away from each other.

- *Sitting Wrestle.* Partners sit on the floor facing each other with the legs bent, feet flat on the floor, toes touching, and hands grasped. The goal of the activity is to pull the other's buttocks off the floor.

- *Upset the Alligator.* One partner lies face down on the floor. On signal, the other opponent tries to turn the "alligator" over. The alligator tries to avoid being turned over.

- *Seat Balance Wrestle.* Partners sit on the floor facing each other with the knees raised and feet off the floor. If desired, they place the hands under the thighs to help support the legs. Start with the toes touching. Each tries to tip the other person backward using the toes.

- *Head Wrestle.* Partners hold each other's left wrists with their right hands. On signal, they try to touch their partners' heads with their left hands, then switch the handhold and try to touch with the opposite hand.

- *Pull Apart.* Partner 1 stands with the feet spread, arms bent at the elbows in front of the chest, with the fingertips touching. Partner 2 holds the wrists of the other and tries to pull the fingertips apart. Jerking is not allowed; the pull must be smooth and controlled.

- *Pin Dance.* Partners hold hands facing each other with a bowling pin (spot or cone) placed between them. On signal, each tries to cause the other person to touch the pin.

- *Finger Fencing.* Partners face each other with their feet one in front of the other in a straight line. The toes on the front foot of each partner should touch. Partners lock index fingers and attempt to cause the other to move either foot from the beginning position.

References and Suggested Readings

American Academy of Pediatrics. (1991). *Sports medicine: Health care for young athletes.* Elk Grove Village, IL: AAP.

Bar-Or, O. (1983). *Pediatric sports medicine for the practitioner.* New York: Springer-Verlag.

Blair, S. N., Kohl, H. W., Paffenbarger, R. S., Clark, D. G., Cooper, K. H., & Gibbons, L. W. (1989). Physical fitness and all-cause mortality: A prospective study of healthy men and women. *Journal of the American Medical Association, 17,* 2395–24.

Bouchard, C. (1990). Discussion: Heredity, fitness and health. In C. Bouchard, R. J. Shepard, T. Stephens, J. R. Sutton, & B. D. McPherson. (Eds.), *Exercise, fitness and health* (pp. 147–153). Champaign, IL: Human Kinetics.

Bouchard, C., Dionne, F. T., Simoneau, J., & Boulay, M. (1992). Genetics of aerobic and anaerobic performances. *Exercise and Sport Sciences Reviews, 20,* 27–58.

Chausow, S. A., Riner, W. F., & Boileau, R. A. (1984). Metabolic and cardiovascular responses of children during prolonged physical activity. *Research Quarterly for Exercise and Sport, 55*(1), 1–7.

Cooper Institute for Aerobic Research. (1992). *The Prudential Fitnessgram Test administration manual.* Dallas: Cooper Institute for Aerobics Research.

Corbin, C. B., & Lindsey, R. (1994). *Concepts of physical fitness with laboratories* (8th ed.). Dubuque, IA: Wm. C. Brown.

Corbin, C. B., & Lindsey, R. (1995). *Fitness for life* (4th ed.). Glenview, IL: Scott, Foresman.

Corbin, C. B., & Pangrazi, R. P., & Welk, G. J. (1994). Toward an understanding of appropriate physical activity levels for youth. *Physical Activity and Fitness Research Digest, 1*(8): 1–8.

Corbin, C. B., Lovejoy, P. Y., Steingard, P., & Emerson, R. (1990). Fitness awards: Do they accomplish their intended objectives? *American Journal of Health Promotion, 4,* 345–351.

Corbin, C. B., Lovejoy, P. Y., & Whitehead, J. R. (1988). Youth physical fitness awards. *Quest, 40,* 200–218.

Corbin, C. B., & Pangrazi, R. P. (1992). Are American children and youth fit? *Research Quarterly for Exercise and Sport, 63*(2), 96–106.

Erickson, D. M. (1980). *The effect of a random running program on cardiorespiratory endurance at the fourth, fifth, and sixth grade levels.* Unpublished master's thesis, Department of Health and Physical Education, Arizona State University.

Glasser, W. (1976). *Positive addiction.* New York: Harper & Row.

Gortmaker, S. L., Dietz, W. H., Sobol, A. N., & Wehler, C. A. (1987). Increasing pediatric obesity in the U.S. *American Journal of Diseases in Children, 14,* 535–540.

Harter, S. (1978). Effectance motivation revisited. *Child Development, 21,* 34–64.

Liemohn, W. (1991). Choosing the safe exercise. *Certified News, 2,* 1–3.

Lindsey, R., & Corbin, C. (1989). Questionable exercises—Some safer alternatives. *Journal of Physical Education, Recreation, and Dance, 60*(8), 26–32.

Locke, E. A., & Lathan, G. P. (1985). The application of goal setting to sports. *Journal of Sport Psychology, 7,* 205–222.

Lohman, T. G. (1992). *Advances in body composition.* Champaign, IL: Human Kinetics.

Macek, M., & Vavra, J. (1974). Prolonged exercise in children. *Acta Paediatrica Belgica, 28,* 13–18.

Macfarlane, P. A. (1993). Out with the sit-up, in with the curl-up. *Journal of Physical Education, Recreation, and Dance, 64*(6), 62–66.

Miller, D. K., & Allen, T. K. (1990). *Fitness: A lifetime commitment* (3rd ed.). New York: Macmillan.

Pangrazi, R. P., & Corbin, C. B. (1990). Age as a factor relating to physical fitness test performance. *Research Quarterly for Exercise and Sport, 61*(4), 410–414.

Pangrazi, R. P., & Dauer, V. P. (1995). *Dynamic physical education for elementary school children* (11th ed.). New York: Macmillan.

Pangrazi, R. P., & Dauer, V. P. (1995). *Lesson plans for dynamic physical education* (11th ed.). New York: Macmillan.

Pangrazi, R. P., & Hastad, D. N. (1989). *Fitness in the elementary schools* (2nd ed.). Reston, VA: AAHPERD.

Pate, R. R., Dowda, M., & Ross, J. G. (1990). Association between physical activity and physical fitness in American children. *American Journal of Diseases of Children, 144,* 1123–1129.

Pate, R. R., & Ross, J. G. (1987). Factors associated with health-related fitness. *Journal of Physical Education, Recreation, and Dance, 58*(9), 93–96.

Payne, V. G., & Morrow, J. R., Jr. (1993). Exercise and VO2max in children: A meta-analysis. *Research Quarterly for Exercise and Sport, 64*(3), 305–313.

Rarick, L. G., & Dobbins, D. A. (1975). Basic components in the motor performances of children six to nine years of age. *Medicine and Science in Sports, 7*(2), 105–110.

Raitakari, O. T., Porkka, K. V. K., Taimela, S., Telama, R., Rasanen, L., & Viikari, J. S. A. (1994). Effects of persistent physical activity and inactivity on coronary risk factors in children and young adults. *American Journal of Epidemiology, 140,* 195–205.

Reiff, G. G., Dixon, W. R., Jacoby, D., Ye, X. Y., Spain, C. G., & Hunsicker, P. A. (1987). *The President's Council on Physical Fitness and Sports 1985 national school population fitness survey.* Washington, DC: U.S. Department of Health and Human Services.

Ross, J. G., & Gilbert, G. G. (1985). The national children and youth fitness study: A summary of findings. *Journal of Physical Education, Recreation, and Dance, 56*(1), 45–50.

Ross, J. G., Pate, R. R., Caspersen, C. J., Damberg, C. L., & Svilar, M. (1987). Home and community in children's exercise habits. *Journal of Physical Education, Recreation, and Dance, 58*(9), 85–92.

Rowland, T. W. (1990). *Exercise and children's health.* Champaign, IL: Human Kinetics.

Slaughter, M. H., Lohman, T. G., Boileau, R. A., Horswill, C. A., Stillman, R. J., Van Loan, M. D., & Benben, D. A. (1988). Skinfold equations for estimation of body fatness in children and youth. *Human Biology, 60,* 709–723.

Smith, L. L., Brunetz, M. H., Chenier, T. C., McCammon, M. R., Hourmard, J. A., Franklin, M. E., & Israel, R. G. (1993). The effects of static and ballistic stretching on delayed onset muscle soreness and creatine kinase. *Research Quarterly for Exercise and Sport, 64*(1), 103–107.

U.S. Public Health Service. (1988). *Healthy people 2000.* Washington, DC: Superintendent of Documents.

Whitehead, J. R., & Corbin, C. B. (1991). Effects of fitness test type, teacher, and gender on exercise intrinsic motivation and physical self-worth. *Journal of School Health, 61,* 11–16.

Wilcox, R. R. (1980). *RRP: An approach to cardiorespiratory fitness of primary school children, grades one, two, and three.* Unpublished master's thesis, Department of Health and Physical Education, Arizona State University.

Williams, D. P., Going, S. B., Lohman, T. G., Harsha, D. W., Webber, L. S., & Bereson, G. S. (1992). Body fatness and the risk of elevated blood pressure, total cholesterol and serum lipoprotein rations in children and youth. *American Journal of Public Health, 82,* 358–363.

Index

Abdominal cruncher, 183
Abdominal development, 166
Abdominal exercises, 166, 180–183
Ability levels, 23
Accident Report Form, sample, 144
Accidents (*see* Injured students; Safety)
Achilles tendon stretch, 176–177
Activity reinforcers, 88
Aerobic fitness, 21–22, 150–151 routines, 195–199
Affective domain development, 62–63
Agility, definition of, 151
Aides for children with disabilities, 113
Animal movements, 167–168
Arm circles, 179
Arm curl-up, 187
Arm-shoulder girdle development, 163–165, 177–180
Arms and shoulders, 193
Arousal, definition of, 36
Assumption of risk defense, 133
Asthma, 125
Astronaut drills, 194–195
Audio assistance in fitness routines, 162
Auditory impairment, 121–122

Back builder, 188
Back exercises, 193
Balance, definition of, 152
Balance and agility, children who lack, 116–117
Ballistic stretching, 173
Baseball, 199
Basketball, 199–200
Bear hug, 185
Bear trap, 188

Behavior, desirable, 86–92 positive reinforcement for, 87–90
Behavior contracts, 96, 97
Behavior problems, 82–86
Behavior skills, 4–5
Bending, 165, 174
Blocked practice, 42
Body circles, 186
Body composition, 151
Body size and motor performance, 20–21
Body torque, 48
Body twist, 177
Body type and motor skill learning, 18–19
Breaking rules, consequences of, 83
Burnout in young children, 24–25
Butterfly, 188

Camelback, 188
Cardiorespiratory development, 166–167
Cardiovascular fitness, 150–151
Cardiovascular problems, 126
Catching objects, 48–49
Cerebal palsy, 126
Challenge courses, 195, 196
Challenging drills vs. threatening drills, 59–60
Changing direction, 46
Children with disabilities, 102–126 least restrictive environment, 108–113
modifying participation, 114–117
screening/assessing, 102–108
specific disabilites, 117–126
Children with wheelchairs, 123
Circuit training, 191–194

Classroom teachers teaching physical education, 6
Closing the lesson, 81
Cognitive development, 61–62
Comparative or shared negligence, 132
Competition, 36
Complexity, definition of, 40
Consequences of breaking rules, 83
Continuity drills, 194
Continuous movement program (CMP), 202–203
Contracts with students, 96, 97
Contributory negligence, 132, 133
Cooperative skills, 4–5
Coordination:
children who lack, 116
definition of, 152
Crab kick, 179–180
Creativity, 60–61
Criterion-referenced health standards, 153
Criticism, 96–97
Curl-ups, 181–182
Curriculum review by administration, 135–138

Decision-making skills, 61–62
Desirable behavior (*see* Behavior, desirable)
Desire to learn, 36
Development levels and progression, 45, 58–59
Developmental skills levels, 34, 58–59
Deviant behavior, 99
Diabetes, 126
Differential reinforcement, 91
Disabled children (*see* Children with disabilities)

Discipline problems, 82–86
Distance curves for height and
    weight, 14
Distance running by children, 27–28
Dividing a class, 78
Drills and skill development, 58–59
Due process guidelines, assessment
    of children with disabilities,
    103–104

Early-maturing children, 19
Early starters in sports, 23–25
Ectomorph body type, 19
Embarrassment, 59, 63
Emergency care plan, 143–145
Emotional disturbances, 124
Endomorph body type, 19
Endurance, 20
Environment of class, 66–70, 85–86
Epilepsy, 118–120
Equal opportunity in sports, 22–23
Equipment, 7–9
    distribution of, 52, 81–82
    installation of, 138
    lack of, 52
    and liability, 138–139
    securing and checking, 51–52
Exercising:
    to music, 190–191
    safety, 25–30
Extended squad formation, 54–55
Extrinsic reinforcers, 88–89
"Eyeballing" the class, 67–68

Fading, definition of, 91
Fast starts, 46
Feedback, 36–39, 54, 70–73, 86,
    158–159
    definition of, 36–37
Finding a partner, 77
Fist pull-apart, 188
Fitness activities (see also Physical
    fitness):
    individualized, 158
    grades 3 through 6, 171–189
    kindergarten through grade 2,
        163–171
    vs. regular activity, 156–158
Fitness routines, 158
    developing, 190–206
    implementing, 161–163
Fitness testing, 154
Flexibility, 151
    and back exercises, 193
    exercises, grades 3–6, 174–176
Flying angel, 180
Follow-through, definition of, 48

Football, 200
Forearm flex, 188
Foreseeability and negligence,
    130–131
Formations, 77–78
Four-corners movement, 170–171

Generalization, definition of, 43
Giving, definition of, 49
Grades 3 through 6, fitness activities,
    171–189
    exercises for routines, 174
    flexibility exercises, 174–176
    harmful practices, 172–174
Group instruction, 85
Growth patterns, 14–20
    percentiles, 16–17
    velocity curve for height, 15

Hand-eye coordination, 48–49
Handicaps (see Children with
    disabilities)
Health standards, 153
Health-related physical fitness,
    150–151, 152–153
Heart disease, 13–14 (see also
    Cardiovascular fitness)
Height, growth velocity curve, 15
Height and weight, distance curves,
    14
Heredity and fitness test performance,
    154–155
Hexagon hustle, 194
Hopping and jumping patterns, 167
Hot climates, exercise in, 26–27
Hydration, 27

Individualized Education Program
    (IEP), 102
    development of, 105–108
Injured students, 66–67, 130, 133,
    143–145
Instruction:
    effectiveness, 56–63
    and liability, 136
Instructional area, 10
Instructional cues, 65–66
Instructional formations, 54–56
Interval training activities, 203–204
Intrinsic motivation, 25
Involving all students, 58

Jogging, walking, 201–202
Jump rope exercises, 170
Jumping and hopping patterns, 167
Jumping jacks, 184, 198

Kindergarten through grade 2, fitness
    activities, 163–171
    animal movements, 167–168
    fitness challenges, 163–167
    fitness games, 168–169
    four-corners movement, 170–171
    jump rope exercises, 170
    miniature challenge courses, 169
    parachute fitness routines, 169–170
    walk, trot, sprint, 170
Knee bender, 188, 189
Knee touch curl-up, 181–182
Knowledge of performance, 38–39
Knowledge of results, 37–38

Lane (file) formation, 55
Lawsuit, minimizing effects of,
    145–147
"Learned helplessness," 23
Learning disabilities, 124–125
Learning the names of students, 80
Least restrictive environment,
    108–113
Leg and agility exercises, 166–167,
    183–184, 192–193
Leg extensions, 182–183
Legal concerns and discipline, 99
Legal liability, 129–147
    areas of responsibility, 133–138
    minimizing effects of lawsuit,
        145–147
    negligence, types of, 131–132
Liability, definition of, 129
Liability insurance, 145
Lifestyle activity, 157
Lifestyle changes in fitness, 13
Lifetime activity, 5, 156, 160–161
Line-ups, 78
Locomotor movements, 169–170
Low-intensity activity, 160
Lower leg stretch, 176

Mainstreaming, 109–113
Malfeasance, 131
Management of students, 75–82
Materials and supplies, list of
    requirements, 9
Maturity level:
    definition of, 35
    and learning motor skills, 35
    and physical performance, 19–20
    and sport skills learning, 22
Medical examination before
    participating, 140
Mental retardation, 117–118
Mesomorph body type, 18–19
Miniature challenge courses, 169

Minimizing effects of lawsuit, 145–147
Misbehaving students, 68, 87
Misfeasance, 131
Mismatching opponents, 140
Modeling behavior, 90–91
Moderation in exercise, 25–26
Mofifying participation for children
        with disabilities, 114–117
    balance, agility, 116–117
    coordination, 116
    strength, endurance, 115–116
Motivating students, 90
Motor skills:
    development of, 3
    patterns common to all children,
        34
    readiness for learning, 35–36
Multisensory approaches when
        teaching children with
        disabilities, 112
Muscular endurance, 151
Muscular strength, 20
Music and exercising, 1990–191

Negative consequences, 92–96
Negative feedback, 70, 86
Negligence:
    and liability, 129–133
    types of, 131–132
Nonfeasance, 131
Nonparticipating students, 80
Nonverbal cues, 90
Novel response, definition of, 43

Obesity, 14
    and aerobic activities, 21–22
Observing class performance, 67–68
Opposition, definition of, 47
Organization, definition of, 40
Orthopedic disabilities, 122–123

PACER aerobic fitness test, 28
Pacing the lesson, 53
Parachute fitness routines, 169–170
Parcourse, definition of, 194
Parental support for children with
        disabilities, 113
Part method of teaching skills, 40
Partner fitness challenges, 204–205
Partner formation, 55
Partner rowing, 175–176
Partner-resistance exercises, 187–189,
        199
Peer teaching, 85
Pelvis tilter, 181
Perceived competence, 23
Personalizing instruction, 69–70

Physical education:
    definitions of, 2
    objectives of, 3–5
    scheduling, 6–7
Physical fitness, 4, 150–205
    attitudes about, 158–161
    fitness routines, 161–163, 190–206
    grades 3 through 6, 171–189
    kindergarten through grade 2,
        163–171
    standards of, 153–156
    types of, 150–153
Physical maturity, 19–20, 22
    and fitness test results, 155–156
Planning the lesson, 56–63
Positive attitudes toward activity,
        158
Positive reinforcement, 87–90
Power, definition of, 152
Power jumper, 184
Practice time, 39–45, 57–58
    length of, 41
    transfer of learning, 43–44
Preinstructional planning, 51–56
Premack principle, 90
Prerequisite skills, definition of, 35
Preseason conditioning, 140
Progression:
    definition of, 44
    and development levels, 45
    teaching skills in, 44–45
Prompting children, 90
Propelling objects, 47–48
Pull-ups, 178–179
Punishment, 97–99
    and liability, 136–137
Push-ups, 164–165, 177–178
    with resistance, 189

Random practice, 42
Readiness and motor skills, 35–36
Ready position, 46
Reclining pull-ups, 178–179
Recordkeeping of accidents, 145
Regular activity vs. fitness activity,
        156–158
Reinforcement, 87–90, 91
Removing positive consequences to
        change behavior, 94
Reprimanding a student, 93–94
Required materials and supplies,
        listing, 9
Resistance (weight) training, 28–30
Reverse curl, 181
Role model, teacher as, 159
Rope jumping, 167
Routines for students, 84

Rules:
    enforcing, 85–86
    planning and implementing, 82–83
Running, 28
    patterns, 167
    in place, 183–184

Safe environment, 66–67
Safe exercising, 25–30
Safety, 141–145
    inspections for apparatus, 67
Safety and liability checklist, 145–146
Scanning the class, 68
Scattered formation, 54
Scheduling physical education, 6–7
Schema theory, 43
Scissors, 188
Screening/assessing children with
        disabilities, 102–108
Seizures, 118–120
Self-concept, 4–5, 61
Shaping techniques (behavior), 91–92
Show-and-tell demonstrations, 60
Side flex, 185–186
Sitting stretch, 175
Size of physical education class, 7
Size of teaching space, 53–54
Skeletal age, 19, 22
Skill development and fitness, 159
Skill performance:
    giving feedback on, 36–39
    and physical fitness, 151–153
    principles, 46–49
Skills demonstration, 64–65
Small-group formation, 55, 78
Soccer, 200–201
Social reinforcers, 87–88
    delivering, 89
Social skills, 4–5
Softball, 199
Specificity, principle of, 44
Speed, definition of, 152
Sport-related fitness activities,
        199–201
Sports program and liability, 139–141
Squads:
    exercises with leader, 190
    formation with leader, 55, 56
    organizing, 78–80
Standing hip bend, 177
Starting and stopping class, 76–77
Starting and stopping the body, 46, 47
Static stretching, 173
Station teaching, 85
Stop signal, 76
Storage of equipment, 8
Strength and endurance, 151

children who lack, 115
Strength and motor performance, 20–21
Strength training, 28–30
Stretching, 165, 173
Student demonstrations, 64–65
Student input, 61
Student-led exercises, 190
Supervision of activities, 134
Swaying and twisting, 165–166

Teacher demonstration, 64
Team evaluation, assessment of children with disabilities, 104
Teamwork, 62
Test instruments for children with disabilities, 104
Time management and lesson, 52–53
Time-out approach, 94–96
Token reinforcers, 88–89

Torts, definition of, 129
Tracking, definition of, 48
Trainability and fitness test results, 155
Transfer of body weight, 48
Transfer of learning, 43–44
Transportation of students, 140–141
Treadmill, 184
Triceps push-ups, 179
Trunk development, 165–166
Trunk-twisting and bending exercises, 184–186

Variable practice, 42–43
Variety in routines/exercises, 158, 161
Verbal cues, 90
Video assistance in fitness routines, 162

Visual concentration, 47, 48–49
Visual impairment, 120–121
Volleyball, 200

Waiver forms, 140
Walk, trot, and sprint, 170
Walking, jogging, 201–202
Warm climates, exercise in, 26–27
Weight and height, distance curves, 14
Weight training, 28–30
Wellness (*see* Physical fitness)
Whole method of teaching skills, 40
Windmill, 186
Withdrawing from participation, 25

Young starters in sports, 23–25